D1539415

MARGARET

The Untold Story

MARGARET

The Untold Story

Noel Botham

BLAKE

Published by Blake Hardbacks Ltd,
98-100 Great North Road, London N2 0NL, England.

First published in Great Britain in 1994

ISBN 1 85782 078 9

British Library Cataloguing-in-Publication Data:
A catalogue record for this book is available from
the British Library.

Typeset by Pearl Graphics, Hemel Hempstead

Printed in Finland by WSOY

1 3 5 7 9 10 8 6 4 2

To Lesley Lewis for her loving encouragement
and Robin Cook – best-selling chiller writer Derek Raymond –
for pushing the pace.

Contents

1

The Little Princess

Princess Margaret Rose of York – heartbreaker extraordinary and the woman destined to introduce sex appeal into the British royal family for the first time – was born during a violent and dramatic thunderstorm in the vast, ancestral pile of Glamis Castle. As befitted her later love of theatricality, lightning flickered across the turrets, towers and battlements and driving rain lashed the leaded windows of her mother's bedroom as the latest grandchild of the King/Emperor George V entered the world at 9.22 pm on 21 August 1930. The baby girl, who would grow up to become the last real princess, weighed 8lb 11oz. Hers was the first royal birth of any importance in Scotland since Charles I was born there in 1600.

Only half a dozen people, including the Home Secretary, John Clynes – who was there to satisfy ancient custom – were in the rambling family castle which had once slept

88 guests and is reputedly home to nine ghosts. Retainers who had planned to light a giant beacon on nearby Hunter's Hill were trapped in their crofts by the wild weather and it was morning before the birth was publicly celebrated – by a 41-gun salute at the Tower of London and a further 41-gun salute performed by the Royal Horse Artillery in Hyde Park.

The bells of St Paul's and Westminster Abbey echoed the joyful peals of church bells throughout the length of Britain and that evening, joined by well-wishers from as far away as Edinburgh and Glasgow, the Glamis retainers were able to fire their great beacon, which was seen across six counties and signalled the firing of hundreds of other beacons nationwide.

The birth of a second daughter to Prince Albert, Duke of York, the younger brother of Edward, the heir presumptive, was seen as a cause for national rejoicing and celebration – in significant contrast to the more recent birth, two generations later, of a second daughter to the present Duke of York!

A week later, when the King, George V, and Queen Mary came to look at their new grandchild, her names had already been chosen – Margaret, after a string of Scottish queens, and Rose for the emblem of the House of York. Three weeks after the birth, the whole family, with nurse Clara Knight, former nanny to Elizabeth, Duchess of York – who, unable to pronounce Clara, had dubbed her Alah – returned to 145 Piccadilly, London. This modest town house, which looked south over Hyde Park Corner, and has since been demolished, was the Yorks' only residence.

Margaret Rose was christened in the private chapel at Buckingham Palace by the Archbishop of Canterbury, Dr. Lang. Her godparents were Edward, Prince of Wales (later to become Edward VIII and later still Duke of Windsor), Princess Victoria, the King's sister, Princess Ingrid of Sweden, Lady Rose Leveson-Gower and David Bowes-Lyon.

A second nanny, Margaret MacDonald, was already working for the Yorks and after Princess Margaret's birth she and Alah were joined by her younger sister, sixteen-year-old Ruby MacDonald. Ruby eventually became the princess's maid and dresser, while her sister, Margaret, became dresser to the Queen.

A year after Margaret's birth, the Yorks were given Royal Lodge, Windsor, a slightly tumbledown property urgently in need of attention, which stood close to the castle. They immediately began the enlargement, repairs and general refurbishment of the house which was to become a favourite weekend retreat and a future love nest for Margaret, who would one day entertain several of her lovers there.

The year 1932 saw the arrival of Princess Elizabeth's governess, Marion Crawford, a 22-year-old Scot, fresh out of teacher training college in Edinburgh. Elizabeth nick-named her Crawfie and she was to remain with the two little princesses until her marriage fifteen years later.

Meanwhile, Margaret was being encouraged to walk and talk by her sister who wanted a play pal. She rapidly learned to mimic what her sister and mother said and by the age of two could sing perfectly in tune. King George encouraged her to dance for him and would allow her to ride on his back while he scrambled around the royal drawing room bellowing with laughter. He liked his grand-daughters to be with him as often as possible, although he tended to favour Elizabeth more than her younger sister. Elizabeth was closer to the throne and also more respectful towards the old king. Sometimes his deafness made him roar at the two girls but this hardly intimidated Margaret at all. She tried to get round her grandpa with hugs and kisses, as she did her father, but he still singled out Elizabeth for special treats from which Margaret was excluded.

Both princesses took part in the King's Silver Jubilee celebrations, seated side by side in an open carriage. Only the King himself received louder cheers than the little princesses, as they were now universally known. In the autumn and winter, when the trees were bare in Buckingham Palace gardens, the King would wave a large, white handkerchief from his window every morning at the same time and the princesses would wave back.

Then, on 18 January 1936, King George V died and started a chain of events that, within a year, was to bring enormous changes to the lives of the little princesses.

Elizabeth went to the funeral, while Margaret remained in the nursery. From then on, it seemed to Margaret that she was destined never to catch up with her sister. She knew the King had died and told Crawfie: 'Grandpa is in heaven now, and I'm sure God finds him very useful.'

That year Margaret began lessons with Crawfie, although these were sometimes interrupted by heated rows between the sisters. 'Margaret always wants everything I want,' Elizabeth would cry. Then she would slap her sister's face and Margaret would bite her. Usually, however, both sisters worked hard at their lessons. Outside interest in their schoolwork was mainly shown by Queen Mary. 'History is as important to these children as arithmetic,' she urged Crawfie. 'They are not like ordinary children.'

At that time the new king, Edward VIII, known to them as Uncle David, was showing that he was not like ordinary monarchs. Within the family and government there was as much growing concern about his involvement with Mrs. Wallis Simpson as for his openly stated admiration for Adolf Hitler. For fear of offending Mussolini, the new king also refused to receive Emperor Haile Selassie of Ethiopia even though it was a British cruiser that had rescued him as the Italian army advanced into Ethiopia, and delivered him safely to England.

In October 1936, Mrs. Simpson was granted a decree nisi against her second husband. It was later revealed that the King had offered her husband a knighthood to ease the divorce smoothly through the courts. Ernest Simpson had enough style and pride left to refuse.

On his knees, Bertie, Duke of York, prayed that his brother would not give up the throne. Shy, easily embarrassed and with an appalling stutter, Bertie considered himself incapable of doing the job for which David, and not he, had been trained all of his life. Bertie said that he felt like the proverbial sheep being led to the slaughter, 'which is not a comfortable feeling'. Although at the time Margaret did not understand why Uncle David should disappear and Papa become king, she was never to forgive Edward VIII for putting self before duty and she later came to blame this turn of events as the cause of her father's premature death.

It was to be another fifteen years before she was able to ferret out the details and extract uncensored accounts of her uncle's scandalous sexual preferences from well-informed courtiers. Mrs. Simpson's fatal attraction for Edward was that she was the only woman who would allow him to satisfy his unnatural preferences on and in her body and the only one with whom he could achieve sexual satisfaction. Edward was homosexual. That, she was told, was what he gave up the throne for, not for love.

Later, when people tried to compare the royal 'love' crisis of Edward and Mrs. Simpson with that of Princess Margaret and Peter Townsend, Margaret would remark icily: 'There were no similarities at all. Mine was real love.'

It was Queen Elizabeth, now the Queen Mother, however, who proved Mrs. Simpson's toughest opponent. It was she who finally engineered the ousting of the detestable Wallis, and Edward VIII too when it became obvious that he would not abandon her. When Bertie finally succeeded to the thorne, Queen Elizabeth personally sacked all of Edward's palace staff and banished his supporters from court. At the end of November, when Edward finally told his brother that he was abdicating, Bertie broke down and cried on his mother's shoulder for an hour.

When six-year-old Margaret was told about it, she wanted to know: 'Will they chop off his head?' Concerned that Grandpa and Uncle David had both vanished within a year and that her father might be in need of special protection, she cautioned him to be careful and asked: 'Do you sing "God save my gracious me", now?'

Only David had been trained for kingship and Bertie had to learn things as he went along. Coping with the new job meant that now he had precious little time for his children. After their move to Buckingham Palace, which Margaret found big, cold and unfriendly, she found that the biggest change was not the new routine but relations between herself and Elizabeth. In under twelve months, her big sister had been promoted from third in line of succession to heir presumptive. Extra teachers were brought in to supplement Crawfie's lessons as the realities of constitutional monarchy were drummed into Elizabeth.

In the vast palace, cut off from their parents by endless staircases and corridors, the little princesses were left almost exclusively in the hands of nurses, their governess and the occasional lecturer brought in to school Elizabeth. Margaret complained: 'Now that Papa is King, I am nothing.'

The result was that, if anything, she paid even less attention than before to her studies and gave up much of her time to mischief.

Worried about Margaret, her sister Elizabeth began to assume a parental role. 'I really do not know what we are going to do with Margaret,' she would exclaim after suffering another of Margaret's pranks. Leaping from behind pillars to scare footmen was one favourite; putting salt in people's tea was another. Buckingham Palace has more than 600 rooms. Margaret claimed to know more than 400 of them through following the official clock winder around the palace to satisfy her curiosity.

When they joined their parents at garden parties, Elizabeth would warn her: 'If you see somebody with a funny hat you must not point at it and laugh.' Yet when Margaret did misbehave, which was often, she was rarely reprimanded. She invented an invisible friend, Cousin Halifax, on whom she put the blame for all her 'little troubles'. However, more often she relied on her quick wits and comic inventiveness to get her out of a tricky situation. She never seemed to be at a loss for words. On one occasion, when she was being taken to a fancy dress party dressed as an angel, her mother said: 'You don't look very angelic, Margaret.'

'That's all right. I'll be a holy terror,' was Margaret's instant rejoinder.

To try to put the girls in touch with ordinary people a little, Crawfie organised a Girl Guide troop in the palace, although Margaret was designated a Brownie until she was ten. Crawfie also took them on rare bus rides, to the pantomime and for walks in Hyde Park, although they were forbidden to talk to other children – a nod and a smile were all that was allowed. None the less, these outings were high adventure indeed for the last real princess, who was able to glimpse a world she barely knew existed.

As the two girls grew older, their curricula became more dissimilar. Elizabeth was being prepared for a life of service and everything concerned with her upbringing and education was overseen by the Queen. Preparing Elizabeth to be queen, say friends, was her mother's greatest achievement. She was taught that duty came first in everything.

Margaret was sacrificed to this ambition. She was second-best all the way and her parents acknowledged it. All the King ever expected from Margaret, he said, was her love. She wasn't ill-treated in any way but many of her very considerable talents were never allowed to develop or even be recognised. It was Crawfie, too, who taught her to read and write and who chose what she would read, which programmes she could listen to on the radio and which games she could play. Margaret is an excellent raconteur and this is chiefly due to Crawfie encouraging her whenever she launched into one of her amazing stories. Under Crawfie's prompting, she would recount a dream or a fantasy, letting her vivid imagination run riot, sometimes for hours on end.

Family friends say that the King would always try to find a little extra time for Margaret and spoiled her considerably. He had learned about the suffering involved in being the younger child of a reigning monarch. As one royal commentator put it: 'He knew she wasn't going to be head girl.' He would say to people that Elizabeth was his pride but that Margaret was his joy. Margaret made him laugh when there was little to laugh about. She would wind her arms around his neck and kiss and cuddle him until he was wet with kisses. Bertie, a rather serious and introverted man, while showing outward embarrassment, secretly confessed to loving his younger daughter's impromptu hug-ins.

Apart from being very affectionate Margaret could also be very endearing and was a natural comedienne. She put on Christmas pantos, organised treasure hunts and played sardines with Crawfie and the young guardsmen – and Bertie forgave her anything and everything.

In July 1939, she witnessed the start of the romance between Elizabeth and Philip, a romance, say family friends, that was, incredibly, orchestrated by Lord Louis Mountbatten and his family right under the noses of the King and Queen. It wasn't that Princess Elizabeth didn't like other boys – she was never permitted to see anyone too often or close up, except Philip.

Lord Mountbatten was the son of Prince Louis of Battenberg, who had anglicised his name, as the King had done, in 1917. His maternal grandmother was Queen Victoria. Mountbatten – eventually to become known among close associates and relatives as the real 'queen' in the royal family, because of his secret sexual preferences, accompanied Bertie, the Queen and the two little princesses to Dartmouth that July. It was Bertie's first visit to the naval college since his days there as an unhappy cadet some twenty years before. Mountbatten's nephew, Prince Philip, forced, with his parents, into exile from Greece, was among the latest cadet intake.

It was Mountbatten who 'suggested' that Cadet Captain Philip be the princesses' escort during their weekend visit. The eighteen-year-old show-off particularly impressed Elizabeth by leaping backwards and forwards over tennis nets. 'How high he can jump,' gasped the thirteen-year-old. Philip went on to steal a place in her heart by being in the last vessel of the tiny flotilla to turn away when they followed the royal yacht out of the harbour. He still rowed on when all others had turned back, until ordered back by the King who was concerned for his safety.

Observers at the time suspected the hand of Mountbatten in this neat piece of attention grabbing. Certainly, Elizabeth seemed well and truly hooked. She talked about the tall, good-looking, blond boy to anyone and everyone. It didn't occur to her, or to anyone else, that he was the first boy of that age to whom she had been allowed to get that close, nor that Philip's subsequent visits to call on the princesses were just as meticulously orchestrated by his uncle! Soon Philip's aunt, Princess Nicholas of Greece, would start to talk about his unrivalled qualifications for becoming Elizabeth's husband.

Six weeks later, nine-year-old Princess Margaret wanted to know: 'Who is this Hitler spoiling everything?'

'He and the rest are brutes,' said Elizabeth, mimicking her father.

The little princesses – by now the best known children in the world – were at Windsor when the Germans forced the British to retreat from France by way of Dunkirk. Whitehall mandarins immediately began drawing up plans for the evacuation of the royal family – the princesses, at least, it was thought, should be flown to Canada.

When the Queen was asked to comment, she said: 'The children will not leave unless I do. I shall not leave unless their father does, and the King will not leave the country in any circumstances whatsoever.'

Bertie installed a shooting range at Buckingham Palace and Windsor and practised with rifle and pistol. He would die fighting, defending his country and people if it came to it, he said. Margaret's reaction was just to carry on being herself, which was all that was ever expected of her.

During the blitz, the girls slept every night in the Windsor Castle dungeons and breakfasted and lunched with officers of the Grenadier Guards who were stationed there. Margaret would sit opposite her sister with an officer on either side. It was during these sessions that Margaret developed her lifelong love of gossip. Endless spicy titbits were collected each mealtime, for consideration and repetition later. Even at that age, her tongue was sharp and she was sometimes seen to leave young officers, ten years or more her senior, open-mouthed at her lightning repartee.

The first wartime pantomime was produced at Windsor. It was *Cinderella* with Margaret in the title role. On the morning of the performance, she had such a bad attack of stage fright that she stayed in bed, missing breakfast and lunch. Ten minutes before curtain up, however, at 2 pm, she was made up, in costume and raring to be the star of the show. This routine was repeated each year. Her stage fright never diminished but her determination to be centre stage always overcame her nerves at the last moment.

In 1942, at the age of sixteen, Elizabeth became honorary colonel-in-chief of her first regiment and began taking on minor public duties. Margaret tagged along whenever possible but was disappointed to find that she was almost invariably cut off the pictures that appeared in the newspapers. Because of a wartime shortage of newsprint, these had been reduced to only four pages.

'I've been censored again,' she would grin, but deep down she was very hurt at being ignored. She believed that the newspaper editors chopped her out because she was just a nobody, not because of shortage of space. It only increased her lasting determination to gain attention.

There were examples enough of Margaret constantly being pushed into second place. Elizabeth received one shilling (five new pence) a week as pocket money until she was fifteen. Margaret received nothing. She was also too young to join the ATS (Auxilliary Transport Service) in which Elizabeth was a subaltern and which allowed her to have trips to London and Camberley while Margaret remained a near prisoner in the castle.

Margaret learned to play the piano and to sing, while Elizabeth learned about constitutional rule. Elizabeth was being groomed for monarchy; Margaret's destiny – as foreseen by her parents – was to marry into the peerage and create her own dynasty. The King always pictured her, grown up, as mistress of a spectacular castle or ancestral home with a vast acreage of land – a mini queen, so to speak, with a mini court. He would not live to see that dream fail to materialise.

Crawfie painted a picture of Margaret's childhood which contradicted most other current versions. She described Margaret as being spoilt, wilful and resentful of being the second-born. Spoilt she definitely was, and the whole family is quick to endorse this. But wilful? That is strenuously denied by the family, particularly by Elizabeth. Margaret, too, has always denied resenting her sister's birthright and there is no outside evidence to support Crawfie's unique, though privileged, view.

Elizabeth was given her own apartment, with private sitting room, when she was sixteen, and went on to have a lady-in-waiting and a private secretary while still a teenager.

Bertie bought her a car of her own when she passed her driving test. Margaret had none of these things but she cheerfully accepted them as being her sister's by right. After all, she argued, the price of these added rewards – life dedicated to the service of the people – was not one that she would be willing to pay.

Parliament had granted Elizabeth a £40,000 a year Civil List allowance, to be received after she reached the age of 21. Margaret was granted only £6000 following her coming of age – and this was merely a parliamentary afterthought because Winston Churchill chose to plead her case personally.

On 5 May 1945, VE Day, Elizabeth and Margaret appeared on the palace balcony with their parents and Winston Churchill to be cheered by the huge throng below. Then they slipped out, unseen, with a group of young army officers and joined in cheering their parents from outside the palace.

Six weeks later came Japan's surrender and in August Princess Margaret and her family travelled north to Balmoral for their first peacetime holiday in six years.

There Margaret celebrated her fifteenth birthday – and said goodbye to her childhood. One of the royal family's guests was the King's equerry, dashing Battle of Britain fighter pilot hero Peter Townsend.

Margaret had decided that she was already in love with Townsend – who was then exactly twice her age.

For the last real princess, the time for real living had begun!

2

First Romance

Princess Margaret was in her twenty-first year when she embarked on her first real love affair, with 36-year-old Group Captain Peter Townsend, a dashing Battle of Britian war hero and Deputy Master of the King's Household. He was also married and the father of two children; a commoner on a modest income and a tight budget.

Other men had vied to be first in this unique enterprise. They were all immensely wealthy, landed gentlemen who were single and considered highly suitable consorts for the King's younger daughter.

The three principal contenders were Johnny Dalkeith, already an earl and heir to two dukedoms, nine years Townsend's junior and owner of three vast estates; 'Sunny' Blandford, the Duke of Marlborough's son and heir to his 11,500 acres; and Billy Wallace, a lanky playboy and gambler who had already inherited millions from his late father, a former Tory minister.

FIRST ROMANCE

Said Billy Wallace:

'The King would have pushed her towards Dalkeith, then towards Sunny. I would have been well down the list. It would have been almost a certainty that she would end up with an aristocratic husband and be mistress of vast estates. The thing with Townsend was a girlish nonsense that got out of hand. It was never the big thing on her part that people claim. I had my chance and blew it with my big mouth, or she would have become Mrs. Wallace: and I would have been able to handle her. Most men didn't stand a chance of coping with Margaret. Townsend less than most. He might have been a war hero but he was too wimpish when it came to dealing with her.

'He had only her. She could choose virtually anyone she wanted.'

The most amorous of her teenage flirtations was with Sunny Blandford, whom Margaret much preferred to the more conventionally dour Dalkeith. She even confided to her mother that she believed Blandford would make her an ideal husband.

'Had Sunny or Johnny proposed at that time then Margaret would have dropped Townsend like a hot potato,' said one member of her circle.

'But Sunny fell for one of Margaret's chums, Susan Hornby, whom he married in 1951, and Johnny began courting a former debutante and very sexy model, Jane McNeill. He spent Margaret's twenty-first and twenty-second birthdays with the princess but then announced his engagement to Jane whom he married in January 1953.

15

'The truth is that before her twenty-first birthday Margaret was already running out of serious suitors. And it was all her own fault. She had been spoilt to the core. Her father had granted her anything it was in his power to bestow, which was a fairly considerable amount, and he had given in to her every whim.

'The only position in which she felt comfortable was centre stage and that is the place she demanded – as her natural right. She was a princess first, second and third and insisted on being treated like one at all times.

'She saw everything in terms of black or white. There were no greys. She loved or she hated. You were good company or you were bad. Her rudeness was worse than anything I have ever witnessed. Her meanness was taken for granted.

'She is a woman who has never owned a credit card and never carried money – except for the church collection plate. She expected to be paid for by her escorts or her hosts. It would never have occurred to her to ask what anything cost. That was of no interest to her. If she wanted something she expected to get it.

'To be familiar – no matter after what length of time – was to face banishment. She had to be called "Ma'am" by everyone outside the royal family. There have not been any exceptions. To refer to "your sister" was an act of gross familiarity. The person would be fixed with an icy glare and told: "I think you mean Her Majesty the Queen".

'Young beaux came and went – usually banished in head-shaking bewilderment for completely misunderstood acts of gross familiarity which, even when explained to them afterwards, left them scarcely less bemused. Just touching her, even by accident, was certain to switch on the ice machine.

'Even regular members of her set occasionally fell foul of her acid tongue, but such was the status of being part of the Margaret "set" in the fifties that no one took umbrage – not even members of some of Britain's most noble families.

'No one criticised Dalkeith, Blandford or the rest for not pursuing Margaret to the altar. Rather, one admired them when they became engaged to others, for eliminating themselves so cleverly from the field.

'No one had any doubts what life with Margaret would be like. Here was a princess brought up in the Victorian mould. She was the last princess never to go to school; the last to be waited on hand and foot since birth. She was impossibly selfish, outrageously demanding and far too grown up and sophisticated for her years.

'She was also unbelievably theatrical. Anything and everything was done or said, so it seemed, for effect. She would touch up her lipstick at the table and smoke no matter where. Her addiction to cigarettes came from her father, Bertie, who was a virtual chain smoker. The tortoise-shell holder was her own affectation and used as a permanent prop.

'Most men were daunted by the mere prospect of trying to control her. They pictured a lifetime of evenings like this spent in the 400 or Les Ambassadeurs or in restaurants or at weekend parties, surrounded by people sycophantically pandering to Margaret's every whim – stretching on to the grave – and they became terrified.

'They would all give it a brief try. For, after all, there

are few men, given the chance, who could resist the kudos which would come from having a romantic fling with a king's daughter, even if they could boast of it only within a very tight circle of friends. But none – with the exception, perhaps, of Billy Wallace, who spent most of his waking moments at gambling clubs and race courses – seriously welcomed the idea of marriage to the princess.

'There had been hot kisses and cuddles exchanged between Margaret and some of her suitors on darkened terraces, in discreetly empty corridors and in starlit country gardens. But until Townsend, no one had managed to ignite sufficient passion in her to make her want to give up her body with total abandon.'

Princess Margaret was to take several lovers during her spinster years. In every case it was they who had to conform to her lifestyle; she never attempted to do things their way. Everything – even love – had to fit around her wants and her schedule.

Elizabeth's duty was to marry and produce a successor. Enviably, for someone at her level, she had married a man she loved and, despite Philip's macho tantrums and rumoured romantic escapades, she had made it endure. With no such obligation to the nation and family, Margaret's leanings to the hedonist lifestyle, with scant or no regard for convention, were not surprising to her contempories. Few expected more of her and none felt cause to raise so much as an eyebrow in criticism.

One of her occasional dates of that time, who has now reached retirement age, still remembers vividly the kisses they shared.

'She had the most incredibly deep blue eyes that, when they twinkled, which was often, promised everything a woman could promise a man. And she had full, soft lips which seemed to be inviting kisses.

'Princess Margaret was a very sensual, sexual woman. She was considered to be the most beautiful woman of her generation and women worldwide copied her in everything. Those who think that the press mania over Princess Diana is excessive today should have witnessed the press mania over Princess Margaret. Twice the number of photographers followed her around the world in the fifties and sixties as chase the Princess of Wales today.

'She was a tough lady who could control herself and everyone around her. But I also thought there was something very vulnerable about her too. She had an almost desperate need to be loved and wanted. She had been number two throughout her childhood. Being number one had become a major – I would say indispensable – prerequisite in her life.'

At the same time she was tightly locked into a system that almost dispensed with human needs. At the highest levels of society, marriages were frequently arranged for a variety of reasons, none necessarily being love. A royal princess could safely select her lovers from among those noble spouses. As her nephew, Prince Charles, could echo three decades later, Margaret's comment back then was: 'They are a part of royal history.'

Townsend, the man destined to be first to set loose all that simmering passion, was described by first-hand observers at the time as being 'too sensitive and gentle' to be typical of the ace fighterpilot genre. They noted an air of vulnerability, even weakness, in him, which appealed to Margaret and which was to become a hallmark of nearly all her future lovers.

Margaret met Townsend when she was thirteen and within weeks had developed a schoolgirl crush on the handsome RAF officer. At seventeen she was still infatuated and frequently showered him with unsolicited kisses after he had been commanded to take her riding.

By eighteen she was in love with him – or, more correctly, say friends, with the idea of being in love – although it took her a further two years to convince Townsend that she was sincere and sufficiently aware of what she was doing for him to allow himself to reciprocate fully. She wanted his medal-filled chest clutched close to her very ample bosom and his hands around her 24-inch waist. As with everything else to date, she got exactly what she wanted. That she was chasing another woman's husband didn't bring her a moment's concern, say those close to her. She wanted Peter; his wife was not a part of that equation. She didn't matter. That was the way it always happened. When Margaret wanted something, she almost invariably got it. Her father had nurtured that in her. At this stage of her need, nothing else mattered at all.

Was Townsend the greatest love of the princess's life or only a convenient and occasional lover who was elevated, by romantically and theatrically motivated visions of martyrdom on Margaret's part, to the role of possible husband – a position they both knew he could never aspire to?

From his memoirs, Townsend clearly believes the first version, that theirs was a great and unfulfilled love story. Some close to Margaret, however, believe she was never that committed. During their affair, she never stopped her amorous flirtations with other men or her contemplation of a suitable husband from among her blue-blooded circle of eligible bachelors. During their enforced separations, she rarely mentioned him and, within weeks of renouncing him, she was unofficially engaged to Billy Wallace.

Margaret was brought up in palaces and had a need to remain in them. The cost of marrying Peter Townsend was to give up her position, prestige and privy purse, probably to live as an exile abroad for at least five years with two step-sons and a modestly salaried husband. Margaret was in love with the idea of being a tragic heroine. Her love of theatre made the role irresistible, but some royal watchers at the time are convinced it was never more than a 'good part'.

The man cast in the role of Romeo to Margaret's Juliet was born in Rangoon in November 1914. In his schooldays he was remembered as being 'unusually keen on poetry' and 'not very good at maths'. This didn't prevent him from entering the RAF training college at Cranwell in 1933 or being commissioned as a pilot officer two years later.

The painfully shy young man with the dark, almost effeminate, good looks developed a virulent nervous eczema during his first posting in Singapore and was sent back to Britain after doctors recommended a complete break from flying. By the outbreak of war, however, he was again in excellent shape and in February 1940, while attached to Number 43 Squadron, based at Acklington in Northumberland, he was credited with shooting down the first German aircraft over England.

By April he had two more *Luftwaffe* kills to his credit and was awarded the DFC. The citation read: 'in each instance he displayed qualities of leadership, skill and determination of the highest order with little regard for his own safety'.

Then, in August, he, in turn, was shot down in the North Sea and rescued by a minesweeper. This incident barely interrupted his fighter base routine and, by September, after shooting down several more enemy aircraft, he added a bar to his DFC to which, in May 1941, having accumulated a total of eleven kills, was added a DSO.

In that summer he was again shot down, having to bale out, wounded and soaked in petrol, at 1,400 feet over Kent. In hospital, a toe was amputated and metal splinters were dug out of his leg. Townsend explained: 'But twenty months of day and night operations eventually reduced me to a nerve-racked, sleep-starved wreck. I was flying more like a tired chicken than an avenging angel.'

Prescribed barbiturates and grounded, Townsend was posted to Hertfordshire with the rank of wing commander. There he became a regular visitor to the house of a local brigadier who, remembering his own youth in the services, invited the young officers from the airbase to Sunday morning drinks. Helping to serve them was the brigadier's daughter, Rosemary Pawle. 'I could not wait to make her my wife, for life in those dangerous days seemed a brief, precarious thing. So, true to that wartime phenomenon, the urge to reproduce, we rushed hand in hand to the altar.' That was in July 1941. 'Exactly nine months later our first child was born,' he wrote.

Before that happy event, however, Townsend suffered a complete nervous breakdown and had to be hospitalised for three months.

After a full recovery and a spell in command of a Scottish-based squadron, Townsend rediscovered the thrill of combat flying and was made leader of a fighter squadron. He defended the English Channel in planes that were barely in a condition to fly and were flown by teenage pilots who had barely enough experience to fly them.

Squadron losses played heavily on the mind of its leader and Townsend developed a new emotion which he felt powerless to combat – fear. He wrote:

'I knew in my bones that I should never again be the pilot I once had been. I had gone too far down the hill ever to get to the top again. In my thoughts and visions I saw myself crashing, over and over again, to a horrible death. I was convinced I was going to die – an abject state of mind exactly the reverse to what I had felt during the heroic days of 1940 when I was convinced that I was going to live.

'The more I flew, and there could be no relenting, the more fear, stark degrading fear, possessed me. Each time I took off, I felt sure it would be the last.'

In late 1942 he was transferred to staff college and, in January 1943, given command of yet another fighter station in Kent. This led almost inevitably to a second nervous breakdown and, after treatment, a complete break with active service. He was sent to Scotland to take over a flight instruction unit.

Townsend was almost certainly saved from obscurity by a revolutionary decision by the King. George VI disapproved of the old tradition of sovereigns' equerries being selected from the privileged upper classes and was determined to modernise the system. He insisted that he should have young men who had proved themselves in any of the three services and from all walks of life.

Air Chief Marshall Sir Charles 'Peter' Portal was given the task of recommending a suitable young hero from his own service and immediately thought of Peter Townsend. He had performed countless deeds of valour on behalf of king and country and had a fighting record almost second to none. It seemed tremendously unfair that such a brave pilot should be more or less pensioned off to command a flying school because his very heroics had caused a crack-up.

On 16 February 1944, Townsend was summoned to Buckingham Palace to be appointed an equerry to King George VI. After being presented to the King, Townsend was being shown out into the corridor by Master of the Household Sir Piers Legh when the two royal princesses came racing from the far end. The King had tipped off his two daughters that a genuine and very handsome fighter pilot ace was in that part of the palace. They were introduced by Sir Piers who told them that Wing Commander Townsend would be temporarily assigned to the King's staff for three months.

It would be another nine years before he was forcibly transferred from royal service and banished to Brussels after his affair with Princess Margaret became public knowledge, although few people are aware that he remained a special equerry to the Queen for more than a decade after his final split with the princess.

According to Nigel Dempster, Princess Margaret remembers: 'My father became very fond of Peter. They both stammered and that was a bond. When he first appeared I had a terrific crush on him, but there was no question of a romance until much later – he was a married man.' With hindsight, that is the correct moral observation to make but, in reality, Margaret and Townsend's romance was being pursued well before his marriage had ended.

FIRST ROMANCE

After three months Townsend was confirmed in his new post and the King showed his growing fondness for his airman equerry by making him a neighbour in giving him a grace and favour residence – Adelaide Cottage – built as a tea house for Queen Adelaide, wife of William IV. The 'cottage' was really a substantial country house beside the Thames and within walking distance of the castle in Windsor Home Park. It was surrounded by trees and high yew hedges. The walls carried trellis work covered with roses and vines.

Princess Margaret quickly became the Townsends' most regular visitor. Sometimes she would spend a few minutes playing with the two boys and sometimes she would pause for a chat with Rosemary but it was obvious whom she had really come to see – Peter.

A woman who worked for the Townsends at the time remembers:

> 'She was only fourteen when she first started coming – sitting astride her big horse and looking wickedly pretty. "Come on, Peter, come and ride with me," is what she would say and if he made an excuse she would keep on at him until he changed his mind.
>
> 'Didn't matter if he had arranged to go out with his family or had urgent things to do in the house, she could always wheedle him into going. And then she would laugh out loud with real pleasure because she had got her own way.
>
> 'By the time she was nearly seventeen, she had the figure of a grown woman and she knew it and had learned to use it. There would always be an extra button or two undone at the neck of her blouse when she came calling on the group captain.

'Mrs. Townsend, I suspected, began to feel quite jealous around that time. And who would blame her. This young girl constantly chasing after her husband. What matter if she were a princess. It wasn't right. He may have said afterwards that he had no interest in her until after his divorce but I know the way he looked at her – and the way they touched each other when they thought no one was watching.

'She would lean out of the saddle to kiss his cheek and call "Thank you, dear Peter", when they returned from their rides. She would deliberately let her horse rub up against his so their legs could touch. She had the hots for him and nothing could have been plainer. He didn't stand a chance – poor love-sick man. It was clear that someone was going to get hurt because of that relationship. I thought it was going to be his wife or children. In the end it turned out to be Peter Townsend himself. One thing is certain. It was never going to be Princess Margaret.'

During the royal tour of South Africa in 1947, a wider audience had opportunity to see the growing affection between the teenage princess and her father's equerry.

Princess Margaret carried with her to South Africa a secret shared only by the closest members of the royal family. Princess Elizabeth had become engaged to Prince Philip who had proposed during a short leave spent at Balmoral the previous summer.

The King had given his permission only on condition that their engagement remained secret. To gain a permanent commission in the Royal Navy, Philip would need to become a naturalised British subject. With the restoration of the Greek royal family imminent, King

George VI felt it would be ill-timed for Philip, one of their number, to give up his Greek citizenship.

Jealous of this unmatchable piece of one-upmanship on her elder sister's part, Margaret determined to enjoy her infatuation for Townsend as best she could. During their 23,000-mile tour, she managed to spend most of her free time in his company, when he was not required by the King, horse-riding or exploring on foot or simply sitting and talking during the five weeks spent, in total, aboard the royal train.

Margaret returned to Britain believing that even if her bid to turn Townsend into her beau had not progressed to a more romantic level in Africa, their friendship had certainly developed. She felt confident she could confide in him totally and believed his loyalty to her to be absolute.

Townsend returned to Rosemary eulogising about South Africa and suggested that it was the perfect place for them to go and make a new life for themselves. She told him she thought he must be unbalanced even to suggest such a nonsensical idea. She and the children were happy in England and that's where they intended to stay.

The King had laughingly made Townsend Princess Margaret's guardian when he first became equerry. Now, as icy indifference began to cause his marriage to Rosemary to disintegrate, Townsend found himself beginning to see his royal charge through new eyes. Many years later he wrote:

'If her extravagant vivacity sometimes outraged the elder members of the household and of London society, it was contagious in those who still felt young – whether they were or not.

'She was capable in her face, and in her whole

being, of an astonishing power of expression. It could change in an instant from saintly, almost melancholic, composure to hilarious, uncontrollable joy. She was by nature generous, volatile.

'She was a comedienne at heart, played the piano with ease and loved to sing the latest hits, imitating her favourite stars.

'She was coquettish, sophisticated.'

Townsend had already begun to fall under her spell. On the family's return from South Africa, it was decided that Margaret could start to undertake more official engagements on her own, taking over some of those formerly handled by her sister.

Philip's naturalisation had finally been agreed and he had abandoned his Greek royal title and settled for Lieutenant Philip Mountbatten. The engagement was announced by Buckingham Palace on 10 July 1947, and he and Elizabeth were married on 20 November.

Meanwhile, Margaret had taken over the almost exclusive usage of Peter Townsend, with the full approval of the King and Queen. They had no inkling that the Townsend marriage was in trouble and trusted him implicitly with their daughter. They congratulated one another that she was in such safe hands.

By now Margaret was in love with Townsend. The childish crush and later teenage infatuation had blossomed into true love and she was determined to get her man – though not in marriage because that didn't occur to her. It was not even a possibility to be contemplated. Said a royal insider: 'She had felt his arms around her on the dance floor a score of times. Now she wanted them there for another reason. She had decided Peter was going to become her lover and once that young lady made up her mind to something, nothing or nobody was ever allowed to stop her.'

In September 1948, Margaret undertook her most important function of the year, the coronation of the new Dutch Queen, Juliana. She had celebrated her eighteenth birthday in August and went to the Netherlands acting, for the first time, as the King's personal representative. She insisted that Townsend accompany her. In her floor-length pink dress and pink ostrich-feather hat, she looked stunningly beautiful. Margaret was the popularly acclaimed people's favourite after Queen Juliana herself and this was acknowledged when the princess, despite the presence of a host of senior European royals, was chosen to inspect the guard of honour outside the royal palace.

Photographers surrounded her and, when she took to the dance floor with her father's handsome equerry, several of them speculated on their possible relationship. Margaret danced with her eyes closed and her head resting on Peter's chest. He said later that he had no idea of her feelings for him until nearly three years later. If so, then he was either the only man in the ballroom that night who did not interpret her feelings for him correctly or he was a simpleton. And whatever else he may have been, Townsend was nobody's fool.

Margaret hardly took her eyes off Townsend during the full four days of their trip and seized every possible excuse to take his arm or lean on him and devour him with looks of love. Back in Britain, whenever he was on duty she contrived to see him twice or three times a day. When he was off duty in Windsor she now commanded, rather than demanded, that he ride with her and there were fewer and fewer excuses why he shouldn't.

Said the Townsend domestic: 'The group captain knew exactly how she felt about him by then. And he was crazy for her. His wife would have been blind not to know it too. But theirs was a marriage in name only by this time and I don't think she really let his thing with Margaret bother her all that much.'

Townsend accompanied the royal family to Balmoral each summer. It was usual for equerries to spend two weeks on the Scottish estate but Townsend purported to like it so much that he would always extend his tour.

The King's Highland castle retreat, set amid over 40,000 acres of heather and grouse moor, has been the royal family's favourite home since Queen Victoria bought it in 1848. Townsend was there for the family's centenary celebrations in 1948. Balmoral was, and still is, used by the royals as a testing place for potential newcomers into their circle of friends. If they can emerge from a visit there without having made fools of themselves or broken any of the weird taboos or rituals that the royals have established over generations – of which there are many and, to make it even harder, none is ever explained to outsiders – then they have a good chance of becoming permanent fixtures in royal family life.

Townsend loved Balmoral and slotted into the often bizarre routine with just the appropriate behaviour and style. He was to be a regular guest and favourite there for the next four years.

In April and May 1949, Margaret visited Italy and Paris and her every action became front page news across the European continent. In Italy she was hailed as 'La bella Margherita' and in Paris every man she danced with at a charity ball was put forward in the press as a prospective bridegroom. But the man chiefly on her mind was in

England and she couldn't wait to see him. So anxious was she to be with Peter again that she had him summoned to meet her plane at London airport on her return, even though this was totally superfluous to his duties as the King's equerry.

When Townsend flew in the King's Cup Air Race later that year, it was in a Miles Whitney Straight entered by Princess Margaret.

During the summer vacation at Balmoral, Margaret suggested that they revive a tradition started by Queen Victoria, who had decreed that a small cairn of stones, within sight of the castle, be built to celebrate particularly happy family events. Each day, on that and subsequent trips to Balmoral, while out riding, they would gather a stone each and lay them side by side on a low hillock. Their cairn still stands as a reminder of what might have been.

3

Days of Wine and Roses

In 1950 Elizabeth may have been heir presumptive to the throne but Margaret was already 'queen' of the West End of London. By her twentieth birthday, her sister had already given birth to a son and a daughter, ensuring the succession and putting Margaret, as she joked at the time, on the brink of royal redundancy.

With a sophistication and presence far in advance of her years, Margaret was already a confirmed hedonist. On VE night, George VI had written in his diary of his daughters: 'Poor darlings, they have never had any fun yet.' Added the Queen: 'We are only young once. We want them to have a good time.'

If she had lacked fun as a youngster, Margaret was determined to make up for it now and with the full blessing of her parents. At last life had really begun for this most extraordinary royal maverick. She became the life and soul of every major society party. A party without her, it was claimed, was not deserving of the name. Theatrical by nature and inclination, she was a born performer. The bigger the audience the better the act. In those heady days of the early fifties, no pop star was subjected to the adulation lavished on Princess Margaret.

She would go to bed at 4 am and languish there until amost midday. She was a prima donna – vastly intriguing to men, full of charm and wit – a natural leader of the pack with a million-volt charisma. Yet there was also a defiant streak in her, which invited conflict and, just occasionally, a glimpse of a little girl lost and looking for reassurance, a strong pair of arms and someone to love her just for herself.

The club owners loved her. Single-handedly she had made night club going not only fashionable and acceptable but fun. Their only regret was that she hated champagne. Had bubbly been her tipple, then sales of that most expensive of club drinks would have rocketed.

At Les Abassadeurs, band leader Paul Adam encouraged her to join in at the piano and sing. On other nights she would be in the 400 in Leicester Square or in the Milroy Club. Sometimes she would visit all three in a single evening.

Most weekends, if not at Windsor, were spent in the country homes of friends – a habit she later returned to after the break-up of her marriage. In some of these rambling old mansions, a good many amorous activities went on and, as she neared her twenty-first birthday, unattached and fancy free, Margaret was not averse to participating in the odd, romantic adventure. On these occasions thoughts of Peter Townsend seemed very far away.

Gossip was the life blood of their night-time existence and, in other circumstances, Margaret's fondness for a juicy story could have earned her a columnist's job with any tabloid newspaper. She demanded to know all the latest titbits, especially the ones featuring herself. The names of a host of young blue bloods were coupled with hers, but no one thought less of her for her escapades. For those who had grown up in and around royal circles, it was considered quite normal behaviour for a young princess to hone her talent for love on her father's highest-born subjects.

Her life became split in two. The nights and weekends belonged almost exclusively to that group of fun-loving, financially well-endowed young aristocrats who were the premier Hooray Henrys of their day and made up the nucleus of the 'set'. The days were for the occasional royal engagement, her beloved papa and Peter Townsend.

In August 1950, the King had rewarded Townsend's hard work and loyalty by appointing him Deputy Master of the Household. This also brought him a large, green-carpeted office in Buckingham Palace and easy access to Margaret just one floor above. Townsend later wrote of that period:

'But what ultimately made Princess Margaret so attractive and lovable was that behind the dazzling facade, the apparent self-assurance, you could find, if you looked for it, a rare softness and sincerity.

'She could make you bend double with laughing; she could also touch you deeply in your heart.

'I was but one among many to be moved. There were dozens of others; their names were in the papers and the papers vied with each other, frantically but futilely, in their forecasts of the one whom she would marry.

'I dare say there was no one more touched by the princess's joie de vivre than I.

'The time was 1951 and with my own wartime marriage disintegrating it gave me what I most lacked – joy.

'More, it created a sympathy between the princess and myself and I began to sense that, in her life too, there was something lacking.'

The one nagging conern for Margaret during this whole period was the health of her father. Although she had always been prone to illness herself and had suffered almost endless bouts of minor ailments: colds, influenza, measles, etc., during her teens she had begun to suffer from recurring and often severe attacks of migraine. Her father's health problems, however, were far more serious and, although the truth about his condition was usually kept from her by his doctors, she was intelligent enough to gather that his recurrent illnesses were life-threatening. At one stage he was ordered to bed for weeks when doctors feared that circulation problems in his legs might cause gangrene and necessitate amputation. Margaret had her piano moved outside his door so that she could play and sing for him.

When Elizabeth married and moved to Clarence House, Margaret had assured her father that she would provide him with as much daily love as if he still had two daughters living with him. She made sure he received his full, daily quota of hugs and kisses. Courtiers who were then close to the King say that he knew of the strong affection by then existing between Margaret and Townsend but chose to ignore it rather than take any action because he believed she deserved the happiness she was experiencing and because he did not think it would ever come to anything other than a passing romance.

A Scottish observer much later revealed how, one day at Balmoral, two picnic baskets were brought out to two waiting estate wagons destined for a visit to Loch Muich. A servant picked up one of the hampers to put it in the back of the second vehicle and the King asked sharply: 'Why aren't both baskets going in my car?'

The Queen answered: 'Margaret and Peter are going for a picnic of their own.'

'Oh no they're not. We're all going together,' was his response, and the King and Queen drove off with both hampers. After a glance at Peter, Margaret shrugged her shoulders and they climbed into the second car and followed her parents.

Bertie very obviously had his own suspicions of what his equerry and Margaret were capable of getting up to if left alone for the afternoon in one of the sunny, rarely visited vales on the moors.

Prince Philip certainly did not share the King's fondness for Townsend, to whom the prince's love of grouse shooting did not appeal at all. He found the RAF ex-fighter pilot too gentle and sensitive by far and sneered at his habit of riding with the women in the morning before accompanying them to the grouse moors to join the men for a picnic lunch. On one occasion Philip was still shooting when Townsend arrived, chattering to the ladies. 'For God's sake be quiet,' he shouted at the hapless equerry.

Said a palace insider: 'Philip never really liked any of Margaret's boyfriends. He said he didn't think there was a stiff-wristed one among them.'

Fortunately, Townsend found himself more in the company of the King and Queen and Margaret than with Philip and his fellow guns. Some years ago, Townsend told renowned Fleet Street columnist Jean Rook: 'It's a great myth that Prince Philip was out to get me. But, if he was, or if he did when I wasn't around, I wasn't aware of it. He's a hard hitting extrovert, not my sort of man, but I liked him.'

The feelings were not exactly mutual. Future events would find Philip not well disposed to their marriage, but in that summer of 1951 the princess and Townsend were oblivious to almost everything but each other. It was almost as though they knew there was a time limit on their shared future.

Occasionally, they couldn't help letting slip hints of their secret romance. Townsend recalls:

'One day after a picnic lunch with the guns, I stretched out in the heather to doze. Then, vaguely, I was aware that someone was covering me with a coat.

'I opened one eye – to see Princess Margaret's lovely face very close, looking into mine. Then I opened the other eye and saw, behind her, the King, leaning on his stick, with a certain look, typical of him: kind, bland, half-amused.

'I whispered: "You know you're father is watching us?" At which she laughed, straightened up and went to his side. Then she took his arm and walked him away, leaving me to my dreams.'

Not watching 'you' or 'me' but 'us' – the sure words of a lover knowing they were a couple being observed.

That same month, Townsend walked into the dining

room to see the Queen frowning at him. He was puzzled at her reaction until he looked at the table-seating board. Someone had taken his card and switched it so that he was placed next to Princess Margaret.

Yet Townsend still maintained in his memoirs that he didn't have the slightest idea of Margaret's feelings for him until after his divorce in December 1952. I can only assume he says this to preserve Margaret from embarrassment. Even the regulars at Balmoral commented on their hand-holding, cheek-stroking activities. 'They were obviously crazy about one another,' said one witness. Townsend and Margaret had been involved romantically for years by then. And their romance was in full spate a year before she was twenty-one.

On the twenty-first of that month, August, two of Margaret's still single favourites, Johnny Dalkeith and Billy Wallace, joined the small family party for her twenty-first birthday celebration and, in so doing, each became strongly tipped to become Margaret's husband.

Wrote Townsend:

'Tommy Lascelles [the King's private secretary] favoured Johnny – with some feeling perhaps, for Johnny's mother, the Duchess of Buccleuch, was a Lascelles. Drily, Tommy remarked to me: "Dalkeith and the princess were making sheep's eyes at each other last night at dinner." That, as far as Tommy was concerned, apparently clinched matters.

'But he was mistaken. The princess had many friends and not a few suitors, yet among none of them had she found the man of her choice. That, incredibly, was the lot destiny had reserved for me.'

DAYS OF WINE AND ROSES

On their return from Balmoral, leading chest surgeon Clement Price Thomas examined Bertie and diagnosed cancer. He recommended an immediate operation for the removal of the King's left lung, to be carried out in hospital. Bertie would have none of it. 'I've never heard of a king go to hospital before,' he complained. He had his wish and the operation was carried out on 23 September in the Buhl Room in Buckingham Palace. Princess Margaret was appointed a Counsellor of State for the first and last time during her father's reign in case he did not survive the operation.

During surgery, Mr. Thomas discovered that the King's other lung was also affected, as were certain nerves in the larynx. The latter were removed, although Mr. Thomas feared that the King might never speak in more than a faint whisper for the rest of his life, which he doubted would extend beyond two years.

In October, the King's recovery was sufficiently advanced for Elizabeth and Philip to go ahead with a planned tour of the United States and Canada, although their luggage included a black dress, hat and veil and a Declaration of Accession in case Bertie should suffer a relapse.

Margaret was with him almost constantly during his convalescence. Confirming the doctor's fears, he could speak to her only in a whisper but she did most of the talking, keeping him up to date on Elizabeth's progress in North America and making him laugh with stories about her society friends.

'An operation is not an illness,' Bertie told Margaret. 'We're off to South Africa again in the spring. Peter will go down ahead and make sure everything is in good shape.'

On 2 December, a day of national thanksgiving was held in churches all over Great Britain to celebrate the King's return to health. After a quiet fifty-sixth birthday with the Queen and his daughters and son-in-law in Buckingham Palace, he travelled with them to Sandringham for Christmas and a much anticipated outing with the guns. There, a section at a time, his Christmas speech was recorded in advance to avoid the stress of a live broadcast.

In January, Townsend flew out to inspect the royal family's official residence in Durban and give instructions for opening it up for the visit of the King and Queen and Princess Margaret, planned for March. Meanwhile, it was decided by Bertie that Elizabeth and Philip should undertake a tour of East Africa, Australia and New Zealand, which he acknowledged would be out of the question for him to make as had been mooted early in the previous year.

On 30 January, Elizabeth and Philip accompanied the King and Queen to Drury Lane Theatre to see *South Pacific*. Peter Townsend, back from South Africa, escorted Princess Margaret to complete the party.

Next morning, in a bitterly cold wind, Bertie stood bareheaded on the tarmac at London Airport (now Heathrow) and waved goodbye to his daughter and heir as she and her husband boarded an Argonaut of the BOAC fleet. Again, in her luggage were the mourning weeds and draft Accession Declaration. This time, sadly, palace foresight would not be wasted. It was to be their last farewell. Elizabeth would return to Britain as its Queen.

On 5 February, the King felt well enough to take part in the annual, keeper's day hare hunt, a traditional Sandringham end-of-season celebration. He took a good bag and was in high spririts when the Queen and Princess Margaret joined him for dinner after an afternoon spent visiting a local artist. After dinner, they listened to a news broadcast about Elizabeth's activities that day in Kenya and then Margaret played the piano as Bertie glanced through some of the newspapers. At 10.30, declaring himself tired after a day with the guns, he kissed his wife and daughter goodnight and went to bed, to read while sipping a mug of cocoa.

The next morning the Queen told Margaret that her beloved papa had died, peacefully, during the night, of a heart attack.

Queen Elizabeth II, who had received the news of her accession atop a tree in Kenya, returned to London the following day to be greeted by her prime minister, Winston Churchill, with tears rolling down his cheeks.

That evening, she travelled to Sandringham where she received her first curtsy from Margaret, who now felt herself to be very much alone. She remembered later that she received little support in her grief. The nation seemed to allot all its sympathy to Bertie's widow and the new Queen. When prayers of sympathy were said in churches around the country, only the names of Queen Elizabeth and the Queen Mother were mentioned; Margaret's name was never included.

A second-born, just like her, the King had showered Margaret with love to show her that she was equally as important to him as his heir. Now events were proving to her that first-born did mean a great deal more after all. With George VI alive, she was in the main stream, a daughter of the ruling king. As sister of the Queen, she was relegated, in her own mind, to second division, a different branch of the family, in her own royal cul-de-sac.

For comfort, Margaret turned to her faith – in which she had retained a simple devotion – and in the months following her father's death she attended numerous Christian lectures, classes and discussion groups, including private sessions with the new Archbishop of Canterbury, to try to come to terms with the changes in her life.

At the same time, she also turned for comfort to Townsend, whose own grief for the King was distressingly and touchingly deep, and who provided a shoulder to cry on.

Amazingly, the Queen and Philip, together with Margaret, lunched with Townsend and Rosemary at Adelaide Cottage in June of that year, although three of those present, the Townsends and Margaret, knew that the marriage was already in the process of divorce. Despite this, the Queen and Philip were not given the slightest hint that anything was other than normal. This subterfuge by omission would be remembered by Philip when the need arose for his powerful support for their proposed marriage.

In December, Townsend was awarded a decree nisi against his wife and given legal custody of their sons, who were, by mutual consent, left in Rosemary's care. John de Lazlo, son of the portrait painter, Philip, for whom the late King had once posed, was cited and married Rosemary two months later.

For the twelve months following the King's death, Margaret more or less withdrew from public life and her nightly ride on the night club merry-go-round. Instead, she took rides of a different kind, and walks too, usually with Peter Townsend. He remembered that they talked while walking on the hills, among the heather, with the breeze in their faces; or riding in the Great Park at Windsor, along the driveways of venerable oaks and beeches, or through the pinewoods and across the stubble. He says that her understanding, far beyond her years, touched him and helped him. With her wit and jokes she, more than anyone else, made him laugh – and, as he pointed out, laughter between boy and girl often lands them in each other's arms.

Townsend concedes that, in the New Year of 1953, he realised he had fallen in love with Margaret, and she with him. This timing puts it conveniently a few weeks after his divorce. He claims he confessed his love to Margaret in the red drawing room at Windsor Castle while the rest of the family were in London. After listening to him pour out his feelings, she is said to have replied: 'That is exactly how I feel too.'

This version suggests that the evidence of friends, servants and courtiers – and even their own families – was incorrect and that their relationship before this date was one of close friendship only, that between a family retainer and the boss's daughter.

The truth, much more certainly, is that this was the first time that marriage was discussed between them. With Townsend now divorced as the innocent party, it must have seemed to both of them that marriage had become, at the very least, a faint possibility.

Its timing also coincided with Margaret feeling at her most vulnerable. She had just learned that she and the Queen Mother were to move at Easter. It would be their final departure from Buckingham Palace, which had been her home, as the King's favourite daughter, for over sixteen years. To this 22-year-old the future seemed uncertain and her own status equally so.

At that moment, marriage to someone whom she had secretly loved throughout her teens and who had played an integral and essentially personal role in her daily life for more than nine years, must have appeared to offer a more secure future than the unpredictable alternative as a single woman.

For whatever reason, one thing is uncontradictable. Margaret chose to go to the Queen and declare her love for Townsend and his for her.

The Queen greeted her sister's bombshell with characteristic calm. She invited Margaret and Townsend to dine with her and Philip at Buckingham Palace that same evening. Margaret remembered that Philip cracked a number of jokes in rather bad taste about their predicament.

Townsend had the feeling that, behind the Queen's goodwill, she must have been harbouring thoughts she did not refer to. 'Prince Philip, as was his way, may have tended to look for the funny side in this,' wrote Townsend. 'I did not blame him. A laugh here and there did not come amiss and that evening we had several.

'If, as has been alleged, he was indeed instrumental in blocking Princess Margaret's marriage to me, he doubtless had his reasons. But he did not raise them that evening.'

The Queen's calm reaction was very unlike that of her private secretary, Tommy Lascelles, who was appalled when Townsend, believing him to be a friend and ally, told of his and Margaret's love for each other. He replied: 'You must be either mad or bad.'

Some say that it was out of a misguided sense of loyalty to the dead King; some say that it was out of jealousy because his cousin, Dalkeith, had not become betrothed to the princess; and some say that it was sheer bloody-mindedness because he did not like either Margaret or Townsend, but it seems that Lascelles schemed and manoeuvred from that moment on to prevent the marriage from going ahead.

Contemptibly, he made it clear to the couple that their marriage was not an impossibility but, behind the scenes, while pretending to smooth their path, he did everything in his power to thwart their plans.

Margaret said later: 'Had he told us there was no chance of us getting married then we would have thought no more about it. Peter could have gone his own way and I mine and that would have been the end of it.' After learning of his treacherous double dealing, Margaret declared her everlasting loathing of the man and swore that she would curse him to the grave.

When the Queen sought his advice on the matter, Lascelles told her that Townsend should be found an official post abroad immediately. Effectively, he should be banished.

Without informing the Queen, Lascelles then scurried off to Winston Churchill and made the same suggestion. The Prime Minister, who saw scandal and a constitutional crisis in the making, concurred with Lascelles and, at his next audience with the Queen, he, too, pressed for Townsend's removal abroad.

However, the Queen was highly reluctant to take away her sister's newly found happiness and decreed that the whole question be shelved until after the coronation on 2 June. Until then, Townsend should stay on in his new post as Comptroller of the Queen Mother's Household. He would also continue to occupy the tiny house between Clarence House and St James's Palace, which contained his office and sleeping quarters.

In fact, the biggest impediment to the marriage was the Royal Marriage Act of 1772. Instigated by King George III, it was specifically designed to prevent undesirable marriages between the descendants of the king and such persons as might bring the crown into disrepute. If a monarch withheld consent to a marriage, then the petitioner, if under the age of 25, must wait. The marriage could go ahead at that age but only if neither House of Parliament, which must have received written notice, objected and if all the parliaments of the dominions consented as well.

Lascelles made it quite clear to the Queen that, being head of the Church of England and Defender of the Faith, because Townsend was a divorced man, she could not constitutionally give her consent to the marriage unless specifically advised to do so by the Prime Minister. Churchill's reply to the Queen was an unequivocal 'No'. He added with typical bluntness that Margaret had best wait until her twenty-fifth birthday.

Because of this decision, the full ramifications of the Act were never properly explained to Margaret until those two years had elapsed. Had they been, she said, she and Townsend would have abandoned all thoughts of marriage right away.

Almost as disgraceful was the way in which the Queen's press secretary, Commander Richard Colville – a former naval paymaster with no experience of dealing with the media, and urged on by his crony Lascelles – kept Margaret and Townsend completely in the dark about what was happening in the foreign press.

In the United States and on the European continent, the affair between Princess Margaret and a divorced RAF officer had become headline news. As had happened in 1936 over the Edward VIII and Mrs. Simpson affair, the British press remained silent. However, as then, this was not a state of affairs that could remain hushed up indefinitely.

Had Margaret and Townsend been properly briefed by Colville, they might have been on their guard but they continued in the belief that their secret was shared only by close members of the royal family, senior advisors and politicians. It only required one telling move or gesture on their part to launch Fleet Street into action but nobody, least of all those whose responsibility it was – Colville and Lascelles – bothered to warn them.

Such a gesture – so utterly simple but so damningly revealing – happened on Coronation Day, 2 June, in the Great Hall at Westminster where a large crowd of royals, peers and commoners had gathered after the abbey ceremony.

As Margaret stood chatting to Townsend, looking, in his words, superb, sparkling, ravishing, she reached out and brushed a bit of fluff off his uniform. This innocent but intimate gesture was just what the many newspapermen, assembled in the hall, had been waiting for to confirm the rumours of romance.

Abroad, the story was headline news the next day. In Britain, royal self-congratulations over the success of the coronation and its attendant celebrations were somewhat premature. For, twelve days later, on 14 June, the *People* newspaper – renowned for its sensation-mongering – used one of Fleet Street's oldest tricks to bypass palace privilige. It printed the foreign stories in order to refute them.

Under a banner headline it thundered:

'It is high time for the British public to be made aware of the fact that scandalous rumours about Princess Margaret are racing around the world. Newspapers in both Europe and America are openly asserting that the princess is in love with a divorced man and that she wishes to marry him.

'Every newspaper which has printed the story names the man as Group Captain Peter Townsend, Equerry to the Queen and formerly Deputy Master of the Household.

'The story is, of course, utterly untrue. It is quite unthinkable that a Royal Princess, third in line of succession to the throne, should even contemplate a marriage with a man who has been through the divorce courts.'

After revealing that it was Townsend who had secured the decree nisi, the *People* concluded: 'But his innocence cannot alter the fact that a marriage between Princess Margaret and himself would fly in the face of Royal and Christian tradition.'

Lascelles and Colville immediately advised the Queen that the rest of the national press could not possibly be expected to remain silent after the *People*'s broadside. Townsend must go, and quickly. After a meeting of the Cabinet, Churchill told her that they were unanimously against the marriage, as were the Commonwealth prime ministers. His advice was the same as Lascelles's. Townsend must go.

Moreover, the Royal Air Force were to be forced to conive in booting one of their own heroes out of the country. Churchill had ordered the Air Minister, Lord de L'Isle, to find an immediate overseas posting for Townsend. There were three vacancies for an air attaché: in Singapore, Johannesburg and Brussels. Townsend argued that, having just obtained custody of his sons, who were to go to school in England, it would be callously unfair to post him to South Africa or Singapore. Fearing a fresh scandal if they objected, the government agreed to his very reasonable request but they had other ways of bringing him to heel.

By now, Margaret and Townsend had accepted that all thoughts of marriage should be put on hold, probably for two years.

On 30 June, Townsend was to have accompanied Margaret and the Queen Mother on a tour starting in Salisbury, Rhodesia (now Zimbabwe). At the last minute, this was vetoed by Lascelles and Townsend was replaced by Lord Patrick Plunkett, who would also succeed him as Deputy Master. When the BOAC Comet took off from London Airport, Margaret was without her lover but his kisses were still fresh on her lips and she could partly console herself with thoughts of the passionate reunion they had planned that morning.

Before finally agreeing to leave on the tour, Margaret had been assured that Townsend would not take up his new appointment abroad until after her return on 17 July. When they kissed goodbye in the privacy of Clarence House on the morning of her departure, they had cheered each other up with promises of a more intimate reunion-cum-farewell on her return.

On the following day, 1 July, Townsend performed his last duty as equerry to the Queen – a visit to Belfast, the capital of Northern Ireland. It was an extremely agreeable visit, he recalled, until, in the middle of the civic luncheon, Colville, either stupidly or maliciously, chose to release a palace press statement announcing Townsend's appointment as air attaché to the British Embassy in Brussels.

For the rest of the visit the press corps photographers

concentrated more on snapping Townsend than the Queen and the announcement of his banishment completely eclipsed the royal visit in the following day's newspapers.

Some believed it was planned this way by Lascelles, aided and abetted by Colville, so that the date of Townsend's departure would be speeded up and he would be out of the country when Margaret returned. It would be difficult for the press to keep a romance alive if the interested parties were in separate countries.

Lascelles told the Queen that the longer Townsend remained in Britain, the more chance there would be of further sensationalised press coverage embarrassing to the royal family.

He was supported by Colville, Churchill and a number of other courtiers anxious to curry favour by climbing on an anti-Townsend and Margaret bandwagon. This kind of spineless individual still exists in the corridors of Buckingham Palace – eager to join the attack on any fringe royal or in-law who becomes unpopular or vulnerable.

In Townsend's case it worked and he was sent into exile in Brussels two days before Margaret returned from her African tour. 'Instead of our final, expected farewell, we were torn apart,' said Townsend. When she discovered how she had been tricked, Margaret's anger was fierce. She telephoned Townsend in Brussels in tears but he advised her that it was too late to do anything about it. All they could do now was wait.

4

Lost Love

The palace had been scared to put any pressure on Margaret to give Townsend up before her trip in case she threw a wobbly and, like her Uncle David, renounced the lot to marry and be damned. Now they had time on their side; time to build an implacable opposition to her marriage plans if they re-emerged in two years' time; time to win the Queen – still undecided – completely round to their way of thinking.

Winston Churchill would lead the attack. He had vowed that nothing should be allowed to detract from the moral and spiritual benefits of this new Elizabethan Age. He was supported by his cabinet, the Attorney General, Sir Lionel Heald, Lascelles and Colville, a handful of faceless courtiers and Prince Philip. The Queen's husband and counsellors were determined that she should fulfil her obligations to the country as they saw them.

Between them, Margaret and Townsend had not a single champion at court.

What the Queen had not told her sister – and it was a sorry omission – was that Winston Churchill had advised her that it was unlikely that Parliament would approve the marriage even after Margaret attained 25. The only way she would ever marry Townsend was by renouncing the right of succession for herself, her heirs and descendants, by forfeiting her (then) annual Civil List payment of £6,000 and almost certainly having to live in exile for at least five years.

Had she known this, Margaret would never have kept a candle (however much it flickered and was nearly extinguished at times) burning for her banished lover over the next two years.

Those close to Margaret believe it was wicked of the Queen not to have laid this establishment declaration before Margaret and Townsend before his departure for Brussels and given them the option of calling the whole thing off.

Although it must be said that the Queen was a raw beginner in her job and was being manipulated by Winston Churchill, one of the most devious and bullying politicians of the century, this did not prevent Margaret from condemning Elizabeth bitterly two years later for holding her tongue and thus prolonging an impossible situation with false hope. She never forgave Lascelles and although he retired to a grace and favour home in Kensington Palace and lived a few yards from her doorstep until his death in 1981, she never spoke to him again.

On the tail of Townsend's banishment, the *Daily Mirror* polled its readers, asking them 'Should they marry?' In answer, 67,907 *Mirror* romantics voted 'Yes'. Only 2,235 said 'No!'

LOST LOVE

Future Labour Party leader Michael Foot, then editor of *Tribune*, wrote in his independent, socialist weekly:

> '*Tribune* believes that Princess Margaret should be allowed to make up her own mind whom she wants to marry. Most other people, we imagine, would agree with that simple proposition. But the British Cabinet does not agree...
>
> 'The incident is not made any more savoury by our knowledge that three members of the present Cabinet (Sir Anthony Eden, Sir Walter Monckton and Mr. Peter Thorneycroft) have themselves been involved in divorce cases.'

However, no amount of words was going to undo what Margaret's enemies, at court and in the palaces of Westminster and Lambeth, had already achieved. By the end of July, as Townsend settled down to an air attaché's life in Brussels, an amendment to the Regency Act, ordered by the Queen, came into force, making Princess Margaret feel even more insignificant. It meant that she would no longer be her sister's understudy. Now, if Elizabeth should die or become permanently incapacitated, it would be Philip who would become regent and guardian of the King, not Margaret.

Four days later, the Queen and Philip left on a six-month tour of the Commonwealth.

By this time, Margaret had a new 'best girl friend' in the shape of Judy Montagu, grand-daughter of Britain's most prominent Jew and merchant banker, Lord Swaythling. Judy, 30 years old and wealthy, was also very funny and very bright and, in addition, brought to the Margaret 'set' Colin Tennant, a 26-year-old aristocrat whose hedonistic tendencies were almost the equal of Margaret's.

They had met occasionally in the past but this introduction into the set proper was to be the real start of what was to prove a lifelong friendship. Within a year, they had embarked on a romance.

That winter, through Judy, Margaret became involved in the production of a charity play, staged in the West End. *Lord and Lady Algy* featured Townsend's successor, Lord Plunkett, Porchester and Raine Legge, then better known as romantic novelist Barbara Cartland's daughter but destined to become Countess Spencer, Princess Diana's stepmother.

It certainly didn't warrant the press coverage it received but that did encourage the company, drawn mainly from the Margaret 'set', and Judy, to plan a more ambitious production for 1954. This time they chose *The Frog*, an Edgar Wallace thriller, and the Queen, Philip and the Queen Mother attended one of the three performances at the Scala Theatre in June. Porchester played a Cockney police sergeant. Billy Wallace had the detective lead. The Duke of Devonshire was a prison governor and Raine Legge was, again, the heroine. There were ten titled players in the cast, including Lord Brooke.

Although prevented by protocol from having an acting part, Margaret was associate director and went on stage at the end of the brief run to announce that £10,000 had been raised for the Invalid Children's Aid Association.

Each night after the performance, the whole cast would gather in the Milroy Club or the 400 to tease or congratulate one another on their acting, or to commiserate on forgotten lines and to drink and dance until 4 am. First to take to the dance floor with Margaret every night, on those and any other occasions, was Colin Tennant. In reviewing the play in his diary, Noël Coward wrote: 'The whole evening was one of the most fascinating exhibitions of incompetence, conceit and bloody impertinence that I have ever seen in my life.' This didn't dampen the cast's spirits or exuberant self-satisfaction in the slightest!

The Townsend affair seemed forgotten by everyone except Princess Margaret. The Queen and the Queen Mother, who knew they could never condone the marriage no matter how sympathetic they felt towards Margaret, reasoned between them that the longer it remained unmentioned, the more chance there was of her falling in love with someone else. Those close to the royal family watched the developing relationship between the princess and Colin Tennant and hoped for the best.

What none of them knew, or even suspected, was that in direct disobedience of Churchill's orders, the last the prime minister gave before his stroke, that he stay out of Britain for a full two years, Townsend was secretly slipping into the country for clandestine nights and weekends of passion with Margaret in the country homes of trusted friends. One such meeting actually took place in Clarence House in July, a month after *The Frog* production and just a few weeks before Margaret agreed to accompany Tennant to the northern estate he would one day inherit from his father.

Margaret herself had plotted and arranged all the details: 'Just like in a spy film'. Townsend, booked in under the name of Carter, flew in from Brussels and went directly to the book department in Harrods. One of Margaret's trusted aides, a brigadier, was sent to meet him there and take him by car to Clarence House. For the first time Margaret's insistence on having her own front door to her apartment within Clarence House was put to good purpose. She was able to spend several blissful hours with him in strictest privacy before he was driven back to Heathrow and his return flight to Brussels. It thrilled the princess that these secret visits did not become known to the press until well after the affair was over.

It was hardly, then, as a tragic, love-starved princess (which observers believed her to be in the summer of 1954) that Margaret, accompanied by her close friend Elizabeth Cavendish, took up Colin Tennant's invitation to stay at Glen, the family's 9,000 acre estate in Peeblesshire.

After a relaxed and, friends rumoured, romantic sojourn there, Margaret asked Tennant to accompany her to Balmoral for her birthday celebrations on 21 August. The two had been a society 'item' for several months. Their growing affection for each other had been noted by close friends and the press. Now, with the Queen and Philip temporarily absent, she deliberately took Tennant to Balmoral where she knew they would be alone on their first night together. Margaret had enjoyed occasional romantic flings throughout the latter years of her affair with Townsend but, until now, had been far more discreet about them.

Within days the press had ferreted out details of the lone guest being entertained by Margaret in the ancient castle and banner headlines on the theme 'Tennant to Marry Margaret' swept Fleet Street.

'For a moment I almost believed them myself,' said Tennant later. 'But an engagement to Princess Margaret was never on.' Soon after her birthday he flew to Venice and Judy Montagu.

That winter saw Margaret firmly re-established as the brightest star on the West End night club circuit. She now had a private, reserved table in the bull position in half a dozen of the top venues in town and no shortage of male escorts to pick up her tab each night. Tennant, Dominic Elliott and Billy Wallace were usually available, as were Porchester, Peter Ward and Plunkett.

Wisely, Townsend ignored all press and personal reports from London and got on with his new life, devoting all his spare time to show-jumping in which he was beginning to earn international recognition. This also brought about an introduction to Marie Luce Jamagne. She was fourteen – about Margaret's age when he first met her – when she tumbled from her horse and was knocked unconscious almost at his feet. Townsend was already 38 and, some thought, too old for Margaret who was sixteen years his junior.

Marie Luce, a Princess Margaret lookalike from certain angles – who became Townsend's wife in 1959 and is still happily married to the not quite so dashing Group Captain, 80 this year (1994) – was then 24 years his junior.

In January 1955, the year of her twenty-fifth birthday, Princess Margaret's special reward from the Queen for withstanding her supposedly long separation from Townsend without complaint, was a four-week sunshine jaunt around the Caribbean in the royal family's luxury, floating hotel, the *Britannia*, a half-million pound a year indulgence of the Queen, which she gladly wanted her sister to share.

On several of the major islands more than 100,000 people turned out to cheer the princess. So warm was their welcome on this, her first visit to the Caribbean, that the indelible impression it left prompted her to return there regularly ever since.

Between the time she flew back to London in March and her birthday in August, there was a steady build-up of press interest. Everyone seemed to assume that now that the two-year wait was up and Margaret was to be twenty-five, an announcement was bound to be forthcoming about her marriage plans. In fact, all that had been arranged was that the new prime minister, Sir Anthony Eden, himself a divorced man, would visit Balmoral early in October for an informal chat about Margaret's status. More ominously, he would carry with him the feelings of the Cabinet.

Dominic Elliott, son of the Earl of Minto, who was Margaret's major flirtation that year, accompanied her to Balmoral. What official comments came from the Buckingham Palace press machine indicated a perfectly normal Sunday – a visit to Crathie church for morning service, followed by a picnic lunch and a birthday dinner in the evening. Anticipating far better pickings, over 300 photographers, reporters, film and TV crews laid siege to Balmoral Castle.

Margaret's twenty-fifth birthday came and went without any announcement being made, as did the rest of August. Early in September, Townsend returned to Britain officially for the first time, to attend the Farnborough Air Show in his capacity as air attaché, helping to sell British products. During his week in Britain, he twice met with Lady Elizabeth Cavendish. She had no good news for him. The position remained unchanged. The prime minister or the Queen would have to feel very charitable towards them if the marriage were to take place.

Over a hundred pressmen were still waiting at Balmoral on 2 October when Sir Anthony arrived with his wife, Clarissa. After lunch, nervous and on edge, Margaret joined the Queen and the Duke of Edinburgh in the main drawing room and waited for the prime minister. He told them that, sadly, nothing had changed since 1953. Her marriage to Townsend would not receive official sanction.

He hated, he said, to be the bearer of such bad tidings, but her only option – if she still intended to marry – was to give up her right of succession and her £6,000 Civil List income (which would rise to £15,000 when she made an approved marriage) and go to live with Townsend in exile.

If she chose this path, which would require a special bill being passed through Parliament, then, apart from affecting her status and income, it would, in his opinion, cause irreparable damage to the crown. He explained that Lord Salisbury, Lord President of the Council and Leader of the House of Lords had, as a High Anglican, threatened to resign from the government rather than assist in passing a bill permitting Margaret to marry Townsend in any circumstances.

Had she not been aware of this two years before, he asked. And wasn't she also aware that if any children resulted from the marriage they would be regarded as illigitimate by the Church of England?

'No,' replied Margaret, devastated by the finality of what she was hearing and both angry and upset that no one had told her the full picture before. She would have known then that marriage to Peter Townsend was out of the question. To follow her heart meant creating serious difficulties for her sister and her sister's government. It also meant sacrificing her very comfortable, financially cushioned life, with its choice of several servant-filled grand homes, chauffeur-driven cars, private night club tables and the social position of being third in line to the throne, to become the wife of a far-from-rich commoner with, as yet, no long term career and no home of his own.

Wrote Townsend: 'It was too much to ask of her, too much for her to give. We would have been left with nothing but our devotion to face the world.'

Philip believed, further, that the late King would have actively opposed the marriage and would have ruled union with a divorcee as out of the question, and so the duke told his sister-in-law.

When the Queen Mother was approached for her opinion, she said that, with infinite regret and though she was extremely fond of Townsend and thought of him almost as one of the family, it was something he could never become. She agreed unquestionably that the late King would never have sanctioned the marriage, much as he had loved his younger daughter.

That, according to the inner sanctum of the royal family, was the end of the matter. Margaret had already made up her mind when she left Balmoral on 12 October that she was not prepared to make the sacrifices being demanded of her in order to marry Townsend. Barring a miracle, that is, a complete change of heart by the government and Church, there would be no turning back from her decision. When she boarded the Aberdeen sleeper for London, with the faithful Elizabeth Cavendish and Princess Alexandra as companions, she knew that marriage to Peter was a non-runner. However, she was in high spirits when she reached Clarence House the following morning, 13 October. Marriage or no, there was still no reason why they should abandon their love affair. Before that day was out, she knew she would feel Peter's strong arms around her and hear his sweet words of love in her ears.

She had been kept closely informed of Townsend's movements since his arrival in London the previous afternoon and had been instrumental in him being lent the use of 19 Lowndes Square, Belgravia, an apartment owned by the Marquess of Abergavenny, a close friend of the royal family. She had sent instructions for Peter to meet her in Clarence House that evening. It was to be their first official meeting for two years.

Tipped off about his arrival in Britain and hardly needing to guess why he was there, the press were out in force. They chased Townsend around town as he enjoyed a shopping spree with Jean Wills, a friend of Margaret's, niece to the Queen Mother and wife of the tobacco millionaire. Could they anticipate any startling development, the reporters shouted. 'I'm not going to answer those kind of questions,' said Townsend. 'I'm here on holiday.'

Jean and John Wills had already invited the lovers to stay the weekend with them on their Berkshire estate, Allanby Park. When Townsend drove himself to the entrance of Clarence House at 6.20, his green Renault was being trailed by a quarter-mile convoy of newsmen. Others, together with well-wishers, were waiting outside Clarence House, hoping to see the couple together. They were to be disappointed. Margaret and Townsend remained in the princess's private apartment for one hour and 40 minutes. It was there, between embraces, friends say, that Margaret broke the news to her lover that there was virtually no hope of them going on. Only the Queen could overrule all their opponents and to do this she would have to put her own reign in jeopardy.

When Margaret and Townsend arrived, separately, at Allanby Park that Friday evening they found the splendid old Georgian mansion under siege by the world's press. A major contingent from the Berkshire police force patrolled the extensive grounds. Margaret's love of centre stage overcame all other feelings and she left the house twice – exposing herself each time to over a hundred cameras and the press aircraft and helicopters which circled overhead –

once with Mrs Wills to go to church and once to visit the Queen Mother. Observers remember that she seemed to be enjoying the massive media attention. So intense was it that the Buckingham Palace press office felt obliged to issue a statement that no announcement concerning Princess Margaret's personal future was at present contemplated.

Townsend, who was emotionally exhausted, did not leave the house the whole weekend. Aware for a month after his earlier visit that things were bad, he had arrived in Britain with faint hope, only to be told there was virtually none. Whatever future they had together was now in the hands of others. At Allanby Park there was little to do except play games, talk or make love. The last, one must imagine, was done in a feeling of desperation rather than blissful enjoyment. The talks destined for the coming week were almost certain to set the limit on their love affair.

A Cabinet meeting, at which their case would be discussed, was scheduled for Tuesday, to be followed by the prime minister's weekly audience with the Queen. Margaret was to dine with the Queen and Philip alone on Saturday at Windsor for a final 'raking over' of the options, although all the participants were already aware of the outcome of all these meetings.

Most royal watchers concur that Princess Margaret left her meeting with her sister and brother-in-law in tears. Philip was adamant that Townsend should go. Duty with dignity was the only acceptable course.

It was an emotional meeting but told Margaret nothing new. Her own mind was already made up. It was not in her nature to make the sacrifices being demanded of her if her love story were to have the happy ending supported by 90 per cent of the population.

LOST LOVE

Wrote Townsend:

'When the Princess agreed to renounce marriage we both had a feeling of unimaginable relief. We were liberated at last from this monstrous problem which had hung like a millstone around our necks.

'At last we could talk without that crushing weight of world opinion – the sympathy, the criticism, the pity and the anger – all the mass of emotion which had weighed so heavily on our minds.

'There remained only the glow, once shared, of tenderness, constancy and singleness of heart.'

On 24 October, *The Times* joined in, predictably on the side of the establishment. 'They were so against us it almost made me change my mind and marry him after all,' Margaret later told friends.

'Now in the twentieth-century conception of the monarchy,' [*The Times* pontificated], 'the Queen has come to be the symbol of every side of life of this society, its universal representative in whom the people see their better selves ideally reflected; and since part of their ideal is of family life, the Queen's family has its own part in the reflection.

'If the marriage which is now being discussed comes to pass, it is inevitable that this reflection becomes distorted. The princess will be entering into a union which vast numbers of her sister's people, all sincerely anxious for her lifelong happiness, cannot in conscience regard as a marriage.'

At four o'clock that afternoon, in Clarence House, Peter produced an outline statement for her which he had scribbled out over the weekend. He had known there would be no last-minute reprieve. It began: 'I have decided not to marry Group Captain Peter Townsend...'

Margaret read it through twice and told him: 'That's exactly how I feel.' There was no great passionate out-pouring of emotion, just a few tears and a lot of affection. The princess explained later that Townsend and she felt thoroughly drained, thoroughly demoralised. Fate had dealt them terrible cards. Now they just had to play them out, with no chance of winning.

On Friday, 27 October, Margaret visited the Archbishop of Canterbury in his study at Lambeth Palace. Calmly she told him of her decision not to marry, but she also reiterated her love for Peter Townsend. In officially informing the archbishop, Dr. Geoffrey Fisher, first of her decision not to wed, Margaret was being far more under-standing than Peter Townsend might have been, for he was aware that, only months earlier, Dr. Fisher had treacherously and deceitfully dismissed their love affair as 'purely a stunt'.

In his memoirs Townsend revealed that the archbishop had given a remarkable interview when he arrived at Cape Town aboard the *Edinburgh Castle* in Spring 1955. A reporter from the *Cape Town Argus* bearded the archbishop in his cabin and, reminding him of the enormous publicity given to the fact that Princess Margaret and Peter Townsend wanted to marry, asked 'Is the fuss justified?'

To which his grace replied: 'The whole thing – and you can quote me – was purely a stunt. And a most offensive one at that,' he emphasised.

Townsend could see no reason for the archbishop to tell

lies but commented: 'It was a sorry thing to see this good man joining the ranks of those who knew the facts, but manipulated them in public as they saw fit.'

It was decided that the announcement would be made on Monday, 31 October, a full week after it had been drawn up. The palace 'old guard' had tried to re-write Margaret's simple statement and twist it to their own thinking. It was even suggested that no announcement be made at all but Margaret dug in her heels and insisted that the wording be hers and hers alone, re-written alone, punctuated with fresh tears, from Townsend's original draft.

The timing of the announcement allowed them one final weekend together. Lord Rupert Nevill, younger brother of the Marquess of Abergavenny, and his wife Micky invited them down to their Sussex home, Uckfield House. They were again under siege from the world's press – most of whom were still expecting a happy outcome – and were confined to the house for their two-day stay. Said a royal insider:

'They were two days of virtual imprisonment but two nights dedicated to romantic fulfilment. These lovers knew they would never be able to spend another night together. It was their romantic swan song.

'The last, certain, opportunity to express physically the real strength of their feelings for each other. And they seized their opportunity joyfully and took every advantage of it.'

Townsend wrote that, without Rupert and John and their wives, he could never have survived those days of attrition.

'It was a goodbye weekend for the Princess and me. Uckfield House was a haven though one which was blockaded and besieged by the Press and the public. Police and their dogs patrolled, reporters perched in trees or hid in ditches: the Princess and I could neither come nor go. We could only walk in the grounds, sniped at occasionally by long range lenses. Meanwhile the world still waited for the decision made days ago.'

On Monday, 31 October, they returned to London separately, Townsend to prepare for his return to Brussels; Margaret to Clarence House. Townsend joined her there for the last time at 6 pm, to share what they later described as 'a very healthy sized drink', and to touch hands and lips one last time.

It was a goodbye with tears but no recriminations, some laughter and a lot of tenderness, a fond goodbye accompanied by gentle kisses and affectionate cuddles – the goodbye of lovers trying to make the transition into friends; 40 racing minutes in which to close the book on eleven eventful years.

Seven o'clock found Townsend speeding out of London under a friendly moon and back towards Uckfield as the princess's announcement was broadcast to the world.

'I would like it to be known that I have decided not to marry Group Captain Townsend. I have been aware that, subject to me renouncing my rights of succession, it might have been possible for me to contract a civil marriage. But mindful of the Church's teachings that Christian marriage is indissoluble, and conscious of my duty to the Commonwealth, I have resolved to put these considerations before others. I have reached this decision entirely alone and in doing so I have been strengthened by the unfailing support and devotion of Group Captain Townsend. I am deeply grateful for the concern of all those who have constantly prayed for my happiness.

Margaret'.

5

Enter Billy

In Paris, the Duke and Duchess of Windsor commiserated with each other that their neice had not followed their example and sacrificed public esteen and honour in favour of exile and love. Anyone close to Margaret could have predicted that from the outset of the affair. She had always despised her uncle for abdicating and had blamed him for the pressures which brought about her father's early death. She would never have seen them as role models.

It was with a feeling of enormous relief that both Townsend and Princess Margaret turned to the business of getting on with their separate lives.

Various epitaphs were written and, on the whole, Fleet Street got it wrong. Noël Coward's comments were to the point: 'She can't know, poor girl, being young and in love, that love dies soon and that a future with two strapping stepsons and a man eighteen years older than herself would not really be very cosy.

'I hope that they had the sense to hop into bed a couple of times at least, but this I doubt.' For once the Master's doubts were unjustified and I hope Princess Margaret took the trouble to tell him so during one of their subsequent meetings!

Townsend himself finally gave the game away in an interview with Jean Rook, when he told her how he had got into difficulties when writing his memoirs, trying not to be emotional but to tell it how it was.

He told her:

'When I did get carried away, or when publishers pressed me to go into intimate details of what happened when the Queen Mother, bless her, left us alone in a room near the end I thought "No. It's not fair. I must stop."

'You can surely imagine what happened between us? If I'd been a journalist writing about me and Margaret I'd have spelt it out.'

Could Townsend and Margaret have enjoyed a happy marriage? 'Who can tell? It's impossible to say,' Townsend admitted years later.

'Since it's no use crying over spilt milk, I'd say probably not. She could have married me only if she'd been prepared to give up everything – her position, her prestige, her privy purse.

'I simply hadn't the weight, I knew it, to counterbalance all she would have lost.

'Thinking of it calmly, all these years after, you couldn't have expected her to become an ordinary housewife overnight, could you? And to be fair, I wouldn't have wanted that for her.

'Let's say I just knew that, if she gave up everything, it wouldn't work out. But what made me really bitter was that nobody told me anything. I was still the man in the street – I had no public relations officer, no detectives, I had to do it alone.'

His first big decision was to embark on a round the world trip, driving himself, alone, in a Land Rover. It was seen by many as a highly romantic gesture. Townsend would roam for almost eighteen months, covering South America, Australia, South East Asia and Africa. It would take him until March 1958 to return to Brussels – and until 26 March to see Margaret again.

The princess's mourning for her lost love seemed remarkably brief. Just four weeks after issuing her historical statement, Margaret became unofficially engaged to Billy Wallace.

Said one friend of that period:

'Her almost indecent haste to get betrothed after the final split with Townsend was an indication of the desperation and panic she was feeling at the prospect of remaining unmarried. She admitted she would far prefer to marry someone she liked a lot – but didn't love – than to remain a spinster.

'And she found herself with very little choice. In fact choice there wasn't. It was Billy Wallace or nobody. He was the only eligible escort left from her "set". Some were already married. Others were engaged.

'Darling Billy used to pop the question to her every other day almost. It was just a question of waiting until the next time and saying "Yes".'

Billy, a gangling, slightly stooped, Bertie Wooster style figure with slicked back dark hair and a receding chin, was the millionaire stepson of Herbert Agar, Pulitzer prize-winning editor from Louisville, Kentucky. He had tried, and failed, to establish himself as a businessman although this was more due to constant ill health than to any lack of ability.

Billy's mother, Barbara, daughter of the distinguished architect Sir Edwin Lutyens, lived with her second husband on an estate near Petworth and here Margaret quickly became a regular visitor.

Captain Wallace had produced two sons by an earlier marriage and three, including Billy, with Barbara. Four of them were killed in the war, leaving Billy the sole heir.

Billy was not the best match Margaret might have made but he was loyal and caring and he understood her life and background. She felt at ease with him and he was rich. He loved the theatre and had a great knowledge of art. She made their engagement subject to the Queen's blessing and told Billy that if this was forthcoming they would announce their betrothal in the summer. She wanted to make quite sure there would be no hidden obstacles barring their way to the altar.

It is accepted by friends at the time that Billy and Margaret became lovers. They had already shared holidays in the Caribbean and Scotland and been jointly invited to the country homes of friends at weekends. It is also known, however, that theirs was not a very passionate relationship. Friendship, rather than sexual attraction, was the basic foundation of their engagement.

So confident was Billy that the Queen would endorse the marriage that he set off on a last bachelor visit to the Bahamas, joining up with old chums Jocelyn Stevens and Tommy Sopwith of the aeroplane company. While away, Billy stupidly embarked on a hot fling with a local beauty, which would have been fine had he left it at that. On his return to London, however, he dined with Margaret at Clarence House and told her all about it. Perhaps he really was stupid enough to believe it wouldn't matter, or perhaps he had changed his mind about the marriage and used this as a way out, but the effect was the same. Margaret threw him out. Billy purported to be surprised and distressed, which illustrated his stupidity more than anything else.

Margaret refused to talk to him for over a year and it was two years before she forgave him enough to use him as an escort again.

In that year several more of Margaret's 'set' married: Lord Porchester to the Earl of Portsmouth's niece, Jean Wallop; Peter Ward to Lord Ashburton's cousin, Claire Baring; Colin Tennant to the Earl of Leicester's daughter, Lady Anne Coke. Margaret and the Queen Mother attended Tennant's wedding at the Leicester country seat. Taking the photographs was one Antony Armstrong-Jones, although Margaret denies remembering seeing him there.

What these weddings did was remove the last eligible bachelors from Margaret's immediate circle. Her answer was to throw herself, at least temporarily, into official work. At home and abroad, she increased her number of royal events.

Her taste in music was also changing. Rock and roll and jazz were all the rage and Margaret took to them instantly. She loved to jive and jitterbug and never missed a big band concert. Her favourites were Count Basie and Duke Ellington and she was a great fan of Louis Armstrong who, on meeting her backstage at one of his concerts, described her as 'one hip chick'.

ENTER BILLY

Three months after her twenty-seventh birthday, Margaret was beginning to believe that marriage might never come her way and showed her hostility to her sister, whom she was increasingly coming to blame for failing to support her marriage to Townsend, by snubbing her tenth wedding anniversary celebrations.

Margaret believed that had the Queen been tougher with her government then she and Townsend might also have been celebrating an anniversary with joy rather than a further two years apart. On the night of the Buckingham Palace ball, Margaret took friends to see *The Bells are Ringing* at the Coliseum and on to dine at the Savoy. She arrived at the Queen's celebration after midnight – well after dancing had started – and stayed less than an hour.

Four months later, in March 1958, Townsend returned to Brussels from his round-the-world trip and immediately telephoned Margaret at Clarence House. On the one day that would be convenient for both Margaret and Townsend to meet, the Queen was scheduled to be in the Netherlands on a state visit. However, the Queen Mother, who had also missed the group captain, invited him to visit on the 26th.

To the press it was as though the previous two years had not existed. The headlines in the evening papers after the Clarence House tea party said it all: 'Together again'.

The next morning the daily newspapers front-paged the story, relegating the Queen's state visit to the Netherlands to the inside pages. The Queen was alleged not to have known about Townsend's visit and he was attacked for his discourtesy in barging in behind her back. Margaret and Townsend claimed that the press furore took them completely by surprise. If so, then they showed remarkable naïvety. Whenever this couple was seen together, any-

where at any time, there was always going to be speculation about a wedding.

Townsend tried to clear the air with a statement in which
he said: 'There are no grounds whatever for supposing that
my seeing Princess Margaret in any way alters the situation
declared specifically in the Princess's statement in the
autumn of 1955.'

Rumours abounded and Townsend advised that it
would be better if they did not meet again. Yet after visits
to Germany and the Caribbean, Margaret returned to
Britain in early May and telephoned Townsend at his
sister's home. The press clearly did not picture her as being
on the shelf quite yet and Margaret secretly admitted to
friends that she was enjoying all the attention and speculation. It was quite like old times. Observers noted that a
sparkle had returned to the princess's eyes and that there
was a new determination in Townsend. Most thought that
marriage plans could very easily be on again.

Margaret invited him to lunch at Royal Lodge, Windsor
and, during his visit, they went for a long stroll in the royal
gardens, something that did not go unnoticed by the press.
They met twice more in May before the Queen ordered her
sister to cool it. Margaret was advised that the speculation
was getting out of hand and could only damage the royal
family if allowed to continue unchecked.

But they had yet to say their last goodbye. This came at
a famous Clarence House tea party on 20 May, which was
again to hit the headlines in the world's press, causing
great speculation at the time – and ever since. It was one
of the most poignant moments in modern royal history.
The princess, the group captain and the Queen Mother
were present at that last goodbye. Only a few privileged
people learned what took place at that most special event

in the princess's life. Much later on royal insiders were to tell the story.

It was only in the early afternoon that Margaret warned her staff that a special guest was expected and that the Queen Mother would be joining them for tea. He would be arriving at 4.30 and he would definitely be on time.

At exactly 4.30 – as the princess had forecast – the huge wooden entrance gates swung back and a green, chauffeur-driven saloon car swept across the forecourt and stopped a few paces from the front door.

To the complete surprise of those onlookers in the court-yard, out stepped the tall, suntanned figure of Peter Townsend.

He climbed out of the car, stood upright, straightened the slightly crumpled jacket of his dark blue suit and adjusted the knot of his maroon tie. Without waiting to be shown inside, he sprang lightly up the front steps and along the corridor leading to Princess Margaret's sitting room.

Princess Margaret and the Queen Mother had heard the car draw up and were waiting to meet him. Never taking her eyes from him for a moment, the princess darted forward away from the restraining hand of her mother and stopped two feet in front of Peter Townsend. They both moved forward a pace then her hands were reaching up to his broad shoulders and she was kissing him on the lips. They lingered a few seconds in this embrace, Townsend's hands on her waist. Then she looked up at him and said: 'Oh Peter. It's wonderful to see you.'

Her dark blue satin dress was crushed against him and as she backed away her hands went down unconsciously to straighten her skirt. In her understandable excitement, Princess Margaret had broken one of the golden rules of royal protocol. It is a royal rule that if the Queen Mother is present, as senior head of the family, she must always be first to greet a guest.

But the Queen Mother, smiling sweetly, barely seemed to notice this affront to her position and, having reached a point a few feet to one side of Peter, her eyes and lips flashed in a welcoming smile as she moved forward past her daughter to take his hand. Margaret, with a slight bow towards the Queen Mother, stepped back, though never taking her eyes off Townsend's face. The Queen Mother held Peter Townsend's hand for a few seconds and then said: 'Peter. It's been a long time.' Then: 'It's so lovely to have you here again.'

Peter Townsend drew himself to attention and then, with an almost imperceptible bow, said: 'Ma'm I'm more than thrilled to be back here. More so to be here meeting yourself and Princess Margaret than to be back in London again.'

The Queen Mother was the first to break the magic spell. She let go of Townsend's hand and said: 'I'm sure tea is quite ready now,' and led the way slowly towards the sitting room.

The Queen Mother, who looked very regal in a straight-skirted, rust satin, afternoon dress with a silver grey fox fur hanging loosely over her shoulder, entered the room first. Margaret, walking a pace ahead of Peter Townsend with her mother's back to her, threw an affectionate glance over her shoulder to him as he passed into the room. He smiled in return but no words were spoken before they closed the door behind them.

At 5 o'clock, the door of the princess's sitting room opened. The three were already standing away from the tea table. Townsend had been sitting with Margaret on his left and the Queen Mother on his right. It was the Queen Mother who led the way into the corridor. Behind her, Townsend and the princess walked hand in hand, their fingers tightly interlocked. The princess was looking up at Townsend with a serene smile on her lips. He studied her face seriously. Neither spoke a word as they walked down the main corridor and joined the Queen Mother at the front door.

Outside, Peter Townsend's chauffeur sat at the wheel of his car and the policemen on the main gate stood stolidly watching for Townsend to move towards his car, the signal for them to open the main gates. The group stood, still silent, about to say their goodbyes. The princess, her royal position forgotten, reacted as any other woman would to this parting.

The three of them stood at the top of the steps in a semi-circle. In the centre stood the Queen Mother with Townsend on her left. For a moment nothing happened. Then, with a deep breath, Townsend turned to the Queen Mother, took her right hand in his and bent to kiss her gently on both cheeks. He straightened, still holding her hand, and said, in a voice charged with emotion, 'Your Majesty, I am so happy, yet so sorry to be leaving you.' She did not reply. With a half glance at Margaret, she stepped back.

Townsend turned to the princess and they gazed into each other's eyes. He took Margaret by the hand, bent down from his six feet two inches and kissed her slowly and deliberately on both cheeks. He seemed overcome. He seemed unable to express in words the feelings which must have been pounding inside him. Once again he was being parted from Princess Margaret. And this time, as far as any of them realised, it was to be for the last time.

As Townsend was kissing the princess, the Queen Mother looked towards them and smiled gently, then turned her head away. It was her regal way of showing that she approved.

As they embraced, Margaret's eyes were closed. Her chin, held high, trembled ever so slightly as she must have fought to hold back the tears that a woman without her royal training could surely not have controlled. Reluctantly Margaret allowed Townsend to draw away and loosed his hand. This was their last goodbye. Still no words were spoken between them. That kiss had spoken volumes.

Townsend, without another glance at the Queen Mother, looked once more at Margaret, paused for a few seconds, turned on his heel and strode down the steps on to the stone courtyard and towards his waiting car. He did not look back.

As he reached the door he took hold of the handle then, impulsively, glanced back over his shoulder to the main door where Margaret and the Queen Mother were standing side by side waiting for him to leave. Along the front of Clarence House many upper windows were opened wide and crammed with royal servants and staff, gazing down trying to catch a glimpse of Townsend.

Townsend allowed himself one, brisk, half-fluttering wave to the two women standing in the doorway. The Queen Mother, still smiling, stood quite motionless. Then she turned her head slowly until she was looking straight at Margaret. The princess gave a little, helpless sort of wave, forced a smile, then she, too, turned, as if seeking help from her mother to see her through the next few heartrending moments. Then, together, they looked across the courtyard again towards the tall handsome figure of Peter Townsend as he stooped and climbed into the back of the car. Without waiting for the car to move off, without a pause, they turned together and walked briskly, with heads held high, back along the great corridor, up the steps, and were lost to view.

In the courtyard, the car pulled smoothly away and swept towards the main gate. Through the back window could be seen the top of Townsend's head. He was leaning against the rear seat looking straight ahead. As the car passed out through the gates the policeman on duty at the lodge saluted. Then the car was among the crowds which, having heard the news of this meeting at Clarence House, had collected outside to catch a glimpse of Peter Townsend as he left. The car passed out of sight and, as it did so, Townsend's head slumped forwards on to his chest. He had held out to the last. If Margaret and the Queen Mother had been standing at the door still, they would not have seen this collapse of Townsend's brave front.

That evening, for the first time in the year they had been there, Princess Margaret dined alone with her mother in the Queen Mother's sitting room. Most unusually, neither had bothered to change from their afternoon clothes to dine.

After dinner, Margaret spent the rest of the evening alone in her own sitting room, drinking whisky and water while smoking and listening to classical records.

That night when she went to bed one wonders if, the Townsend affair finally laid to rest, she fell asleep gazing at the three photographs on her bedside table, photographs that were never removed from their place, even throughout her romance with Tony Armstrong-Jones. They were close-up portrait shots of Peter Townsend taken from three different angles. One was a full-face picture of him looking straight into the camera. The others were opposite profiles.

The following day, breaking completely with tradition, the Buckingham Palace press office issued a denial to a report that Margaret and Townsend's engagement was imminent.

Twenty years later, when he set his own account and thoughts down on paper, Townsend wrote: 'The denial, though timely, was in the event a parting shot. Continually watched, reproached for "forcing" the princess's hand, my only wish was to clear out once and for all.'

Of their final meeting he wrote:

'There and then we resigned ourselves to the fact that, as long as we could not meet without provoking speculation, it would be better not to meet at all.

'Public curiosity killed our long and faithful attachment. That evening, Princess Margaret and I, warmly, affectionately, said adieu. We have never seen each other since.

'I have no feelings for her now. It was all so long ago.'

In fact, there was to be one further sequel to that meeting, one last goodbye, over 30 years later, when an old man came to lunch with Margaret in the summer of 1992.

He was in London to attend a reunion of those who had travelled to South Africa with the King and Queen and the two princesses in 1947. To avoid press attention, Margaret declined an invitation to the reunion but invited Townsend to lunch at her home in Kensington Palace.

Townsend, nearly 80 years of age, white-haired and stoop-shouldered, chatted to her and the friends she had invited to give her Dutch courage, as though the three decades had not intervened.

To Margaret, perhaps it was a final reminder of what might have been. To Townsend, still dedicated to his young wife, Marie Luce, it was the last, real goodbye to an old and dear friend. As one chum explained: 'He lives in France and rarely comes to England. And one must remember, hard as it is, that he is now an old man with perhaps not too many years left to him. That lunch-time meeting will, though with none of the poignancy and emotion of the previous one, almost certainly turn out to be their final farewell.'

6

The Russian Plot

The detailed, but patently untrue, account of an alleged relationship in the late fifties between Prince Philip and Princess Margaret is almost certainly among the explosive material responsible for certain government papers from 1963 remaining sealed for another 70 years, according to a former top Russian spy.

The key Russian in the Profumo affair – former GRU spy Captain Yevgeny Ivanov – claimed Stephen Ward had hard evidence and photographs of this and other royal shenanigans involving Prince Philip, which ended up in government and British Security hands in 1963 after the arrest and suicide of Stephen Ward. Though the claims were certainly untrue, they could possibly have caused serious embarrassment to the royal family.

Ivanov also claimed to have copies of such information and says it was filed by him from London, where he was then acting as deputy naval attaché, to the Main Intelligence Directorate of the General Staff of the Soviet Army for use as possible blackmail material against the royal family.

A former senior member of MI5 confirms that his department was aware at the time that the Russians had targeted the royal family and were claiming to have discovered highly provocative information about a relationship between Prince Philip and Princess Margaret, though the British believed Ward's and Ivanov's claims to be highly suspect and unreliable.

Said the former MI5 source:

'Much of what Ivanov sent back was romanticised or fictionalised material and the royal files were generally believed to be in this category. Some of his stories were quite outrageous.

'The information, and supposedly photographs too, went back to Moscow Centre and must, presumably, still be on file there. We knew that from Stephen Ward who was working for us in a minor capacity and admitted feeding information to Ivanov before he committed suicide. But no attempt was ever made by the Russians to use this compromising material for blackmail purposes.

'Ivanov met Princess Margaret and Lord Snowdon socially on several occasions and he also met and talked with Prince Philip and the Queen.'

Ivanov, who retired in 1989 and lived, until his death earlier this year (1994), in a modest Moscow apartment, was known by his western counterparts to exaggerate or fabricate many of his reports to Moscow, although he loved to boast of his alleged triumphs in London.

He alleged: 'Sex has always been a powerful weapon of political blackmail and espionage, especially when it involves very top people.'

He told me:

'My access to the information came through Stephen Ward. I was introduced to Stephen in the Garrick Club by the *Daily Telegraph* managing editor Sir Colin Croote, in 1960, soon after my arrival in London as a Captain 1st Rank in the GRU. History has already recorded how, through Stephen Ward, I met Minister of State for War Jack Profumo, Lord Astor and Christine Keeler, with whom Profumo and I shared a bed.

'Ward's claimed knowledge of Prince Philip came out after he had been commissioned by Bruce Ingram, editor of the *London Illustrated News*, to do portraits of the royal family. By that time, Ward's artistic talents had become widely known in London's high society but I was not aware of his long-term connections with royalty. He told me: "You know, Eugene, this commission was not quite unexpected. Prince Philip and I are friends of long standing. We have known each other for fifteen years since I returned from India and started practising in London."

'By talking about his acquaintance with the Queen's consort, Ward gave me a chance to return to it again and again, under different pretexts, but with the same aim, of ferreting out whatever Ward knew about the royal family. He boasted that he knew quite a lot.

'In 1961 Ward did a series of portraits of the royals, in particular portraits of Prince Philip, Princess Margaret and Antony Armstrong-Jones. I was to meet them all later. I don't mean at official ceremonies and parties like the Buckingham Palace tea parties. I sought, and succeeded, in meeting them personally.

'On one occasion – a Royal Geographic Society dinner – I was seated on Prince Philip's right but, despite trying every gambit I had ever learned in training at Moscow Centre, I couldn't get him to say anything of note on any subject. He was evasive or non-committal on every topic I introduced.

'When I told Stephen Ward it had been like a conversation between two deaf mutes, he said: "The Duke of Edinburgh and Philip Mountbatten are two different personae. I remember him before he married the Queen and I know him as he is now. I can compare these two persons. You talked with the statesman who tried to appear wise and cautious. Before, he was an easy-going person with, outwardly, nothing to concern himself about.

'"The Duke of Edinburgh needs to dominate Philip Mountbatten. That's what he was doing at the dinner of the Royal Geographic Society when he was talking with you."

'I told him: "It's not just here it happens. Power and responsibility change people in any country.

'Ward asked me if I remembered a photographic album he had shown me. I said I did.

'"Look again," he said. "You will see Prince Philip there, and his cousin David, together with the rest of our merry bachelor group."

'I certainly remembered the album and the photographs but I hadn't thought them important at the time, although I did recollect that the photographs had been rather candid. Stephen went to a cupboard and produced the album. This time, however, as we talked through it, he identified the people in the photographs.

'When he went out to the kitchen to make coffee, he left the album on the table. I think he left it there deliberately, believing it might earn me kudos from my masters in Moscow Centre.

'Obviously I couldn't just steal the photographs but, as always, I had my Minox camera with me and I carefully copied five or six of the photographs. When Stephen returned with the coffee, he told me about some of the riotous nights out he had enjoyed with the group.

'He told me how they had enjoyed themselves incognito in Soho pubs, about parties in the homes of friends and about visits to clubs for the select few.'

But this was all small time compared, he said, with what had happened recently, only eighteen months before, when Prince Philip began paying too much attention to Princess Margaret.

'The Queen, Ward said, let it be known she would be happier if Princess Margaret married.

'In May 1959, Antony Armstrong-Jones, who Margaret knew little more than casually, was invited to Clarence House for the first time and so promoted, despite his rank of commoner, with the absolute support of the Queen Mother, as principal suitor. In that same month, to every-one's surprise, and afer a ten-year gap, the Queen became pregnant with "a late-marriage love child" – Prince Andrew.

'No doubt there was much interesting speculation among Special Branch and MI5 officers after Stephen Ward approached the Tories in 1963 and came clean about the Keeler/Profumo/Ivanov affair. All his notes, documents and that very interesting photographic album would have ended up with the security services, if not before, then certainly after, his arrest in 1963.

'That evening, after conferring with my London chief, the *rezident*, General Anatoly Pavlov, scientific counsellor to the Soviet Embassy, I forwarded the photographs and my report to Moscow Centre. Later General Pavlov demanded I establish closer contacts with Princess Margaret and her husband. This I achieved during the Henley Regatta when, for two years, I managed to be invited as a guest on their boat.

'Meanwhile Stephen Ward, court artist, osteopath and royal confidante, supplied me with choice titbits from his proverbial well of news. Everything went to Moscow Centre where, should they ever wish to use it, they now had more than sufficient material.

'I once queried with the *rezident* if Moscow Centre were disappointed in my supplying such royal information, which was so far removed from military intelligence. General Pavlov told me we were doing the right thing in collecting this information. "Eventually," he said, "it will be used by the GRU or the KGB. It is invaluable. And our superiors in the General Staff, as you know, are not averse to trading information with Lubyanka."

'The KGB had always been far more adept at using sex in their blackmail scenarios than the GRU and most were devised at their Lubyanka headquarters.

'In January 1963 the Keeler/Profumo scandal was about to break and Moscow Centre thought it wiser to return me to headquarters and a post in the academy. After Profumo's resignation in June, Stephen Ward was put on trial at the Old Bailey a month later, charged with supplying girls like Christine Keeler and Mandy Rice-Davies to rich clients for money.

'It was an outrageous lie, yet it was an accusation which successfully distracted the attention of the public from high-ranking officials who did not want to be involved in a public scandal. Stephen could not stand the treachery of his ex-friends who had made a scapegoat of him. He would not defend himself by accusing others, or even wait for the verdict. He committed suicide on 30 July 1963 by taking an overdose of sleeping pills. It was a shock for me. They had killed my friend. They had actually forced him to die because he was in the way. They feared his revelations. He knew too much, things that must never be revealed. And so he was removed from life, forever.

'But his secrets did not die. They are still on file in GRU Headquarters in Moscow. They are, I am convinced, on file with the British security organisations and they are, almost undeniably, among those 1963 papers which will not be revealed to the public until the year 2063, when no one involved or affected by the events will still be alive.'

7

Developing Passion

Within only a few years of her marriage to Tony – some who were close to them both would say months – Princess Margaret knew she had made a terrible mistake.

It was a mistake which, for a long time, she believed could only be corrected by the death of either herself or her commoner husband, for in the 1960s she would not have dared contemplate the public scandal of an official separation. Nevertheless, she knew that in marrying Tony Armstrong-Jones she had been guilty of the greatest imaginable folly.

Even before their engagement had been publicly announced, she had experienced clashes of will with her stubborn, artistically temperamental suitor but, like most brides-to-be, had closed her eyes to any apparent imperfections in her man, believing they would evaporate at the altar. But evaporate they did not.

89

Part of the problem was that when Tony was thrust into the international spotlight, the glare of which Margaret had always known, he found it almost impossible to come to terms with.

Margaret's childhood friends had been carefully selected for her by the King and Queen. Her escorts and companions during the fifties were almost all from an aristocratic background – wealthy, idle gentlemen with inherited riches, who had been brought up from birth to feel at ease in the company of royalty.

She had rarely handled money and had never needed to question the cost of anything. Tony, on the other hand, was the son of a working barrister who, in his post-university days, had lived in comparative squalor with a series of Bohemian friends. His only income had been what he made himself and he had been welcomed into high society on the strength of his skill with a camera. His casual, constantly changing affairs had been with girls of all kinds and backgrounds although, perhaps significantly, none of them aristocratic.

Several of Margaret's friends had gently questioned her choice and advised her, if not to cancel her engagement, at least to delay the public announcement and the wedding. Until the last minute, Tony's father begged that the marriage should not take place. Three of Tony's closest friends told him the union was bound to fail and advised him to call off the wedding.

When it came to the crunch, the Queen and Queen Mother both supported the match but, having denied Margaret the chance of happiness with Townsend, friends say, they could not possibly deny her their approval and blessing this second, and possibly last, time.

In the end, it was Margaret's own inherent contrariness

which worked against her. One man had been denied her. When Townsend decided to remarry (and told her so in advance in a secret letter sent to Balmoral), then no amount of objections from her family and friends could have made her renounce her second choice. Perfect he was not, but she sincerely believed he loved her. She did not love Tony in the same way, that she admitted later, but she trusted him when he swore he was in love with her.

Other circumstances were working against Margaret. She was nearing her thirtieth birthday and was determined not to end up a middle-aged spinster. At that moment, marriage, even to someone she might not have loved completely, seemed more attractive than the endless years of spinsterhood which appeared to beckon. It was a decision she was to regret bitterly and one that would lead her into a number of adulterous relationships in her thirties and forties, to compensate for her marital misery.

Princess Margaret's first remembered meeting with Tony took place at Cheyne Walk, Chelsea at the home of the mother of her close friend and lady-in-waiting, Elizabeth Cavendish, shortly after her return from Balmoral where she had celebrated her twenty-eighth birthday.

They had been placed next to each other at table and remember talking animatedly thoughout the meal. With all his deepest instincts, Tony belonged to the new, and off-beat, generation and made no attempt to disguise his real feelings and personality. These, say those who knew him, had been deliberately and painstakingly developed. His very considerable charm and non-conformist, Bohemian extrovertism masked an explosive temper and a not readily perceived cooler side to his personality.

He was then freelancing for *Vogue* and *Queen*, owned by

his old pal from Cambridge University days, Jocelyn Stevens, and his photographs were appearing regularly in the national press – principally in the *Daily Express*.

Tony had become hooked on photography at Cambridge and had left, without a degree, to take up an apprentice-ship with top society portrait photographer Baron in his Mayfair studio. This had been financed by Tony's father, Ronald, who also paid £1,000 for the lease of 20 Pimlico Road, a former ironmongers with a ground floor and basement which Tony had converted into a studio and tiny apartment.

He had taken the official photos at Colin Tennant's wedding the previous year but Margaret hadn't noticed him there, although she did know of his twenty-first birthday photographs of the Duke of Kent and those of Prince Charles, Princess Anne and the Queen and Philip.

The only yardstick Margaret had by which to measure this unconventional fellow dinner guest was her meetings with various jazz musicians and actors. Tony disdained the standard dress of three-piece lounge suit and tie in favour of a casual-smart mode – he was already style-setting for the beckoning sixties. Unlike all her other escorts to date, who had been strapping six-footers, he was only inches taller than herself – eye to eye even when, as on this occasion, she was wearing high-heeled shoes.

At this stage he had been living in a very on-off way for eighteen months with beautiful, sloe-eyed actress and model Jacqui Chan whom he had met when she was just eighteen. Photographs of Jacqui, sultry star of *Teahouse of the August Moon*, had helped to win him his deal with *Vogue*. She came and went as she pleased from 20 Pimlico Road and slept with him when it suited her. There was a strong affection between them but no talk of marriage.

DEVELOPING PASSION

Jacqui, part-Chinese, part-Russian, had followed another Eurasian beauty as Tony's girlfriend. The discovery of explicitly sexy pictures of that girl had led to the rapid exit of one of Tony's rather prudish receptionist assistants.

The majority of visitors and guests at Tony's parties, however, were men, several of them known homosexuals, and this had inevitably led to certain rumours about his sexuality, which were just as inevitably passed on to Margaret. Years later, according to Nigel Dempster, when she was asked how Fleet Street had been bamboozled into believing that there was nothing between her and Armstrong-Jones, although their names had cropped up together on several occasions, Margaret replied: 'Because no one believed he was interested in women.'

Margaret's second, remembered, meeting with Tony came a month later and was again in the company of Elizabeth Cavendish. They went to take tea in Tony's studio. On her first visit there, Margaret was fascinated by the dolls' house proportions of Tony's home and work-place. The basement sitting room, reached by way of a spiral staircase designed by Tony, was painted white and filed with bric-à-brac, theatre props and Regency antiques gathered mainly from London street markets. There was an antique bicycle propped against the wall and a large mirror on one wall on which guests had scrawled their signatures with a specially sharpened diamond.

When Margaret suggested adding her own, Tony cautioned her against it. Too many journalists among his visitors might be inclined to make something out of it, he said.

Margaret was proud of her daring in pursuing her strange new friendship. It may seem slightly ridiculous now but at that time Princess Margaret had rarely spent more than a few moments alone with an 'ordinary person'. Apart from Peter Townsend, who was a royal equerry, none of her circle even had to work for a living. Tony both amused and intrigued her. He was different at a time when she desperately needed something or someone different in her life. She wanted to get on with life and Tony appeared to offer an interesting way forward.

She was still extremely cautious, however, and their relationship was only allowed to progress slowly, at her chosen pace. Yet, by November, as Tony left for New York with Jacqui, and Margaret prepared for Christmas with the royal family, she was able to tell her mother and sister that she had met someone she quite cared about and whom she intended to see more of.

Initially, the Queen and Queen Mother were secretly delighted. Anyone who could bring back a happy smile to the princess's face was worth having in her circle. They awaited developments with hopeful expectancy. Both had noted a lightheartedness in her of late, which had been missing too long. A real sparkle had returned to her eyes and they prayed that, in this, the closing year of an eventful and emotional decade for the royal family, the beginning of real and long term happiness might await Princess Margaret.

After two years, Margaret was well settled in Clarence House. She lived a life completely alien to that of Tony Armstrong-Jones; a cosseted, privileged life in which everything and everybody were dedicated to serving her. Tony was still not well enough known and established to be invited inside this royal world. That particular milestone in the development of their romance still lay several months in the future as 1959 dawned.

The untold story of that amazing year has never been

properly revealed until now. It was the year in which Margaret was transformed from the world's most eligible young woman into the wife of an almost unknown commoner. It was a vitally significant period in her life in which the gregarious star of London's night club and party circuit became, as the object of a new suitor's love, satisfied with much simpler pastimes. It was a time when Princess Margaret and Tony Armstrong-Jones were able to pursue their romance in secret, without a single rumour making its way into the newspapers.

This little known period in her life can only now be fully told.

8

A Life of Luxury

Life in Margaret's home, Clarence House, was as strictly controlled and predictable as the changing of the guard outside her sister's palace just along the Mall.

The day started with the princess's dogs being walked in the garden. There were three of them and they slept in baskets in one of the servants' rooms. There were no kennels and Princess Margaret refused to have them in her bedroom. A servant was also delegated to bath two of the dogs – the Sealyhams, Johnnie and Pippin. The third dog, a chestnut-brown and white King Charles spaniel, named Roly, was the princess's favourite and she always bathed this one herself. He was washed in the royal bath adjoining the princess's bedroom, much to the annoyance of her dresser, Mrs. Ruby Gordon.

Margaret would prepare a jug of perfumed shampoo and stand it on the edge of the bath. Then she would kneel down at the side of the bath before dumping Roly in the water and scrub him vigorously with her nails. The princess would wear a tiny pinafore over her afternoon dress on Roly's bathday but she admitted it was never enough protection and she would get thoroughly soaked by the time it was all over. She dried him with a towel and then, while he stood in a corner of the bathroom, the princess plugged in her hair dryer and played it over his long fur, sitting cross-legged on the floor while combing him with a wide-toothed comb and flicking his curls into position.

Margaret's were not the only dogs in the house. Queen Elizabeth, the Queen Mother had her own two corgis and a miniature dachshund called Billy, Joe and Ricky. None of them wore a collar. The royal dogs are the only dogs in Britain which are not obliged to wear collars when outside the house. In Clarence House they were allowed the run of the building. They would scamper between people's legs and were the cause of many minor mishaps. This was particularly true of the dachshund, Ricky, who had one particularly annoying habit, for which the princess loathed him. He was always jumping up and laddering her nylons and eventually she would not allow him to come near her.

Princess Margaret always took the same breakfast. It consisted of a plate of fresh fruit: bananas, grapes, an orange and perhaps a peach. She never ate anything else and, more often than not, would not even touch any of this. Her breakfast would include a pot of weak China tea in a yellow and white china teapot with milk and sugar. Her tray would be carried from the ground floor pantry to the princess's second floor bedroom in the royal lift. This lift was out of bounds to everyone except the royals and their guests and their personal servants. The Queen Mother had her suite of rooms on the first floor directly beneath those of the princess.

Opposite the lift on Margaret's floor were two doors leading to the rooms occupied by the Queen Mother's dresser and Princess Margaret's dresser, Mrs. Ruby Gordon, a Scotswoman in her forties who had been with her since soon after the princess was born. Further along the wall on the same side as these doors were two high wardrobes in which Mrs. Gordon kept the princess's vast collection of dresses. Between them was a door leading to her bathroom. Finally, at the far end of the corridor on the nearest side, was the door to Princess Margaret's bedroom.

When the breakfast tray was delivered, Mrs. Gordon would knock on Margaret's bedroom door and, without waiting for an invitation, wheel it in on a trolley. She parked it on the right-hand side of the bed and, not speaking to the princess, pulled back the curtains.

But if the princess had an engagement to fulfil and it was necessary for her to be up, Ruby would tell her: 'Come along now, Margaret. It's time to get up.'

Then she would take away the dress the princess had worn the night before, together with her shoes, cigarette lighter and holder and any other items scattered around the room. The shoes, lighter and holder would be sent downstairs to the pantry for cleaning. Her shoes, all of them hand-made, were not marked with a size, but were fives and easy to clean. The lighters would be cleaned and filled and the holders were scoured with a pipe cleaner and white methylated spirit.

Between 9 and 11 am, the princess would lie in bed listening to the radio and reading the newspapers which

The young princess was acclaimed one of the world's most beautiful women.

Above: The princess, with first lover Group Capt. Peter Townsend.

Opposite top: Townsend holds the cushion and Margaret looks on as King George VI holds an investiture during the 1947 South African tour.

Opposite below: Townsend tails discreetly behind the two princesses during a walkabout in South Africa.

Top: At the races with Peter Townsend in attendance.
Below: Princess Margaret faces the press at the height of the Townsend affair.

The princess at a royal function. She complained she found some of them 'incredibly boring'.

Top: Princess Margaret made it acceptable for women to smoke in public.

Below: She was a great fan of the Fab Four and loved to dance to the Beatles' music.

Top: The princess and Elizabeth Taylor each enjoyed the love of various men, and shared the same stunning violet-blue eyes.

Below: Frank Sinatra has always been her favourite singer and she rarely misses one of his concerts.

Prince Philip opposed her bid to marry Group Capt. Peter Townsend but he and Margaret have remained good friends.

were left scattered all over the bed and floor. In those days she loved to smoke in bed and there would invariably be two or three cigarette stubs in the ashtray on her breakfast trolley when the cleaners arrived. At eleven, she rose and went to the bathroom adjoining her bedroom, where Mrs. Gordon had run her bath.

The relationship between Ruby Gordon and the princess was a very intimate one. They often dressed in the same style, adopted the same mannerisms and even followed each other's fashions in hair style. Mrs. Gordon was roughly the same height and build as the princess and, not unnaturally, the princess often gave her suits and dresses which she had worn only once or twice.

They were on Christian name terms. Mrs. Gordon was the only servant who ever addressed the princess as 'Margaret'.

She would rely on Ruby to choose her clothes for the day and, at the age of 28, would still call out to her dresser when she got soap in her eyes while bathing. And Ruby would hurry into the bathroom to help.

Mrs. Gordon had been with the princess for so long that her advice on clothes and make-up was accepted by Margaret on most occasions. Mrs. Gordon would select a dress, and shoes to match, from the princess's wardrobe and lay them on the bed. And, with very few exceptions, these were the clothes she would wear that morning. It would usually be a cotton or wool dress, always with stockings and always a handbag for her arm. At other times it would be a pleated skirt and a shirt-type blouse. When she was not going out to a function, the princess would wear a double-strand pearl necklace and an occasional broach. Margaret had, and still has, an impeccable dress sense and when she emerged at about 12.30, she never looked less than beautifully groomed, fresh and crisp. Of course, being a princess meant never wearing her clothes more than once at a time. After she had changed her day dress, for instance, it would be sent by Mrs. Gordon to be either cleaned or pressed and hung away again in a wardrobe, perhaps to stay there for another six months, when she would wear it again and then, possibly, if it had been worn to different functions, have it sent to some charitable organisation.

The head office of the Distressed Gentlefolks Association, an organisation which cared for landed gentry down on their luck or financially crippled by taxes and death duties, would regularly receive a brown paper parcel of dresses and other items of clothing. The Queen Mother was its patron. Evening dresses, which the princess wore about twice, were sent back to the makers for alteration and renovation.

It was generally thought at the time that Princess Margaret, one of the world's most fashionable women, was showered with clothes from every international couturier. The reality was that she had to pay for every stitch of clothing she wore.

The laundering of Princess Margaret's blouses, night-dresses and towels was done by a London laundry appointed by the royal household. They collected the wicker laundry hamper from the back door of the house. The princess's underclothes were washed by Mrs. Gordon herself in a washbasin in the dresser's bedroom. They would be hung on a clothes horse to dry in front of a small electric fire. She chose white, nylon underclothes, flimsy and frilly.

Mrs. Gordon would carry a clean set of underwear into the princess's bathroom each morning. Margaret would spend about half an hour there before going back to her bedroom. After dressing she would do her hair and make-up. These she always did herself. Even when going out for a big occasion, she applied her own make-up and would brush her hair into the style she had chosen with two big silver hairbrushes. Her hairdresser was only called in to make the final touches if she was attending some state engagement.

The princess normally went down to her sitting room at about 12.30. On her desk would be waiting her mail – which had been vetted – and a large glass of fresh orange juice.

Her morning mood was always difficult to predict. Sometimes, after a late night, she would not be in such a sweet temper and would stride straight from the lift to her sitting room and slam the door. It was the type of behaviour Mrs. Gordon remembered so well from the nursery. With Margaret nothing changes. It was on such stormy mornings that she would ring for a bottle of vodka to go with her orange juice. It was one of her favourite lunchtime drinks – and, according to friends, worked as the ideal pick-me-up. One was enough to clear that morning after feeling. In those days, however, she rarely over-indulged and her moods of bad temper were few and far between.

One woman who knew the princess well in the fifties said:

'She was so outrageously spoilt and selfish. She let her feelings show like a child – and had to be indulged in just the same way. Her cigarette smoking was a perfect example. She lit up when she wanted and where she wanted.

'The convention then was that no one was allowed to smoke until after the loyal toast. The joke with Margaret was that she would arrange for the loyal toast to be announced after the soup course. A lot of people were very happy when she finally quit smoking in 1992. One of them probably being Keith Waterhouse, the writer. He once saw her with an inch or more of ash on her cigarette in danger of falling and reached across in front of her, palm upwards, to grab an astray.

'She simply flicked her ash into his open palm as it passed. All Waterhouse could mutter was: "Thank God she hadn't decided to stub it out."'

The princess's plans were worked out days, or even weeks and months, in advance. But extra instructions were left for her staff in handwritten notes before she went to bed. These were simple instructions: to order a car or take her undeveloped photographic film to the camera shop she used. This job was later to become a trip to the Pimlico Road studio of Antony Armstrong-Jones.

Even at this stage the princess was a keen photographer and loved to take snaps of the royal family, dogs or those guests who were invited to share family weekends at Royal Lodge, Windsor. She used two cameras in those days: one a French miniature type, the other a Japanese-made reflex.

Margaret's personal mail was always sorted for her by one of the staff and certain items sifted out. She had a particular loathing for that section of the outside community for which she reserved the special name of 'crankpots'. These are the people who write her begging letters, ask to meet her or who want her to assist, in some way, with their domestic or financial problems. This pile of mail, from all over the world, often comes from mental institutions – from demented men and women posing intimate questions about her private life and offering various pleasure that might be afforded her if she would let them visit her. As well as these, there were, and still are, half a dozen proposals of marriage each week, most from men claiming they are fabulously rich, with offers of a home in luxury for the rest of her life. Perhaps the most loathsome mail was the tiny packages that used to arrive at the house addressed to Princess Margaret and marked personal. At one stage, she had opened one of these packages, containing stripper-style underwear, and been disgusted by it. She had ordered her staff that on no account must they ever bring her packages that had not been carefully checked beforehand. She wanted them disposed of if their contents seemed in any way questionable.

Of the twenty or more letters that arrived each day, no more than five or six would find their way into the princess's sitting room and on to her desk. To help in the sorting, envelopes and postal markings from previous crankpot letters were kept on file, against which each incoming letter could be carefully checked.

The letters that were genuine could be spotted immediately. All her friends knew the code to adopt when writing to the princess. After addressing their envelopes, they would write their initials discreetly in the bottom left hand corner. It was WW for Billy Wallace, DE for Dominic Elliott, P for Lord Plunkett and later TAJ.

Ten or a dozen times a week her secretary would be called by an anxious switchboard girl to be asked: 'Does the princess know a Mr...?' Often these calls were from as far away as America or Africa. Sometimes they posed as relatives, saying they wished to speak to Princess

Margaret on a purely personal, family matter. Then the whole household would buzz for a few minutes while frantic calls were put through to her lady-in-waiting, Iris Peake, to discover if the princess really did know someone of that name.

Should the call obviously come from a crankpot, the person, usually a man, would be told by the switchboard operator, or the duty policeman in the lodge, that the princess was not in residence and advised not to call again.

Genuine calls were put through to the princess either in her bedroom or sitting room. Margaret has always been an almost obsessive user of the telephone and sometimes spends hours each day chatting and gossiping with friends.

But there was one crankpot, in her pre-marriage days, for whom the princess had a soft spot. Regularly, until her wedding day, he would send her a modest bunch of flowers every Monday morning, which was carried up by messenger boy. Attached to them was a card which read simply: 'With all my love and best wishes. E'. The message never varied. These were always placed in her sitting room, where she would see most of them, as the princess had grown fond of this charming but harmless gesture. She would tell all her visitors: 'These are from Ernest, my very good crankpot friend.'

Most of the flowers decorating Clarence House were brought up from the gardens of Windsor Castle. But they were not free. The Queen's household would make a modest profit by selling them to the Queen Mother. They came up on Mondays and Wednesdays every week and, though lovely, never lasted more than a couple of days, even though the water was changed every day.

Another regular sale was the dozen fresh eggs, quart of milk and pat of newly churned butter brought from the castle to the house every morning. These were used exclusively for the Queen Mother and Margaret.

By the time the princess had finished reading her mail, it would be almost 1 o'clock and she would walk from her sitting room to the morning room. Already assembled in here would be the princess's lunch companions, the members of the household, including her lady-in-waiting, the Honourable Iris Peake, Lord Adam Gordon, her press secretary Major John Griffin, the Queen Mother's lady-in-waiting and the Queen Mother's private secretary Colonel Martin Gilliat. They would be standing in the morning room, having helped themselves to drinks, waiting for the arrival of the princess and the Queen Mother.

The morning room was large, about sixteen feet by twenty-four feet, light and airy, tastefully furnished in pale blue and cream. A huge, crystal chandelier hung from the ceiling and pale grey, wall-to-wall, fitted carpet covered the floor.

When Margaret and the Queen Mother joined the company, one of the men would pour the princess a gin and tonic from the drinks tray and the Queen Mother would have the same. They had time for one drink before a page announced lunch in the library. He slid open the doors in readiness and other servants would already be in the library waiting to serve.

Led by the Queen Mother and the princess, the chattering party would walk into the library and take their places around a full-sized round table in the centre of the room, which stood directly beneath the chandelier. Bookcases covered the lower part of three, cream-painted walls and, on the fourth, to the left of the main door, were two large windows divided by a large marble table. A deep-pile, grey carpet covered the floor and a tall standard lamp stood in the corner. Apart from this, the room was bare, relieved only by three large porcelain vases on the marble table which were never used for flowers.

The royal servants would take it in turns to walk the 50 yards through the huge sliding doors, across the dining room reserved for official luncheons and dinners, and down the old, wooden staircase to the basement kitchens. The return journey would take about ten minutes, there being no hot plate within easy reach of the library.

Conversation at lunch revolved around plans for forth-coming engagements and Margaret would often entertain the company with witty comments about engagements which she had fulfilled and the various people she had met. She is brilliant at mimicking different accents and the people in her stories really seem to come alive, say her luncheon guests. In those days, these stories would often earn her a quiet 'Oh, Margaret', from the Queen Mother and a meaningful glance would be exchanged between the royal officials. Occasionally, when politics was introduced into the conversation, Margaret and the Queen Mother would be anxious to change the subject, politics being officially outside the sphere of their interests.

The princess would always enjoy these informal get-togethers around the library luncheon table. Lunch was served from silver dishes and the company, including the Queen Mother and the princess, helped themselves to whatever took their fancy.

These meals were always prepared to Princess Margaret's taste. Earlier she would have received a suggested menu and ticked those dishes she wanted. Lunch, which usually ran to four courses, including fruit and various cheeses, for which she had a special affection, was normally accompanied by a liberal amount of white wine, chosen at the steward's discretion. Red wine was never served.

The princess would then sit smoking while the others enjoyed a sweet. It was rarely that she joined them in this course and she never excused herself for smoking while they ate, said one regular diner. 'Margaret would take a generous helping of meat but always refused potatoes. Apart from this one fad, she was a hearty eater.' Her habit of smoking so much did result in certain accidents. Said the Clarence House guest:

'I have seen her ruin more than one skirt and top with burning ash falling from her cigarette. She would use the cigarette and holder as a prop, waving it wildly in the air to make a point or flicking it on the side with her thumbnail when she was angry. Once at lunch at Clarence House the stub of her cigarette flew out of its holder and burned a hole in the tablecloth.

'It didn't phase her in the slightest. She just fitted a fresh cigarette in the holder and left it to someone else to cope with the smouldering cloth.'

Lunch over, at about 2.15 the princess would again retire to her sitting room and spend a couple of hours catching up in her diary, writing personal letters or perhaps slotting pictures into one of her personal photo albums. These were albums full of pictures she had taken herself, either at the Royal Lodge or at the homes of freinds. Many of the pictures were of her dogs. She took pictures of them when she exercised them in Green Park or St James's park. She kept her albums in a cupboard in the sitting room and prized these thick, maroon, leather-bound books very much and kept the cupboard locked.

The princess also took advantage of this lull in her routine to rehearse the speeches she wrote for official functions. Even from outside the door passers-by could hear her small voice. She would be saying: 'It gives me great pleasure to be here...' or 'I declare this building open...' or the like.

At about 4.30, tea would be served on a cloth-covered wooden tray placed on a small table in the centre of her room. It was usually a pot of scented China tea, a plate of paste or foie gras sandwiches and two or three fancy cakes. She was nearly always alone for tea and never joined the Queen Mother, who also ate alone in her first-floor sitting room.

About an hour later she would take the lift to her bedroom to make her first, perhaps even her second or third, change of clothes for the day. With the help and advice of Mrs. Gordon, the princess would select her dress for the evening. This would be either a simple cocktail dress or a more flamboyant evening gown which Margaret so revelled in wearing. After re-doing her make-up and brushing her hair, the princess would once again take the lift down to the ground floor and return to her sitting room.

While the princess was upstairs, a drinks tray would have been prepared for the evening. First item for the large silver tray was always a decanter of Scottish whisky. This would be accompanied by a large, sealed bottle of Malvern water – a still mineral water which the princess invariably uses. Sometimes difficulties arose because of her insistence on this particular kind of water.

During the early evening, the princess would sit quietly smoking and listening to her records until the first of her guests – or as was more usual – her escort for the evening, arrived.

A LIFE OF LUXURY

A decanter of gin and a few tonic waters were put on the drinks tray for her visitors, but Margaret never drank anything else in the evenings except whisky.

Occasionally she would spend the evening alone, lounging on a settee with her feet up and her shoes kicked off, listening to records. Alongside would be a glass of whisky and water and the inevitable cigarette in its holder.

If she stayed in, she would have a simple meal served in the room, on a coffee table, at about eight. She often ate with a brightly covered paperback novel propped up on the table in front of her. At such times she never took wine with the meal but poured herself another whisky and water.

Between eleven and twelve, she would go up to her bedroom where, Mrs. Gordon remembered, she had already laid out a nightie.

This was a day in the life of Princess Margaret at Clarence House in the late fifties – but at that time that sort of evening alone was pretty infrequent.

Very often during the morning, and the afternoon too, Margaret had official engagements to perform. Many of these were pleasant chores, but very often the princess would not be able to disguise her look of gloom and boredom after returning from a stodgy and tedious engagement. Sometimes, after such affairs, the Queen Mother would be waiting at the front door to see Princess Margaret return. One well-remembered rainy day, the princess came back from a more than usually boring function and the Queen Mother was waiting just outside the half-open main door of Clarence House with friends, having just let the dogs out into the garden for a run.

As sweetly as ever, the Queen Mother asked: 'Did you enjoy yourself, darling?'

Margaret scowled and said: 'Honestly, Mother, I was bored stiff.'

The Queen Mother raised her eyebrows, shrugged and said: 'Well never mind, darling. You must always remember to look interested even if you are not.'

Margaret lifted her shoulders huffishly and stomped off down the corridor leaving the Queen Mother looking after her with just the glimmer of a smile around her lips. She was probably remembering her own younger days when banquets and state occasions seemed relentlessly boring, said a palace visitor.

There were very few occasions like this when Margaret and the Queen Mother met inside Clarence House, except for lunch. Though they often stayed in their rooms alone in the evenings, Margaret and her mother rarely met to talk or listen to Margaret's vast collection of records. For the most part, these records were popular songs and melodies. Although she had a good collection of classical music, it was seldom heard. One of her favourite singers was Frank Sinatra and when she had visitors to her sitting room in the evenings, one of his latest discs was usually on her record player.

Both the Queen Mother and the princess were linked by the house telephone service and had only to pick up the receiver and dial the right code number to speak to each other or any member of staff. If wishing to communicate, however, both preferred to do so by means of little handwritten notes, which were sealed in envelopes and addressed formally to either Her Majesty Queen Elizabeth or Her Royal Highness Princess Margaret. The royal mother and daughter would initial their envelopes in the bottom left-hand corner.

The princess was able to speak to her sister at any time.

There was a white telephone on her sitting room desk – and an identical extension by her bedside – which were connected, just as today, from Kensington Palace straight through to the Queen's sitting room in Buckingham Palace.

By far the most popular way of spending an evening for Margaret was to head for the bright lights of London's West End theatreland with one of her many escorts. The current favourites were: Billy Wallace, the Mayfair millionaire man-about-town, forgiven by then after his engagement fiasco with the princess three years earlier; Dominic Elliott, the handsome young son of a Scottish earl and a Mayfair playboy; Lord Plunkett, Deputy Master of the Household to Her Majesty the Queen; and Christopher Lloyd, a wealthy young bachelor. All these were acceptable to the royal family and several had their names romantically linked with the princess's after the Townsend affair.

Sometimes, escorted by one of these men, the princess would join a theatre party to see a new show and afterwards the whole company would be invited back to Clarence House to have a late dinner. These dinner parties often did not start until after 11 o'clock and could continue into the early hours until Margaret retired, which could be at dawn.

Dinner with the Margaret set was always a very lively affair. After their meal in the official state dining room, the party, often of a dozen or so people, would troop along to her sitting room and there they would have a ball, explained one of their number. On went the records. Their shoes were kicked off and, with brandy and cigars in quantity, the 'set' would let their hair down. However, even in their liveliest moments, in the early hours after one of their wilder parties, none of the guests would ever dream of addressing Princess Margaret by any other name but 'Ma'am', said a friend.

After these parties, the bubbling princess, usually still smoking, would trot barefoot down the long main corridor to wave her guests farewell from the front door, calling her goodnights to the departing company as they made their way out of the house and courtyard, through the police lodge gates.

These usually spontaneous parties were always followed the next morning by late rising on Margaret's part, although her whole staff were still expected to be up at the crack of dawn.

During these late night sessions Margaret would often entertain her guests at her grand piano, accompanying herself expertly as she worked her way through a selection of new songs. She sang in a clear, soprano voice, which her guests applauded but which, when she practised during the afternoon, did not get such an appreciative reception from her dogs, explained a visiting observer. Roly, the King Charles spaniel, would always join in in a high-pitched whine, with his head cocked high in the air, almost drowning out Margaret's singing.

When expecting one or other of her escorts, Margaret would take slightly longer than usual in changing and making-up. The prospect of a night out on the town in a new dress would be enough to make her bubble over with good humour. On occasions, she would trip down the stairs holding the skirts of her dress and admiring herself and her 'pretty clothes', sometimes observed by an escort who had arrived early.

Her favourite escort at the time was Billy Wallace who was always about fifteen minutes late. He would arrive in his tiny bubble car. She would greet him affectionately with a quick, glancing kiss on either cheek and the words: 'Hello, darling Billy'. He would reply 'Good evening, Ma'am,' and give a slight nod of the head. It was a ritual, known to all her escorts, which never varied. Usually they would go to a theatre, followed by a London night club. The police guard on the main gate regularly recorded them as returning to the house at after 2 o'clock the next morning.

In that year of 1959, nights out on the town were the normal thing for the princess. For her it was a whirl of theatres, parties, night clubs and social engagements. Almost every night, one of the escorts would drive up to Clarence House or arrive by taxi to whisk her away to the bright lights of London. Midnight was early for her to return. More often than not she would drive back with her escort, laughing and bubbling in the highest of spirits. The only staff still up would be the security men who recorded her every movement in and out of Clarence House, noting it down in the log book in the police lodge. More than once it was noted that she came in with the morning newspapers. From outside the main gate would come the 'peep-peep' of Billy Wallace's bubble car. The duty policeman would hurriedly straighten his uniform and spring to the gate. When he opened it, in would drive Billy and Margaret, obviously enjoying the look of amazement on the policeman's face. On one such occasion, Margaret, wrapped up in a fur coat, with Billy in a, by now, crumpled dinner jacket, chattered away as they drove to the front door. They stopped for a minute or two, still talking, then Billy leaned across the princess's knees, released the catch on the front of the car and swung the glass forward section open. Margaret climbed out slowly and stretched upright in a languorous and feline way. She waited for Billy to scramble out and they walked together up the front steps. They did not kiss or even shake hands. The princess, with a stifled yawn, smiled: 'Thank you, Billy, I enjoyed myself thoroughly. I'll call you later.'

As Billy Wallace returned to his car, Margaret slipped her mink from her shoulders, revealing a pale blue, flared, satin cocktail dress and its creased skirt. She looked pale and ever so slightly red-eyed. Her make-up, which she had applied with such care the previous evening, was almost gone. Significantly perhaps, none of her lipstick was left. She went straight up to bed and, reportedly, did not rise that day until gone one o'clock.

The princess's nights out, always at the most expensive places, had to be paid for. Many a restaurateur would have loved to have footed the bill to have Margaret dining there, but none would ever be allowed to do so. The escorts always paid – with a generous tip of course. The princess herself never carried money with her. Her handbag contained only her lighter, cigarette case and holder, make-up and hankies.

Said one of her former 'set' members:

'It was a fortunate thing that all her friends in those days were quite rich. The privilege of taking out Margaret for the night did not come cheap. Her escort had to foot the bill for dinner and drinks afterwards in a night club. No ordinary working man could have afforded those prices.'

She had her own bank account, of course, and would write out cheques whenever she had been on a shopping spree. Occasionally, she and her lady-in-waiting, Iris Peake, would drive into London's West End and walk into a big store to look around. If they bought anything, Mrs. Peake would pay.

It was because the princess never had any cash that she was sometimes involved in amusing incidents. For one thing, she always had to be provided with money to put in the collection plate whenever she went to church.

On Sunday mornings at Windsor Lodge or when she was away staying with friends, she always asked on Saturday night for her church money. A member of staff would leave it on her breakfast tray on Sunday morning, in a little envelope with the edge of a pound note showing. It amused staff and family alike to see how Margaret loved to have cash in her pocket. She used to go to great lengths to make sure she had a couple of shillings to rattle. Then she would put them in the pocket of her dress or coat and walk around jingling her change, just like a small child.

One weekend at Windsor, when she had planned to go to the royal chapel, she asked as usual for her church money and a pound was left in an envelope on her tray. But she wasn't going to give it all to the collection plate. She rang for the household steward, who had come down with the Queen Mother, and, as he revealed later, asked: 'Can you change a pound for two ten shilling notes?' The steward dug in his pocket and produced the notes, handed them to the princess and took her pound. It was a week before anyone knew what she was planning. That Saturday night she did not ask for her church money.

At 11.25 on Sunday morning, she was ready to go to the chapel, dressed in a dark grey costume with a pleated skirt and a white, petalled hat. It was only when she was half-way down the drive that the steward realised she had no collection money and foresaw the embarrassment which might be caused if the princess had to pass up the collection plate without contributing to it. He ordered a servant to chase after her with a pound note.

When the running servant came within hailing distance he shouted without any formality: 'Have you got your church money?'

Margaret turned in her tracks and said happily: 'Yes, thank you', and continued on her way.

The whole household was intrigued to know where she had got it. Eventually it was Mrs. Gordon, her dresser, who solved the puzzle. When she explained, everyone roared with laughter. Mrs. Gordon had seen the princess go, almost guiltily, to her dressing table, rummage in her handkerchief drawer and bring out a ten shilling note. It was one of those changed for her by the steward the previous weekend.

Margaret loved to work these little tricks to get herself some loose change. One of her 'set' at the time explained: 'She loved catching out her close friends and staff, usually on very simple things. And she would roar with laughter if she succeeded. But if one tried the same on her she never saw the funny side. She would explode.'

The princess in a paddy was a lovely sight to behold. Her big, deep blue eyes flashed and she tossed her hair like a Thoroughbred filly. But she usually simmered down after a few minutes. It was when she went quiet and coldly regal that she was really formidable. No doubt it was occasionally used to good effect with some of her escorts. Undoubtedly the favourite, until Tony Armstrong-Jones became more in favour in the spring of 1959, was Billy Wallace. No matter how much he may have let her down over their engagement, this man, more than the others, was on almost intimate terms, not only with the princess but with the Queen Mother. He had the necessary quality, possessed by the others to a lesser degree, of always having something to say when in the company of Margaret's mother.

The ability to do this was most essential. The Queen Mother, for all her charm, was not a great talker with the younger people. And many is the young man who has 'died' in her presence. For if the conversation flagged, there would be a great silence and the Queen Mother would break it only by making excuses – taking her dogs out for a walk or something like that – and leaving.

But Billy could make her laugh. Dominic Elliott and Lord Plunkett also chatted away quite freely to her and their meetings were generally lively.

The princess always addressed Billy Wallace as 'Billy'; Lord Plunkett was 'Patrick'; and for Dominic Elliott she reserved the special nickname 'Dom-Dom'. For each of them, when they called, she would have a kiss, but only a sisterly one and always on the cheek. They would, in the house at least, always address her with the rather formal 'Ma'am'.

Lord Plunkett was a little different to the other two. Although he was frequently her official escort for the night, they rarely went out together alone. She confided to some of her friends that she was never quite so fully at ease with 'Patrick' as she was with the others.

There were many speculative rumours in the press linking the princess's name with Wallace, Elliott and Plunkett. But her confidantes dismissed most of these rumours as mere idle gossip. The relationship between Margaret and her three most popular escorts was one of friendship, based on a mutual interest in good conversation, good food, good music and the arts. Before the appearance of Tony Armstrong-Jones, Margaret spent many weekends in their company at house parties in Royal

Lodge, Windsor. She was rarely seen at Clarence House at weekends. If it wasn't Royal Lodge, Windsor, then it would be visits to friends in the country or trips to Balmoral or Sandringham as a guest of the Queen. However, it was at Royal Lodge that Margaret really relaxed. On these weekends, Margaret indulged in her favourite pastimes of riding, dancing in the lounge, swimming in the open-air pool or just wandering in jumper and slacks through the wooded parkland in Windsor Great Park.

It was on one of these weekends away – to the Devon home of her cousin, Mrs. Ann Rhodes and her husband – that it became clear how strong was Margaret's insistence on Malvern water with her drink. On the evening of her arrival at the house, the princess and her host and hostess, together with other guests, were about to take pre-dinner drinks. The drinks tray was on a table and Mr. Denys Rhodes, as the host, was offering drinks. He asked the princess what she would have and she said she wanted whisky and water. He poured the whisky into her glass and lifted the crystal jug of water to add to it. But the princess interrupted him by saying: 'No, Denys. I want water.'

'This is water, Ma'am,' he said.

'No,' said Margaret firmly, 'that is tap water.' She beckoned her own servant over. 'You know what I mean,' she said. 'Fetch me my special water immediately.'

Mr. Rhodes looked perplexed as the servant left to go to the kitchen to sort out the crate of Malvern water and Margaret's favourite brand of whisky, which she always took with her. When he returned, the guests were still waiting for their drinks, and Mrs. Rhodes was saying: 'But Margaret, water is water wherever it comes from.' The servant took the bottle to her and showed it to her. It was still sealed – she insisted on this – and, on seeing it, she nodded her head. He undid the seal, placed the bottle on the drinks tray and the party went on.

'That is water,' she said. It was the last word on the subject.

Though Margaret was not prepared to 'rough' it with ordinary water, she was quite able to put up with other discomforts or inconveniences if the occasion warranted it.

Friends recall the weekend the princess paid a visit to Mrs. Rhodes's mother, Lady Elphinstone – 75-year-old sister of the Queen Mother – who lived in a gaunt, ramshackle mansion near Musselburgh in Scotland.

This rather eccentric lady lived alone in the house, her only servants being a cook and a daily cleaning woman, and, when the royal party arrived, everyone, from the princess down, was astonished to find no electric light bulbs in the house and no heating.

A chauffeur was sent down into the little town to buy two dozen bulbs and then he helped to get the electric generator started. Meanwhile, as the princess chatted politely to the old lady, Mrs. Gordon was shown Margaret's room. She was horrified and returned to complain that it was dark, damp, dreary and cold. Eventually, much to Mrs. Gordon's disgust, the chauffeur installed a smoky, soot-covered paraffin heater in the room. It had obviously not been used for years because, when it was lit, clouds of smoke belched out.

Dinner was served in the library – the dining-room on the first floor being completely covered in dust sheets. As no one on Lady Elphinstone's staff seemed capable of serving dinner, it fell to Margaret's own staff to cope. After fitting one of the newly available light bulbs into the single socket in the ceiling and examining the table, it was obvious to them that dinner could not be served on it because it was sticky with damp. A white table cloth was spread over it and a search made for the cutlery. All that could be found was an old, bone-handled set which, it was thought, would not do for the princess.

Reported friends:

'One of the servants approached Lady Elphinstone, put his lips within a foot of her ear and roared: "Where is the cutlery, M'lady?"

'She said it was all in the kitchen, so bone handles it had to be. The table was set for four: the princess, Lady Ephinstone, the lady-in-waiting, Lady Cavendish, and the princess's private secretary, Major Francis Leigh. However, search though they might, the servants could find only one knife, one fork and one spoon apiece. Consequently, when the party had eaten their grapefruit – with the soup spoons – someone had to rush to the kitchen and wash them in time for dessert.

'The meal was eaten in gloom. There was only one cruet set which shuttled back and forth across the table in a most unroyal way. They shared a single half-bottle of table wine among them and the princess sat hunched in her chair with a thick woollen cardigan wrapped tightly around her, glancing now and then at the huge, empty and unlit fireplace and the window with its thick, iron bars fixed to the frame.

'"It was the shortest meal ever served to the princess," remembered the source. "The whole thing was over in twenty minutes flat and they retired quickly to the drawing room."

'A fire had previously been lit in this room when the guests went upstairs to change for dinner. Now it spluttered and crackled despondently in the hearth. The cook had warned against building it up too high in case the chimney, unswept for decades, caught fire.

'Margaret must have seen the funny side of this evening for, after dinner, she enlivened the group with jokes and stories which kept them all amused until they went to bed at eleven.

'The bedrooms were reached by walking along a stone-flagged hall where one's footsteps echoed in a ghostly way around its tall, white-distempered walls and ceiling.

'Out of earshot of her hostess, the princess said that she would not like to stay there for any length of time. But as it was for only one night, she was prepared to grin and bear it. After all, it was better than sleeping on a train in a siding.

'That night, huddled under their blankets and trying to keep out the cold, I doubt there was one member of the princess's party who agreed with her. They all spent a restless, draughty night, wishing for the luxury of a warm British Rail berth in a siding.'

The following morning the whole party rose early and, after a quick, spartan lunch, the princess and her guests left the house.

This was one side to the lively young princess which members of the public and press did not know. These informal weekends with her friends; her 'Let's get away from it all' attitude, when she managed to escape for a few days from the seemingly endless list of royal engagements.

There was nothing Margaret loved better than a party. Occasionally, she would invite a few friends into her sitting room at Clarence House when she was in the party mood and keep them there until well after midnight. When she gave these parties, the champagne would flow freely. But newcomers, who had read in the diary columns of the newspapers that Princess Margaret was very fond of champagne, never saw her touch a glass. During the evening when the champagne was poured, she would take another whisky and water. It was the only drink she really enjoyed in the evening.

Said one of her occasional guests:

'Margaret could handle her liquor well in those days. But like anyone else she would sometimes have too much – and then one had to watch out.

'It's a difficult enough thing to persuade an ordinary person to go to bed because they've had one too many. With a princess it is virtually impossible. The rule was that no one could leave until she went to bed and she wouldn't go to bed if she was enjoying herself.

'I remember one night about ten people being there and Margaret was in her cups. The party dragged on and on until, in the end, most of the guests, about eight of them, had dozed off. Finally, at dawn, she announced: "You people really aren't much fun" and went off to bed – much to everyone's utter relief.'

The princess was really in her element when she could dress up in a new gown and spend the evening dancing. Soon after her return from the annual trip to Balmoral in 1959, where the whole royal family go every year for the grouse season, the Queen Mother decided to hold an informal dance at Clarence House.

Two hundred and fifty people were invited, because even an 'informal' dance was a grand occasion; the men in dinner jackets, the women in their evening dresses sparkling with diamonds and other jewels.

What none of the guests realised was that this was a secret celebration of Margaret's engagement to Tony Armstrong-Jones. Her friends and the press were still speculating on just who would be the most suitable boyfriend for Margaret to take to the altar – and she was already betrothed to the man considered the least likely suitor of them all.

9

Dancing the Night Away

Only a handful of people were aware at the time that Margaret's decision to marry Tony Armstong-Jones was taken as early as October 1959 during their Balmoral holiday. Or that she told Tony she would become his bride just hours after receiving a letter from Peter Townsend telling her that he had decided to marry.

For the strongest personal reason, her own pregnancy, the Queen had ordered the couple not to mention their betrothal outside the family until the following spring. But when the Queen Mother suggested an informal dance at Clarence House as a way of celebrating her daughter's unofficial engagement, the Queen gave her permission.

The Queen herself attended but Prince Philip did not as he was away on a private engagement. The Queen Mother, Princess Margaret and Princess Alexandra completed a fabulous royal quartet.

DANCING THE NIGHT AWAY

All day preparations were made for the dance, held in the huge, chandelier-lit, first-floor drawing room. For days, crates of drink and hampers of food had been arriving. The Persian carpets were rolled back and the settees pushed against the walls and a dozen tables were placed in the corridor outside laden with drinks.

One hundred and twenty bottles of champagne were kept on ice for the champagne bar. At the liquor bar, hundreds of bottles were stacked up. Extra staff from the palace were recruited to help out there and in the buffet in the ground-floor dining room.

The servants wore their semi-state liveries of scarlet-tailed coats with gilt buttons and gold epaulettes hanging from their left shoulders, white ties and black trousers. On an occasion like this at Buckingham Palace, the servants would have had to wear full state livery of scarlet coats, blue velvet knee breeches, white stockings and black patent shoes with silver buckles. When this was worn, servants had to plaster their hair with a white paste in place of the traditional powdered wigs. This was an economy on the part of the royal household, for wigs were terribly expensive and harboured moths. Thus, the poor servants had to walk around all day with a gluey mixture in their hair, being compensated for the discomfort by the princely sum of threepence a day extra – in old currency, a little more than one penny today. They had to rise at 7 o'clock, smarm the paste on their heads and brush it well in, then leave it there all day until washing it out before going to bed. When there was an official state visit at Buckingham Palace, they would sometimes have to go through this routine for three consecutive days – all for ninepence! However, the semi-state livery did look very impressive when worn, as on this occasion, by the whole serving staff.

After sleeping for an hour in the afternoon, Princess Margaret and the Queen Mother arrived together at the first-floor drawing room at 7 o'clock.

Margaret was positively bouncing with excitement. She looked beautiful, said a guest, in a full-length, oyster-pink satin gown with an off the shoulder neckline and a priceless necklace of diamonds, diamond pendent earrings, a diamond bracelet and gold wrist watch. She had called in her hairdresser that evening to give her dark locks a final setting, and her make-up, as always, was perfect.

One guest who saw the princess with the two queens midway through the dance said:

> 'The Queen was sipping a drink and had just been joined by the others. The Queen Mother and her two daughters made a charming picture as they stood talking animatedly above the noise. I saw Margaret lead them in a burst of boisterous laughter, holding on to her sister's arm as she did so. They looked incredibly happy. It's remarkable that it wasn't until months later that any of us realised the significance of that dance.
>
> 'We all saw Margaret dancing with Tony – several times – but no one thought anything of it. No one thought she could be the slightest bit interested in him.'

All four royals danced for hours, returning occasionally from the drawing room flushed with excitement and high spirits. The highlight of the evening was a fantastic sight. The Queen Mother had requested the band leader, Ray Ellington, to play a conga. Then, urging the Queen, Margaret, Alexandra and the rest to follow her, she led a swaying, laughing, noisy conga line around the room.

DANCING THE NIGHT AWAY

Out of the room they went, along the corridor and down the stairs. Round and up again they jostled in the greatest display of letting down their hair that anyone had ever seen in a royal residence. Holding on to one another's hips, they coasted back to the drawing room and broke up in howls of laughter.

This glorious sight literally stopped the dance for a few mintues and the Queen and her mother went to the bar again with Alexandra. This princess wore a startling, tulip-style dress of orange with a green fern motif. She and Margaret danced constantly with an ever-changing variety of partners.

The dance went on until close on 3 o'clock, when tables were arranged in the ground floor main corridor with portable cookers. From then on, bacon and egg breakfasts were served to order, taken with either champagne or black coffee, depending on the stamina of the guest.

By 4, the princess and the Queen Mother were standing at the front door, seeing off the guests personally. Dozens of cars were waiting in convoys to take them away and the front door was a confusion of people still talking at the tops of their voices and footmen trying to persuade them, gently, to go to their cars.

When the last of them had departed, the princess and her mother still had spirit and energy enough to walk around the house saying their thank yous to the servants before retiring to bed.

At daybreak, the house snapped back into routine and the Queen Mother was called, as usual, at 7.30 but the princess slept on until midday.

At the back of the house the dustbins bulged with broken plates, glasses, scraps of food and literally hundreds of empty bottles – the usual sort of debris from any party – only tenfold.

This evening came towards the end of Margaret's 'escort era' when, the Townsend episode out of her system, she threw herself into a hectic round of high life in the night clubs and at the parties of the upper set. By the time the royal family returned from Balmoral that year, the short, dapper figure of Antony Armstrong-Jones had begun making regular appearances at Clarence House.

He had been with the princess at Balmoral and the fact that he had been invited there alone, had, for her very closest confidantes, confirmed the suspicion they were developing that there was some deeper feeling between Margaret and Tony.

Margaret had known Tony for about a year by this time. He had taken her out occasionally and had been seen as a fringe member of the Margaret 'set'. No one seriously linked the name of the princess with this society photographer. A friend, perhaps, but still a commoner and no match, they thought, for the princess. Usually, people thought he was with the party as official photographer and didn't even place him as a guest.

However, as one of the very few even to suspect a budding romance put it: 'In the last half of 1959 when one began to see more and more of Tony and less and less of the old crowd – the Wallaces, the Elliotts and the Plunketts – one came to feel that one was, unknowingly, sharing a secret.'

In those months, there were very few witnesses to most of the charming, funny, touching and serious moments which paved the way to their final decision to marry. And when that decision was taken, they were banned from announcing it.

It was already known in October that the Queen was pregnant again and the birth was expected in February. No engagement or marriage plans could be broadcast until after that event. Such was royal protocol and etiquette.

The first time the man who was to become Princess Margaret's husband even set foot inside Clarence House was on the occasion when the Queen Mother threw a formal lunch for the High Commissioner for Rhodesia and Nyasaland in July 1959.

This was just three months before Tony and Margaret became unofficially engaged!

It was held in the huge drawing room on the ground floor of Clarence House, a room hung with gold drapes. Being a formal luncheon, the table was laid with the Queen Mother's silver-gilt dishes and cutlery and those serving at table were wearing semi-state livery.

It must have been rather awe-inspiring for Tony to attend such a formal royal occasion. The sunlight streamed in through the four large windows of the room as the guests took their places. Tony was sitting on the right-hand side of Princess Alexandra, Margaret was four places along to the right of him.

At the time, never having seen him before, most people did not know who he was. One of those present said:

'He attracted my attention by the way he kept looking around the room and at the other guests and eyeing the servants in their liveries in a sort of obvious wonder.

'During luncheon he was talking most of the time to Princess Alexandra, speaking in a soft, slightly effeminate voice and with a great deal of gesticulation. Sometimes he waved his arms across the table when he turned to talk to Iris Peake, seated on his right. As far as I could tell they were shooting questions at him about photography, but he interspersed his answers with what must have been amusing stories, for he tended to giggle a lot.

'At the time he was wearing a navy blue suit with a white shirt and plum-coloured tie. His fair hair was well groomed in a characteristic quiff. During the meal he threw occasional glances along the table at Princess Margaret but she was busily engaged in conversation with the official guests.

'After the luncheon, the guests rose to go into the morning room and it was then that I noticed he walked with a strange springheeled step. This, I later learned, was caused by him having one leg shorter than the other.

'This slight deformity was hardly noticeable under normal circumstances because he had his left shoe built up and the difference then became negligible.

'I watched him as he walked out of the room, his slim figure emphasised by the tightness of his trousers which tapered away to sixteen-inch bottoms.

'He did not have his car with him but walked away through the main gates to the right-hand side of the police lodge and I saw him stroll off in the direction of the Mall. He was off to the Victoria Palace to photograph the Crazy Gang – one of the Queen's favourite comedy teams – or so I had heard him say over lunch. I learned later why Tony got on so well with Princess Alexandra. He had seen her on several occasions when visiting Kensington Palace to photograph her brother, the Duke of Kent. This, supposedly, is the reason why he was first introduced to Margaret.

'Tony had seemed perfectly at ease talking to the Queen Mother with his hands tucked inside his

trouser pockets. This was probably due to his experience with other, lesser members of the royal family
during the previous ten months when he had been on
the fringe of the Margaret 'set'.

It was only after Tony had been visiting Clarence House
for several months that some pepe learned he had been a
fairly constant escort of the princess, though one who had
never been to the house before that formal July lunch. In
retrospect, friends often speculated why the princess had
never introduced him to Clarence House before that
luncheon party. But no one appears to have been able to
find the answer to that question.

Shortly after this party, the initials TAJ began to be
noticed more and more on Princess Margaret's letters.
Letters were also delivered to the house by hand and, with
them, there often came brown paper packages which
usually turned out to contain photographs. Some were
landscape and portrait shots of Princess Margaret,
obviously products of the Armstrong-Jones studio. It was
an unusual fact that, at this time and throughout their
courtship, no one remembers seeing a photograph of
Armstrong-Jones in the princess's possession or even in
Clarence House.

About a fortnight after the luncheon party, Tony
received his second royal invitation. This time it was much
more informal – a weekend down at Royal Lodge,
Windsor.

Margaret travelled down to Windsor in the Rolls-Royce
and Tony found his own way there in his shooting brake.
The house party included Tony Armstrong-Jones, the
Queen Mother, Lady Elizabeth Cavendish who had first
introduced Margaret to Tony, Lady Elizabeth Basset,

lady-in-waiting to the Queen Mother, Colonel Gilliatt, the Queen Mother's private secretary and, of course, Margaret.

At this, his first weekend at Royal Lodge, Tony was valeted by the Queen Mother's personal footman. He found himself the centre of conversation at dinner on the first night at Royal Lodge. He was questioned closely by the princess about his photographic work and the Queen Mother also showed great interest both in that and in his theatre design work, for which he was making a name.

Tony was seated on the right-hand side of the Queen Mother who was at the head of the table. Margaret was seated at the other end of the table which made it impossible for them to have any kind of private conversation. However, throughout the meal Tony and the Queen Mother chatted together and it was obvious to other guests that he had made a hit with her. She seemed to approve of him as a friend for Margaret and, of course, had something in common with him because of her great interest in design and décor.

The following morning (Saturday) after the dinner party, the royals had their first experience of Tony's late rising habits. He did not get up that morning until about 11.30. The princess had already drunk her early morning vodka and orange juice and had wandered down to the stables to look over her horses. When Tony finally came down, he went straight to the lounge and sat for three-quarters of an hour reading the morning newspapers. Then he went up to his bedroom to fetch a camera and strolled out into the garden at the front of the lodge.

Revealed one guest later:

'He wandered around the gardens looking for a suitable subject for his camera. Just before midday the Queen Mother, who had been out in the park exercising her dogs, came in and asked after some of the guests.

'She was told that Tony was in the garden. I watched the Queen Mother go out into the gardens, the dogs still in tow, and walk over to Mr Armstrong-Jones. He showed her his camera and she nodded in answer to one of his questions. Then, side by side, still talking, they strolled around the garden in the sunshine. She clearly enjoyed his company to have sought him out like that.

'That afternoon, the whole party went out on to the terrace and sat in wicker sun chairs and deck chairs. Some just sat relaxing in the warm sunshine, others were reading, and I saw the princess looking often at Mr Armstrong-Jones who still had his camera around his neck. Every few minutes he would glance up from the magazine he was reading and look at the princess. Their eyes would meet and a meaningful smile would pass between them. Then, unnoticed by other members of the party, they would return to their reading.'

The following week, Tony turned up for escort duty for the first time. He arrived at Clarence House in his grey, Borgward shooting brake at about 7 o'clock.

They spent an hour in her sitting room listening to music on the stereo record player. This was the Princess's favourite way of spending the early part of the evening.

At about 8 o'clock, the couple walked out hand in hand to Tony's waiting car. He climbed into the driving seat leaving Margaret to walk round to the other door by herself. It stunned onlookers that the usually imperious princess didn't even mention this incredible display of bad manners. Tony obviously meant a great deal to her.

The following week Tony called for Margaret three times. Twice they went out by themselves, but the third night – again a Thursday – they stayed in. This evening was to be the first of their many visits downstairs to the private Clarence House cinema in the basement.

The cinema is a small affair, intimately lit with soft wall lights. It has a sloping floor and can seat about 50 people in armchairs arranged loosely in rows. Unlike the more luxurious Buckingham Palace version, it had not been fitted with a wide screen. When Tony and Margaret arrived in the cinema everything had been made ready for the showing of the film *The Wild One*, which had been banned in the rest of the country. The star was Marlon Brando, one of the princess's favourites.

They sat down in armchairs at the back of the cinema with cigarettes layed out on coffee tables alongside. The princess and Tony sat for an hour and a half in their red plush armchairs. After watching the film they went out to a restaurant for a quiet meal alone.

The following weekend, he was again a guest at Royal Lodge, Windsor, arriving after the princess but far more self-assured than on his previous visit. This time there was nothing formal or restrained about their greeting.

Said one witness:

'Margaret was obviously thrilled to see him. They held hands in front of them and kissed. But it was no royal escort's kiss. Rather a full-blooded lover's embrace, full on the lips. It was the same sort of heart-felt kiss the princess had offered to only one man publicly before – Peter Townsend.

'After what seemed an age they parted and stepped back, still holding hands. The princess was the first to speak, saying – "Tony, how wonderful it is to have you here."

'He, still remembering such things as the correct form of address, answered: "Ma'am it's delightful to see you." But all the formality in the world couldn't have disguised that kiss. In the space of just seven days sizzling, raw passion had exploded between these two. This was for real.'

The following weekend saw Margaret on her way to Scotland for the start of the traditional Balmoral holiday. She was in a particularly awkward mood for the short drive to Kings Cross main line station, where she was to join her own, private train. She always looked with loathing at the stations she travelled from for little was ever done to disguise the general filth and debris which used to litter our rail terminals.

Her face would flinch when she glanced around her, although, thoroughly trained as she was in royal behaviour, she never took the smile from her face, although she was often heard by her travelling companions to mutter, 'These awful stations. They nauseate me.'

This time her ill-humour owed more to Tony's absence than to the state of King's Cross. She was missing him dreadfully already she admitted. And she didn't know if she could survive the two weeks until he was due to join her in Balmoral.

10

Tony's Rude Awakening

Princess Margaret had not awaited a guest so eagerly at Balmoral since the Townsend years. Even the Queen commented on her sister's restlessness, but was clearly unaware of the cause. It is remarkable, looking back, how Tony was drawn by Margaret into gradual acceptance by the rest of the family without them realising just how close had become the relationship between the two of them.

Tony arrived as a guest of the Queen though, of course, this was at Princess Margaret's suggestion. It was Tony's first meeting with the Queen and Prince Philip and from the start he never seemed quite at ease with the top branch of the royal family tree.

If this was a kind of initiation ceremony for Tony, it was a pretty tough one. It must have been very hard for him to get into the swing of things at Balmoral. After all, the royal family are essentially a simple, energetic and sporting family who like nothing better than rising early, dressing in thick clothes and boots and going out on to the moors for a day's hard shooting or fishing or stalking. This, of course, was not the kind of thing that Tony had been trained for.

In his own way, he took part in the activities, but never actually carried a gun, as did the other men led by Prince Philip. He would stand unhappily in the butts, seeing to it that he was near to the princess as much as possible.

He even looked out of place in his dress. He tried to match them when he joined them on the moors. He produced a pair of plus fours – bulky trousers that laced tight just below the knee – and wore them with thin stockings and suede boots. Above, he usually wore a corduroy jacket and a sharp-brimmed cap. But fellow guests remembered that he always looked slightly awkward and ill at ease whenever he wore the 'uniform'. He only looked like the old Tony at night, when all the men changed into dinner jackets.

However, one thing was spared him in the way of dress. Being of Welsh extraction, he was debarred from wearing the kilt. Tony must have been very thankful for that at least.

If there was one single thing which undermined any efforts Tony might have been making to join in the spirit of the holiday, it was his love of bed – or, rather, his loathing of getting up.

He was always the last down. The other men were invariably down early to eat a very full breakfast before their long day in the open, but Tony rarely appeared until well after they had finished. Breakfast for him those mornings was a hasty affair, bolting his food so as to catch up with the party. Many a time the Land-Rovers would be waiting outside for fifteen or twenty minutes for him and it was after half-a-dozen of these late rising demonstrations that Prince Philip finally blew his top at him.

Recounted an eye witness:

'The prince had been sitting at the wheel of his vehicle with two companions, waiting for Tony. Then he started pressing the horn button and generally looking agitated. At last, he turned to one of the other guests and snorted: "Where the hell has that bloody man got to? Still in bed I suppose." As he spoke, out of the castle rushed Tony, his coat tails flying, and he clambered into the vehicle, full of apologies.

'Those days on the moors were purgatory for Tony, at least until the ladies arrived for lunch. It was Townsend repeating itself.'

Lean-to marquees were set up on the moors, under which they had lunch. These were quite rough-and-ready affairs, consisting of cold meals packed in hampers and served by the ladies of the party, including the Queen and the princess. They always packed everything away again afterwards, leaving it to the servants to take everything back to the castle.

These picnic lunches provided Tony with some respite at least.

Said the insider:

'Philip's patience with Tony was little better than with his predecessor. Tony always appeared to drag along behind Philip and his friends, being at ease only in the company of Margaret. Indeed, she seemed to spend a lot of the time explaining to him just what the

138

other men were doing. Apart from this, they both carried their cameras wherever they went and spent a lot of time taking photographs of the party, the wonderful views and of each other.

'After he had left, he sent quite a number of packets of prints to the princess, of pictures they had both taken, and she showed them to everyone with apparent delight.

'After dinner in the evenings the royal family and their guests played games, talked and drank and occasionally danced to the music of a record player. Tony could usually be found standing on the fringe of the circle around Philip, smiling and nodding as required, but taking very little active part in the conversation, which was dominated by the prince's booming, masculine voice.

'The princess did her best to draw him into the flow, but Philip somehow seemed to brush him aside. However, with the ladies Tony was quite at home and appeared to be genuinely popular.'

About Princess Margaret's feelings there seemed no doubt and these were subjected to the ultimate test when the special delivery letter came from Peter Townsend to explain, in advance of a public announcement, that he was intending to marry in December – and to a girl less than half his age.

Margaret's instinctive reaction was to hit back at her former lover in kind. Later she was to admit that she was probably not completely in love with Tony at the time, but that afternoon she told him that she wanted to marry him.

She informed the Queen and the Queen Mother that same day that Townsend was to marry and that she intended to marry Tony the following year. No announcement could be made until after the birth of the Queen's third child in February but the decision to wed had been taken.

When Tony left he was seen off by the Queen, the Queen Mother and, of course, the princess. Between the princess and Tony, when they said goodbye, there was simply a handshake, none of the show of affection which they displayed in more intimate surroundings.

Off went Tony to be driven the 50 miles to Aberdeen to catch the London train, with a packed lunch of chicken, provided by the household, in his baggage. More sustaining, one would imagine, was the knowledge that he had the promise of the hand in marriage of the late King's younger daughter.

Thereafter, Princess Margaret stayed on at Balmoral and life there went on in the same round of shooting, hunting and strenuous open-air activity which the family love. Margaret, like all the other ladies, abandoned her dress sense and wore whichever old thick tweeds she could. She looked terrible in the big floppy hats – they called them pea-picking hats – favoured for their daily excursions, but it was tradition and she didn't give a damn.

She spent a lot of her time in her suite of rooms at Balmoral, writing letters and pasting up the photographs that she and Tony had taken there.

At last came the time to return home and a reunion with Tony. Margaret travelled in her own train, which was two luxuriously converted carriages coupled to the end of the normal service train. It was beautifully carpeted and Margaret had her own bedroom, dining room and bathroom.

Back in London, a final Townsend drama still had to be

played out. It was the last time Peter Townsend's name was brought up at Clarence House. It was the day, in mid-October, that his engagement to the lovely Belgian girl, Marie Luce, was announced in the evening newspapers.

Although she had received the news first and in his own words at Balmoral, then it had been private. Now, she would have to face everyone in the world knowing that her ex-lover had fallen for another woman who would finally erase the princess's place in his heart. Perhaps she felt it a betrayal that he was the first to take that step.

It is now known that Margaret first knew of the public announcement that sunny autumn afternoon when she read it in the stop press of the evening papers.

Said a close friend:

'She was very upset by it. She had known it would have to come out at some stage but she still wasn't properly prepared for it. It was the final slamming of the door on her past. But it was Townsend and not her who was doing the slamming, and for someone like Margaret that was hard to take.

'She would have loved to have rushed into a public announcement of her own engagement before his hit the papers, to show that she had found a replacement partner before him.

'She was hurt and angry and one would have expected her to have called Tony and fought off her mood in his company. But she didn't. Instead she did the totally unexpected. She phoned Billy Wallace and asked him to take her out.'

Which is why, just after seven, late as usual, Billy Wallace arrived in his bubble car to go out on the town. Gone was all the anger and sadness of her earlier mood. This was the real Margaret, the young woman bubbling over with gaiety and happiness. She leaned forward and kissed him lightly on the cheek and stood back, almost hopping with enthusiasm.

They walked across the courtyard to his pale blue bubble car arm in arm, chatting and joking between themselves. Margaret was clearly looking forward to her evening out, probably at a night club in London's West End.

To observers, it looked slightly ridiculous her being whisked away in a bubble car rather than the usual Rolls-Royce. But she seemed perfectly content. He lifted the hood and clambered in ahead of the princess. He had to go first as the car had a left-hand drive and he would have had to step over Margaret if she had sat down before him.

The princess stepped daintily in after him with all the royal dignity she normally used to enter an official car. Then, letting off the handbrake and pulling the hood down over them, Mr Wallace drove off round the house. On these informal outings, Margaret's escorts rarely used the main gate. They usually passed behind the house and went out through the tradesmen's entrance. This was a ruse originally planned by Margaret when she first moved in – to escape the crowds that were invariably waiting outside the main gates.

The police lodge recorded that Margaret returned at the same time as the morning papers, which were full of the Townsend marriage story.

Why she chose Billy Wallace as an escort that night in preference to her new love, Tony, will probably never be known. Perhaps she wanted the companionship of some-one who had known Peter Townsend, to whom she could talk about it. Or perhaps she simply wanted the comforting arms of a former lover to take away the hurt.

However, after that night Margaret and Tony were to be almost constantly in each other's company and nearly every weekend was spent at Royal Lodge, Windsor.

As each weekend passed, Tony felt more relaxed and at home in the most informal of the royal residences. But he was still able to make mistakes. One of these brought him into conflict with the cook at Royal Lodge and involved breakfast in bed. Within days, Tony's *faux pas* was the main talking point of all the royal households.

A breakfast tray was delivered to him, as ordered the previous evening, at 10 am. The bedroom had been in darkness, the curtains still drawn and the windows shut tight. This was normal procedure for Tony, who never slept with his windows open, even in midsummer.

When woken, Tony had groaned, and, so the story goes, turned over and pulled the bedclothes over his head. Two hours later, he had rung his bell and ordered a new breakfast. The other, naturally, was cold.

Said a Buckingham Palace insider:

'When given the order the cook exploded. She turned on the duty servant and stormed: "Breakfast? I can't do breakfast. Go and tell him I'm cooking lunch now and if he's too bloody lazy to eat his first breakfast he can go without. I'm not going to start preparing another breakfast at this hour of the day."

'The servant asked her: "Do you really want me to go and tell him that?"

She said: "Yes, I do."

'When the servant returned and reported his subsequent encounter with Tony, the cook had virtually to be restrained from charging upstairs with her meat cleaver. For, after receiving the message from the kitchen Tony had, goes the story, kicked off the bedclothes and, stark naked, made a rude gesture saying: "That to the cook." Nature had been very generous to Tony Armstrong-Jones in endowing him magnificently in his most private appendage. This he had grasped and pointed in a very suggestive way, went the story, which was soon recounted throughout London.

'It was only when she was told that the servant had already gently chastised Tony by telling him: "Please, sir. Remember who you are and why you are here," that she calmed down.'

The chosen few who shared those weekends with Margaret and Tony at Royal Lodge still remember that summer and autumn of 1959 as a glorious season, prolonged by a wonderful Indian summer, when the air in the gardens hung heavy with the scent of thousands of flowers. As the year wore on, the runaway weekends became more and more intimate and those who shared them inevitably became drawn more and more into the slowly and secretly entwining lives of these two people.

They were happy, carefree days. Only once did Tony experience the full blast of Margaret's temper when the princess went into one of her notorious states of haughty, white-faced, regal fury. It was triggered off by a terrible gaffe Tony made in her presence and, like his previous gaffe over breakfast, it involved one of the staff and became the hottest below-stairs story in the royal households.

Only the evening before he and the princess had been dancing barefoot in the lounge until well after midnight to the strains of romantic music from the radiogram, oblivious to the presence of others or to a world outside the softly lit room.

The following morning, preparing to go back to London and Clarence House, Margaret was sitting cross-legged on the floor behind one of the high-backed settees in the lounge, sorting out some records to take back with her. Went on the story, recounted by a Buckingham Palace source:

'When she had established one pile, she rang for a servant to carry them to the car. He was halfway towards the door with the records in his arms when Tony burst in and, throwing up his arms, said: "I've been looking for you. Be a darling and..." Tony had failed to see the princess on the floor behind the settee. But he was cut short by the sudden rustle of the princess's skirts when she jumped up from the floor. She glared at him, having gone white-faced with rage.

"Be a darling? What on earth do you mean, be a darling? Who are you talking to?"

'Tony was visibly shaken at this unquestionably icy interrogation. He blushed scarlet and hopped from one foot to the other. "Oh, Ma'am," said Tony at last. "I had no idea ... I didn't see you. I wanted him for something."

"And what do you mean by 'darling?'" asked Margaret again, fiercely. "Is that the way one man should refer to another? A normal man that is."

"It's an expression used often in the theatre world, ma'am," he stammered. "I'm afraid I have picked it up..."

'Margaret said nothing to him but turned to the servant and, in her most imperious voice, said: "You may go."

145

'Half the household had heard the screaming and the story of the lovers' first quarrel was being retold in Buckingham Palace before Tony and Margaret had driven back to Clarence House in his car – in silence – and was the source of speculation by most members of the royal households.'

One of Tony and Margaret's most ardent supporters from the start was the Queen Mother. Perhaps it was her own memories of her younger days which prompted her tacit acceptance of Margaret's romance with Tony. She obviously knew that Margaret and he were spending every available weekend down at Royal Lodge because she herself was going down less and less often, probably because she had guessed that they had become lovers and wanted them to have the privacy to explore their relationship fully.

The Queen Mother was no prude and knew from her own observations what antics the couple got up to in Windsor. Like the way they would suddenly decide to change from evening clothes to swim suits and also, as their detectives occasionally observed, went 'skinny-dipping' for a midnight plunge.

As always happened in the midst of a love affair, Margaret was at her slimmest and healthiest during that year. Guests and detectives alike were moved to comment on the stunning loveliness of the 29-year-old princess. Her picture, looking so beautiful and fresh and full of life, dominated the front pages of the world's press. Speculation continued unabated as to who she would choose as a husband. The one name that was never mentioned was that of Tony Armstrong-Jones.

11

True Love

Throughout that long, warm autumn the royal couple became more and more deeply involved in their love affair. By mid-autumn Armstrong-Jones was Margaret's constant companion. The other escorts, though still receiving their kisses when they called at Clarence House, were slowly being discarded.

The pair spent many evenings alone in Clarence House, dancing to romantic music on the record player or just sitting with the windows open, hand in hand on a settee, smoking, chatting and planning. It was a source of great amusement to friends when Margaret sang or played anything special for Tony. He would sit and listen attentively and make all the right, appreciative noises and remarks. But the truth was, he was tone deaf, although, as far as anyone is aware, he never confided this information to Margaret.

147

Hardly a day went by without him calling at the house, writing or telephoning the princess. Often a letter would arrive in the morning post and he would deliver one by hand later in the day, sometimes following this up with a visit in the evening. By this time he was 'Tony darling' to the princess and he was always greeted by her with a big kiss, usually full on the lips.

Some six months before their wedding and some time after Tony and Margaret had become unofficially engaged, a most unusual conversation took place at a Clarence House luncheon. Princess Margaret was sitting next to her lady-in-waiting, Lady Elizabeth Cavendish. The luncheon was going well and there was the normal animated chatter when a nearby observer heard Lady Elizabeth say casually: 'Have you heard the news, Ma'am?'

Margaret carried on eating and replied: 'What news?'

'Why your dear cousin Pamela is to marry that person Mr Hicks.'

Margaret's fork dropped with a clatter on her plate. 'Oh no', she exclaimed. 'She couldn't. Does she realise what he is?'

She was obviously shocked that her cousin, Lady Pamela Mountbatten, was contemplating marrying an interior decorator. Lady Elizabeth continued: 'It's true, Ma'am. After all, they are two of a kind.'

Margaret frowned and said: 'I really must remember to have a word with Pamela before she goes any further with this.' There was an embarrassed silence at the table for a few moments, then Margaret quickly changed the subject and the chatter started up again.

These seemed very odd remarks coming from Margaret, who, before long, would be announcing her own engagement to a commoner, a photographer.

TRUE LOVE

The Queen Mother was in on their secret, as was the Queen but she could have had only the slightest idea of the true intimacy of their relationship, and the general impression was that they thought she would not have been too pleased if she had known, for if ever the Queen visited Royal Lodge during one of their runaway weekends, Tony would go into hiding.

The window of his bedroom overlooked the Royal Chapel which the Queen, and perhaps Prince Philip and the children, would attend from Windsor Castle on a Sunday morning. This, of course, was a great advantage. Revealed one weekend guest:

'Whenever the Queen dropped into the Lodge for a drink with her sister, the main guest in the lodge would hide quietly away in his bedroom, coming down only when he saw the Queen and the royal party move off down the drive.

'Nothing, as far as I know, was ever said about this habit, but Princess Margaret would expect Tony to come down as soon as she had seen the Queen away. And they would carry on as if nothing had happened'.

The garden at Royal Lodge involved another of Margaret's little habits, one which put her in the bad books of the Royal Lodge gardeners. She liked to walk around the garden, looking at the hedges, bushes, rose trees and flowers, with a pair of pruning shears in her hand. Explained one of her weekend guests:

'One would spot her in the garden working the shears in the air until she found something to chop. Then she would hack away like mad, leaving a pile of little

149

clippings on the grass. Any plant which took her fancy would get a royal crew cut and she often walked deliberately beneath an out-of-the-way tree to see if she could find an excuse to lop off a low twig or two.

'But one day she went too far. Watching the princess altering the garden layout was like watching a silent comedy. It was hilarious. She had evidently decided that one of the hedges, which divided the garden, was much too long. In fact, to reach one of the spacious lawns did involve walking right to the end of it, turning at the top and walking back along the other side. Margaret tackled the job with utterly feminine determination.

'She inspected the hedge two or three times, walking up and down on both sides with a frown creasing her forehead. Then she made her decision and trotted away. She came back with a pair of large hedge shears in her hands.

'Without further ado, she started hacking away at the middle of the beautifully groomed hedge until she was standing calf-deep in snipped branches. She worked away with fierce determination and, when she was done, she stepped back over the debris to survey her work. She had hacked a wide, ragged hole in the hedge to make a short cut. It was enough to make the gardeners weep but the sight made me cry with laughter.'

The gardeners grumbled like mad about it when they had to get to work to tidy up Margaret's handiwork and make the hole neat. They also complained loudly that their beloved potting shed had been turned upside down, with rakes, spades, forks and other garden tools strewn about the floor.

It was also to the poor gardeners that Margaret complained about the swimming pool. They always drained it the day she returned to London and refilled it with fresh water the day she got down again to the lodge. She once marched two of them out by the pool and told them the water was 'filthy'. 'Look at that,' she said pointing to the surface of the water. It was two autumn leaves!

The gardeners scooped them out but still the princess was not satisfied. That afternoon, while Tony lounged in a wicker garden chair by the edge of the pool, Margaret scuttled off, reappeared with a long-handled scrubbing brush and spent an energetic twenty minutes scrubbing the sides of the pool. Only after she had completed the full circuit of scrubbing and inspecting did she throw down the brush and splash into the water.

Visitors during those months usually found something to amuse them at Windsor Royal Lodge. It was as though Margaret wanted every day to be a fun day. One royal insider remembered a very amusing incident during a weekend there when Margaret and Tony had gone on to the terrace to take photographs.

She heard howls of laughter wafting in through the open french windows and, after a particularly prolonged gust of laughter from Tony and the princess, she let her curiosity get the better of her.

'There was Princess Margaret wearing a pair of old grey slacks, a red checked shirt, man's shoes and a brown trilby hat pulled rakishly down over her eyes. Her hair was tucked away under the hat and she was standing in a manly pose against the balcony.

'But even more startling than the princess was Tony Armstrong-Jones. I just stood there grinning from ear to ear. Margaret too was shaking with laughter at the sight of Tony's spindly bare legs protruding from beneath her brown pleated skirt.

'He had on one of Margaret's long-sleeved white blouses and an enormous floppy picture hat. His feet bulged in a pair of her delicate, open-laced sandals.'

The intimate evenings at Clarence House continued towards Christmas, as did the secret dinner parties in Pimlico and in Tony's rented rooms across the river in Dockland. They had even taken the Queen Mother across to the Dockland hideaway where they played the piano and sang until after midnight. Yet the newspapers, although occasionally mentioning Tony as being in a party with the princess, had not seriously linked their names and usually only publicised the bigger nights out when the princess went out with a crowd.

She did not always enjoy publicity. Arrangements for her to go to the theatre, for example, were made by a lady-in-waiting, using her own name to book seats, but it sometimes happened that these outings did make the papers. Occasionally, Margaret would be furious about it.

One night, after what must have been something of a mêlée of photographers outside the theatre where she had been to see the Brendan Behan play *The Hostage*, the princess returned to Clarence House in a fury. She marched straight out of her car and stormed into her sitting room, where she summoned her detective, Chief Inspector Crocker.

The poor detective had been an impotent witness while Lord Plunkett had pushed aside the photographers to make way for Her Royal Highness. When she had reached her car, the photographers had crowded round, trying for a picture. The princess, quite out of character, was so enraged that she apparently put her hand over her face to prevent them taking pictures. She told Crocker he would have to be more careful or make better arrangements when she went out. Quite obviously the theatre people knew him, she said, and they expected to see her when he arrived. He really would have to do something abut it, she told him. She could not have scenes like that whenever she went out for the evening.

Poor Crocker could only agree, of course, and was dismissed from the room in disgrace. On that occasion, however, it had been the theatre management who had tipped off the papers but Crocker still had to take the full blame.

Like any woman celebrity, the princess was never entirely happy with the hundreds of pictures of her that appeared each year in the papers and magazines. She would often complain to her friends about how awful she looked in the papers, or would ask, resignedly, why they couldn't have used a better one.

Once the princess turned to a lady-in-waiting and, holding up a picture of herself in the *Daily Mail*, said: 'Look at that. Isn't it terrible. That's that awful man Rothermere on the warpath again.' She believed that Beaverbrook and Rothermere both had it in for her personally.

However, it was no longer the big occasions that the princess looked forward to. She seemed happiest when she and Tony were alone together, doing the simplest things, although going off to his flat alone for the evening struck those of her friends in the know as possibly the most startling departure from the rigidity of royal protocol. About a dozen times Tony returned Margaret's hospitality by taking her to his home for supper.

He would collect her in his car, brown paper bags of groceries on the rear seat, and drive the mile or so to his little, studio-cum-flat in the Pimlico Road or across to Rotherhithe and the docks.

The princess loved these occasions. It was the sort of thing she had never done before. They were like two care-free children off on a picnic. In the shopping bags Tony brought with him were packets of frozen food, steaks, perhaps a few slices of smoked salmon and sometimes a bottle of wine.

On one November day they drove down to spend a weekend with Jeremy Fry and his wife at their home near Bath. Tony and Jeremy had known each other since before the chocolate tycoon was married. It was during this weekend that Tony confided to Jeremy that he was going to marry Margaret and asked his old chum to be best man. No one believed then that a 1952 homosexual conviction and a pending charge would come to light and make it necessary for Jeremy to stand down.

That winter – her last as a single woman – one saw the absolute beauty of Princess Margaret. She was the spirit of happiness personified, a lively, exciting young woman who was giving her whole soul to the job of being in love. The romance had blossomed within a mile of London's West End club land, under the noses of her 'set', yet even at that late moment only a handful of people were aware of what was happening. The royal romance between Tony and Margaret was running as hot as the weather was, suddenly, running cold.

12

A Wedding
to Remember

The Queen was aware of her sister's marriage plans shortly after the question was popped at Balmoral in October 1959. Elizabeth was one of the first to be shown the engagement ring – a ruby set in gold and surrounded by diamonds – which Tony gave Margaret before Christmas.

It was decided at Balmoral that no formal announcement could be made until after the birth of the Queen's new baby in February. Elizabeth appeared determined that nothing would be allowed to sidetrack the public's attention from her own happy event.

It was not until exactly one week after Prince Andrew's birth – on 26 February – that the world was stunned to learn:

'It is with the greatest pleasure that I can announce the betrothal of my beloved daughter, the Princess Margaret, to Mr Antony Charles Robert Armstrong-

Jones, son of Mr. R.C.L. Armstrong-Jones and the Countess of Rosse, to which union the Queen has gladly given her consent.'

It was signed Queen Elizabeth, the Queen Mother.

The day before, Tony had cabled the news to his old friend Jocelyn Stevens in the Bahamas. The two men had not spoken since Tony had revealed his romance with Margaret the previous year. Stevens was utterly opposed to the affair and had heatedly argued with Tony, advising that to continue further with the relationship was madness. Stevens's succinct reply to Tony's cable read: 'Never has there been a more ill-fated assignment.'

Other friends were even more pointed in their reactions. 'Have a bloody good affair with her, but for God's sake don't marry her,' was the concensus of opinion.

Inevitably, there were those who questioned Tony's suitability as a husband for the princess. After all, he was the first commoner to wed the daughter of a British monarch in 457 years. Surprisingly, Margaret's most powerful ally came from an unexpected source, Prince Philip, who was devoting himself more and more to his position as the Queen's chief supporter and principal counsellor. The couple were consolidating their marriage in every possible way, noted royal observers.

Philip overrode the objections in typically pungent language, particularly concern about Tony's father, twice a divorcee, who had recently taken a lovely young air hostess to be his third bride. According to some, Mr. Armstrong-Jones Senior's divorce court record would have barred him from contact with the Queen on most occasions. To hell with protocol, decreed Philip. If the fact that the bridegroom has three mothers is a problem, then sort it out.

Armstrong-Jones Senior had a much more practical answer and had already communicated it to his son – begging Tony to call off the wedding. 'It can only end in disaster,' he warned.

Ronald Armstrong-Jones was in Bermuda, on his third honeymoon, when the announcement was made. 'I wish in heaven's name this hadn't happened,' he is reported as saying. 'It will never work out. Tony is a far too independent sort of fellow to be subjected to discipline. He won't be prepared to play second fiddle to anyone. He will have to walk two steps behind his wife and I fear for his future.'

A more tangible problem appeared on 18 March when it was announced that Jeremy Fry would be best man at the Westminster Abbey wedding. Rumours began circulating almost immediately about a conviction in 1952 involving a homosexual offence.

On 6 April the chocolate company heir issued a statement from his home. He regretted that he would not be able to attend the wedding of Princess Margaret and Tony Armstrong-Jones due to a recurrence of jaundice, from which he had suffered periodically since childhood. Ninety per cent of the world did not believe it, but Fry actually retired to his bedroom and gave interviews to pressmen propped up in his massive bed, looking fit and deeply suntanned after a winter holiday. (Fry and his wife eventually separated and divorced after thirteen years of marriage and five children.)

When Jeremy Thorpe was proposed by Tony as his second choice for best man, and the security services advised that he, too, was homosexually linked, Prince Philip was moved to ask whether there were any heterosexual contenders for the role of best man.

Tony produced a short list of other possible candidates and a somewhat distant friend, neurologist Dr. Roger Gilliatt, whose father was surgeon gynaecologist to the Queen, was chosen as the most suitable. It caused considerable head-scratching in the newspaper offices of the world. They searched their files for him – and found nothing. Plans for the 6 May wedding went ahead.

The world had scarcely digested the revelations of the Fry scandal when news of a less serious, but potentially just as embarrassing, situation began to trickle through to the royal family.

In their determination to make Margaret's wedding a really big show of family unity, invitations had been sent out all over the world. One of the prime objectives had been to gather together as many of the reigning monarchs of Europe – many of them relatives of the Queen and Margaret – as possible, under the great, vaulted roof of Westminster Abbey.

Duly, the gilt-edged cards, styled by the finest calligraphers in the world, popped up in the pick of Europe's palaces and stately homes. 'The Lord Chamberlain is commanded by Her Majesty, Queen Elizabeth the Queen Mother to invite...' they read. But they were received coolly by the crowned heads of Europe who seemed to show no great eagerness to attend the untitled photographer's wedding to Princess Margaret. One by one, the apologetic rejections, supported by a variety of 'previous engagements', were delivered by stony-faced embassy officials to Clarence House.

In the Netherlands, Queen Juliana had announced that she would be attending celebrations commemorating the anniversary of the Dutch Liberation. Her daughter, Crown Princess Beatrix, had excused herself because the wedding clashed with her visit to a tiny country town. A statement from Juliana's household: 'It is the wish of the Royal Family to say nothing at all. You must draw your own conclusions,' had already been released.

In Norway, King Olaf would be at the two-hundredth anniversary celebration of the Royal Norwegian Society of Science. His son, Crown Prince Harold, would be away on army exercises. It was stated by a palace official as being 'sheer nonsense' that they would not be attending because Tony was a commoner.

In Sweden, the royal family had declined the invitation because of the state visit of the Shah and Queen of Persia, which was due to begin the day before the wedding.

In Belgium, King Baudouin had pointed out that he was due to attend a concert at Antwerp Opera House on 6 May. His refusal to attend the wedding was polite, but firm.

Probably the most humiliating refusal came from the present King Juan Carlos of Spain, then Don Juan Carlos, Pretender. He replied from exile in Portugal, declining the invitation. He explained that May was a very busy month as many Spaniards visited the Fatima shrine celebrations in Portugal on 13 May and took the opportunity to call on him!

Publicly, the royals smiled their regrets but privately they seethed with anger and embarrassment.

Meanwhile, as the wedding arrangements shambled forward, the Archbishop of Canterbury, Dr. Fisher, showed his disapproval, already privately voiced, by not turning up for the rehearsal with Tony and Margaret but leaving it to a stand-in.

Tony found himself virtually a prisoner in Buckingham Palace. Ostensibly there as the Queen's guest so that he could be on call for discussions about the wedding, Tony found that his movements were seriously restricted. This was best illustrated by his stag party. He had intended it to be two nights before the wedding, just like Prince Philip's stag night before his wedding to Elizabeth. However, on the night on which the party had been discreetly arranged, the shuttered windows of his old home and studio in Chelsea remained darkened. That morning he had telephoned friends to say the party was off. Far from playing host at the anticipated binge, Tony was enduring a rather strained dinner party at the palace with Margaret, Philip and the Queen. He was packed off to bed at 11 o'clock.

On the morning of 6 May the fabulous glass coach, with its four smart carriage horses, swept from Clarence House in bright, early summer sunshine and turned towards the Mall. The clatter of hooves was instantly drowned in the tumult which swept along the Mall as the dazzling coach wheeled into the centre of the road beneath the crowned arches, entwined with thousands of red roses. Even someone as used to crowds as Margaret looked in wonder at the delirious thousands – many of whom had waited all night – who jostled and screamed their good wishes to their favourite princess.

Worldwide, millions of eyes watched this first ever televised royal wedding as the coach, flanked by its escort of stiffly mounted Household Cavalry, came to a halt beside the red carpet leading into Westminster Abbey. Moments later, leaning on Prince Philip's arm, Margaret was gliding along inside the abbey, decorated with thousands more flowers, marguerites and roses in honour of Princess Margaret Rose.

It was a glittering, stylish and regal wedding, outdoing Hollywood, and, to the mystified onlookers, only one facet of it produced a puzzled reaction – the behaviour of the Queen, whose expression of distaste seemed to leave no room for doubt about her attitude towards the wedding. Three hundred million people were witnesses – through the eyes of the TV cameras – that she plainly seemed to wish she were elsewhere.

Throughout the ceremony, which momentarily touched the hearts of even the most sturdy opponents, she looked daggers at everyone. Foreign journalists reported that she seemed scarcely able to concentrate on the procedure and looked about her with thunder on her face. British journalists have another name for this expression by the Queen. They call it 'po-faced,' and it was firmly in place when Margaret and Tony, now man and wife, rounded the altar after signing the register and came in sight of the Queen. Margaret halted and dropped a pretty curtsy to her sister, while Tony bowed slightly and stiffly from the waist.

The Queen looked at them coldly, responding to the curtsy and bow with only the smallest nod of her head. Her 'po-face' was fully operational.

Even close friends of the royal family have disagreed as to why the Queen was in such a savage mood that day. Some claim that she was happy for Margaret to be marrying at last, but critical of the man she had chosen. Some say that the sight of Margaret walking down the aisle on Philip's arm had roused memories of her own wedding which, coming so soon after the war, had been a far more austere affair, so that her main emotion was envy. Others say that she was just plain jealous of her sister marrying a good-looking, fun-loving young man with whom she could enjoy a future that was not rigidly defined by duty. If there was a single, simple explanation, I have not been able to discover it.

The wedding breakfast at Buckingham Palace over, the couple made their appearance on the balcony overlooking the Mall. There was no doubt about the feelings of the crowd. Margaret and Tony were greeted with a roar of approval which was heard half-way across the capital.

Four miles away, on the Thames by Tower Bridge, Vice Admiral Peter Dawnay, on board the Royal Yacht *Britannia*, was in his sea cabin. His sealed orders lay open and charts of the West Indies were not far from hand. Half an hour later, Margaret and Tony were aboard, being ushered by two impassive stewards to their vast state room, which occupied the whole of the superstructure above the deck towards the stern. Seconds later, from the deck came the sounds of shouted orders, the hoot of ships' sirens and, from beneath them, the first gentle throb of *Britannia's* engines.

The honeymoon had begun. The first 4,000-mile leg across sunlit seas was to take the 5,769 ton, £2,000,000 yacht to the island of Tobago. From then on it was Margaret's ship to do with as she pleased. She knew the islands well from her official tour in 1955. Now, only she knew which of the lovely, palm-fringed bays she would choose to land in.

For the honeymoon couple the worries, hitches, scandals, family rows and general confusion surrounding their wedding were forgotten as they lost themselves in each other.

On shore, however, the snipers were still at work. Although their honeymoon was less than 24 hours old, it had already cost the taxpayers nearly £1,000. And this staggering bill, the equivalent of a bank manager's annual salary in those days, would continue to increase by the same amount each 24 hours throughout their 40 days of bliss.

A WEDDING TO REMEMBER

A week earlier, arguments about the cost of the honeymoon had reached Parliament. In the Commons, the secretary to the Admiralty had been forced to admit that the weekly pay bill for the 236 crew and 21 officers on the *Britannia* totalled £4,000 alone, without fuel and catering expenses.

Such was the public outcry that the Queen Mother, always ready to spring to the defence of her daughters and the family's honour, had been moved to offer £40,000 from her own purse to finance the honeymoon.

The critics, shamed by the Queen Mother's generous offer, stilled their gossip for a time. Prime Minister Harold Macmillan advised the Queen that it would be politically inexpedient for the Queen Mother to pursue the matter, 'It would', he told her pointedly at their weekly meeting, 'be playing straight into the hands of Your Majesty's Opposition.'

For Tony and Margaret their leisurely cruise among the islands in the sun was a peep into paradise. A small piece of that paradise had been permanently reserved for Princess Margaret by her former escort Colin Tennant, now married to Lady Anne Coke. The year before, after selling a small estate in Trinidad, Tennant had invested the money in buying the private Robinson Crusoe island of Mustique, close to St Vincent. It measured three miles by one and a half and had a tiny, resident, black population. Tennant had offered Margaret an ocean front plot as a wedding present and he and Anne flew down to join the royal yacht to give them a personal tour of the island.

They visited several palm-ringed coves but decided to put off making a final choice of site until they could study maps back in London. From the outset, Tony was against Tennant's gift and wary of Tennant himself, perhaps envying him the easy familiarity with his wife which came from more than a decade's friendship and which included a well-known romantic fling.

Tony cautioned that her patronage would give the island a terrific commercial boost and could benefit Tennant to the tune of millions. Tennant later admitted that her association was 'obviously helpful' in promoting the venture but that when he originally made his offer he had no plans to develop the island commercially.

In 1977, Tennant sold the island he had bought for £45,000 for undisclosed millions and, today, more than 50 homes there are owned by millionaires who are pleased to have Princess Margaret as a neighbour.

Tony, despite his great love of sun, sea and palm-fringed beaches, thereafter refused to be associated with Mustique, turned down Margaret's request to design her house there and never visited again.

13

Married Life

On 18 June, a scorching summer day, the *Britannia* steamed majestically into Portsmouth harbour. The couple returned to London by train and, two hours later, after changing in Clarence House, were on their way to Windsor Royal Lodge.

That night, they dined with the Queen, Prince Philip and the Queen Mother at Windsor Castle and Margaret recalled later: 'It was one of the happiest family meals I can remember.'

There was more laughter the following day when Princess Margaret informed Tony: 'Someone has stolen you from my side.' Prince Philip had telephoned the Royal Lodge to report that someone had stolen Tony's effigy from the Tussaud waxworks in London. The news that the effigy had been carried from the waxworks was the joke of the weekend but, soon enough, more serious business arose. They returned to Clarence House for a temporary stay until their grace-and-favour, ten-roomed house in Kensington Palace was made ready for them, at a cost to the Treasury of £6,000. Tony talked incessantly about design and décor while Margaret busied herself in conferring with Clarence House officials about suitable servants. Among those proposed for the job of butler was one Thomas Cronin – and more trouble was on the way.

Princess Margaret's purse from the Civil List had automatically been raised to £15,000 a year when she married. As Tony had repeatedly insisted that he was not a member of the royal family, only married to one, who was determined to pay their household expenses out of his own earnings, it was then queried why her Civil List payment should more than double.

The explanation was simple. For eight years Margaret had lived, and shared expenses, with the Queen Mother in Clarence House. Now she was moving into a home of her own and needed a private staff to enable her to carry out her duties. This, unbeknown to or guessed at by Margaret, was to create the first of a series of adjustment problems for Tony. Margaret had been used to being surrounded by servants all her life. Tony, who had thoroughly enjoyed being waited on hand and foot at Clarence House, Windsor Royal Lodge and other royal residences, was not used to handling servants. He had never had to share his home with anyone who wasn't a lover, a friend or an assistant.

Five weeks after their return from honeymoon, the newlyweds moved into 10 Kensington Palace. With them went the butler, Thomas Cronin, Princess Margaret's maid, Ruby Gordon, the housekeeper, Nora Foley, plus a cook, a footman and a chauffeur. Princess Margaret also had a private secretary, who came in daily, and shared a press secretary, Major John Griffin – who had accompanied them on honeymoon – with the Queen Mother.

A little under a month later, the peace of the palace was shattered late one August afternoon with the arrival of a taxi outside No. 10. Out of the house stormed its intended passenger, Cronin. 'I'm damned if I'll work for them,' he roared, throwing his two suitcases into the back of the cab. With a venemous glance at the red-brick house, he gave the taxi driver an address in Notting Hill and drove off, into a blaze of publicity.

Cronin talked, long and loud, to the *People* newspaper and its legendary editor, Sam Campbell, about the way Tony had behaved on becoming master of his own household. He complained that Armstrong-Jones made it impossible for him to do his job of running the household properly, by taking it upon himself to account for every shilling spent.

Cronin called it interference because he was told what wines to order, what rates to pay the cleaners and asked to give an account of all the money spent. Tony even suggested that, with Cronin's help, he could build wine racks himself to cut expenses.

However, the butler, quietly backed by Princess Margaret, had secretly ordered wine racks and a selection of moderately priced wines. When confronted by Tony, he explained that, with the Queen liable to dine with them, a certain minimum standard was expected in the wine cellar.

When Cronin spent £20 on servants' cutlery and requested a £100 float for daily tradesmen's bills, Tony exploded. He cut the float to a quarter of Cronin's figure, explaining that it was his hard-earned money that was being spent. He wasn't going to pay more just because his wife had a title. Cronin quit.

Margaret's answer, unthinkingly, was not to teach but to take over, which she did in almost every area of their lives within three months of marriage. Margaret's public duties took her out several times a week and, to begin with, Tony insisted on tagging along as escort. At first he quite enjoyed playing royals, walking the regulation one pace behind his wife and adopting the typical hands-behind-the-back pose of all the royal males.

Said a royal observer of the time:

'Tony quite liked the glamour and being the centre of attention. But that soon wore off and he discovered that what he was doing, both on and off duty, was playing second fiddle to his wife.

'In public she was in complete charge. And to many – which gradually began to include Tony – she was in charge at home as well. Certainly, nobody who went as a guest had a chance of getting out of there until one or two in the morning; often much later. Tony would start trying to steer people out around midnight, but Margaret, with years of experience at not going to bed until the early hours, would bully people into staying and no one could quit, including Tony, until she decided to go to bed.'

Sometimes the strain would tell and there would be whispered, snarled words between them but their body language shouted the news that they were a couple still compulsively physically involved.

Said one old friend:

'It was the last thing to die in their relationship. Had it not been for the sex, their marriage would have collapsed far sooner. They had an incredible lust for each other. They would touch and squeeze each other in front of friends and strangers alike. There were times when they couldn't keep their hands off each other and one could sense them straining at the bit in their eagerness to get to the bedroom.

'There may have been rumours about their stormy relationship but theirs was a very passionate and physical marriage and she certainly didn't go short in that direction.

'When she did turn to other lovers during her marriage, it was because of his indifference and that she suspected him of chasing other women, not because she had been sexually disappointed.'

Another subject on which they found themselves in total accord was the question of a title for Tony. The Queen had broached the subject before the wedding and Tony had politely, but positively, turned the offer down. He still wanted to be respected in his own right, he said. Margaret had been just as adamant. Tony should not be given a title – still a distinctive honour in those days – simply for marrying a princess who happened to be the Queen's sister.

Despite this, Margaret privately admitted that she loathed being called 'Mrs Jones' by the media. Officially, she remained Her Royal Highness, the Princess Margaret.

After the announcement of their engagement, Tony's agent had released sets of his royal photographs which had earned substantial amounts in royalties worldwide.

However, after their marriage Tony found his career put on hold. Within months he was finding life in the royal goldfish bowl unremittingly boring. Areas of social concern provided material for documentary work but Tony missed his true vocation. It was repeatedly explained to him that he could not return to his old life as a photographer as his new position would give him an unfair advantage over his competitors and the Queen would frown on his connection with the royal family being commercially exploited.

Tony's consultancy at the Design Centre was unpaid and a commission accepted from Regent's Park Zoo, to design a new aviary, was hardly going to provide the kind of income he would need to pay what he considered to be his share of household bills. When Margaret announced, in April 1961, that she was pregnant there loomed the added financial burden of supporting a child. Tony was determined not to become a kept man but recognised, realistically, that the money he had amassed as a photographer before his marriage was not going to be sufficient to live off.

To her credit, Margaret recognised the need in Tony to be self-sufficient and, even more important, usefully employed. Sorting things out with the Queen was her department. Tony, she declared, should look for work as a photographer. It was what he was best at and loved best.

Thus it was that, towards the end of 1961, four significant events in the Armstrong-Jones household occurred almost simultaneously. The first was the question of Tony's ennoblement. The Queen was eager to honour her brother-in-law and Tony and Margaret both recognised that a baby altered matters. He or she would be fifth in line to the throne. The ordinary 'Master' or 'Miss' titles would not really suffice.

170

It has been suggested that Princess Margaret was disappointed when Tony was not offered a dukedom as Philip had been and felt that she was again being restricted to second best. However, Margaret denies this and says she was perfectly content with the earldom he was granted. 'I know my place,' she told biographer Christopher Warwick. An earldom carries a courtesy title of viscount for a son and lady for a daughter.

After much research, Margaret and Tony opted for first Earl of Snowdon, in honour of his Welsh ancestry, and named his subsidiary peerage after his maternal grandfather, Linley Sambourne, a famous *Punch* cartoonist.

The announcement was made on 3 October. One month later, on 3 November, Viscount Linley of Nymans weighed in at 6lb 4oz.

Six weeks later he was christened David Albert Charles in the music room of Buckingham Palace. His godparents were the Queen, Lord Plunkett, Lady Elizabeth Cavendish, Lord Rupert Nevill and the Rev. Simon Phipps, later to become Bishop of Lincoln.

The birth of David raised the immediate problem of a larger home for the Snowdons. The solution was just a stone's throw away. No. 1A in Clock Court, Kensington Palace was a 21-room home on four floors which had been left empty and decaying since the previous occupant, Princess Louise, Duchess of Argyll, the fourth daughter of Queen Victoria, had died there in 1939 at the age of 91.

Some of the rooms had not been decorated for nearly a century. There was also a certain amount of bomb damage from World War II which hadn't been repaired. The whole building had been left to rot.

The government allocated £55,000 for the restoration work, on top of which the Queen donated a further

£20,000. However, this didn't prevent a Commons attack, accusing wastage of public money. MP Willie Hamilton referred to Margaret as 'a kept woman', but the public and press refused to endorse the Commons whingers and the furore was over in a couple of days.

Much of the renovation work was undertaken personally by Lord Snowdon. He also supervised the installation of an office, dark room and studio in the basement; for which he negotiated a separate rental and rates deal for himself. It was to take almost two years, however, before the place was habitable.

Between the two events a twin-pronged approach to the *Sunday Times* was made, seeking a job for Tony. Princess Margaret's effort came in a private chat with Jocelyn Stevens who was asked to whisper in the ear of *Sunday Times'* editor, Dennis Hamilton, that Tony would not turn down the right job offer.

Tony, meanwhile, was having similar talks with old friend Mark Boxer, who had been hired by the *Sunday Times* to launch its colour magazine.

Whichever approach was responsible, it resulted in the newspaper's owner, Roy Thompson, having a meeting with the new Lord Snowdon and offering him a £5,000 a year job as artistic advisor on the embryonic magazine. He would receive generous expenses and there would be plenty of international travel.

Told of the job offer at one of his weekly meetings with the Queen, Prime Minister Macmillan raised no objections. They agreed that the *Sunday Times* must not unfairly obtain royal exclusives because of Tony's family connection, nor should his name be used for promotional or advertising purposes. Additionally, said Harold Macmillan, he must keep away from politics.

MARRIED LIFE

The announcement of Tony's *Sunday Times* appointment provoked an immediate backlash, but not before another incident had angered press and public alike and caused an end to the honeymoon period between them and the royal couple. It involved the Snowdon's infant son, David, and, as well as earning the criticism and disapproval of the British public, it was also the cause of Tony's first major disagreement with Margaret.

It all stemmed from Margaret's decision, two months after the birth of Viscount Linley, to leave the baby in Britain and fly off with Tony for a holiday in the West Indies. A quarter of a century later, Princess Diana and Fergie were both to experience the same hostile reaction from the public when they travelled abroad without their babies, but this was 1962 and Princess Margaret was undisputed star of the royal family show.

Tony had been overjoyed when his son was born in Clarence House, the Queen Mother's home, on 3 November. He spent every available moment with his son and took hundreds of pictures of the baby. 'I am the world's happiest father,' he told friends, and meant it.

Princess Margaret, however, although an adoring mother, was less inclined to spend all her time with their child. She, like all royal babies up to that time, had been cared for from birth by a nanny and reared by a nanny and a governess. She had seen her mother before nursery breakfast and her parents together in the late afternoon. For Margaret this was the way things should be.

After recovering from the birth, her first thoughts were to seek the sun and escape the confining regime which every new mother knows is essential to the smooth running of the nursery and the well-being of her baby.

It was mainly to avoid these restrictions – and the necessary four-hourly feeding sessions with her son – that she elected not to breastfeed her baby. Even before the birth she had voiced her decision to take a three-week holiday almost immediately afterwards.

Tony, too, had been raised by a nanny, but his mother, Anne, until her separation from Ronald Armstrong-Jones when Tony was three, had rarely been parted, even for one night, from her son.

He believed that for a child to grow up happily, it should have the company of its parents every day, even if only for a few hours. Margaret's decision to leave their baby and fly 4,000 miles to Antigua wasn't what he had expected. 'How can one bear to spend three whole weeks without seeing the baby?' was his very middle-class reaction, one that amused Princess Margaret who explained that the nanny, Verona Sumner, and her nurse assistant knew far better how to take care of him than she did. Little David wouldn't know who was feeding him when his parents were not there. After all, she had been the one who had had to carry him all that time. She needed a holiday.

When news of their departure on holiday appeared in the British newspapers, public criticism was almost universal. 'Cruel' and 'heartless' were typical of the comments aimed at the fly-away parents, but Margaret appeared unrepentant. The criticism was ignored as she lay sunning herself on a West Indies beach.

Tony, who had anticipated the hostile reaction, was more concerned about the public's attitude. Despite the calm meteorological conditions, several stormy moments hit their Antiguan hideaway. This was one of the first real intimations that, perhaps, the marriage was not quite as perfect as it had seemed.

The press attacks had barely abated when the announcement came of Tony's appointment to the staff of the *Sunday
Times*. While Thompson preened, *Observer* editor David
Astor wrote: 'It will inevitably seem unfair to rival newspapers and magazines that the Queen's close relative is
used for the enlargement and enrichment of the Thompson
empire.' On television he claimed it was 'potentially
harmful to the standing of the monarchy'.

Thompson retorted by saying that he had employed
Tony because 'I don't know of a better unemployed photo-
journalist.'

Poison-pen letters began arriving in the morning mail at
Kensington Palace but, as usual, they were sifted out
before Margaret saw them. However, the combined furore
over their holiday and Tony's job lasted only a few weeks
and soon Tony had settled down to a return to his old life
as a photographer, while Margaret concentrated on the
refurbishment of their new home.

In August 1962, Princess Margaret, representing the
Queen, sat on the throne in Kingston, Jamaica, with the
Earl of Snowdon at her side, and officiated at the independence celebrations which signalled the end of 307 years of
British rule. Tony, who had still not become totally bored
with playing escort to his wife on ceremonial occasions,
fully participated in the four-day visit and, together, they
gave events a glamorous sparkle which had been sadly
lacking on the post-war royal front.

1963 saw the move to their new home in Kensington
Palace. Their second child, Lady Sarah Frances Elizabeth
Armstrong-Jones, was born there on 1 May the following
year.

One of the godparents at the Buckingham Palace
christening, six weeks later, was Anthony Barton, an old

chum of Tony's from his Cambridge days. Barton, together with his Danish wife, Eva, and their two children, lived in Bordeaux where he had inherited a family wine business. Within two years, as his own flirtatious escapades became more emotionally complex, Tony did nothing to discourage a close relationship developing between Barton and the princess. It led to her falling in love with her husband's close friend – with explosive consequences.

However, in 1964 Tony and Margaret still made a sparkling pair and, on the surface at any rate, mutual disillusion had as yet produced no tarnishing effect.

In August the couple flew to Sardinia as guests of the Aga Khan, Prince Karim, the Ismaili spiritual leader, in his private Falcon jet. The young prince, known to his friends as K, put them up in one of his hotels in Porto Cervo and placed his fabulous yacht, *Amaloun*, at their exclusive disposal.

Tony, who had accused Tennant of exploiting Margaret over Mustique, seemed unconcerned that they were providing international publicity for K's fabulous new holiday resort on Sardinia's Costa Smerelda in exchange for their luxurious freebie holiday.

In the mid-sixties Tony and Margaret – or Tone and Pet as they called each other – had become the darlings of swinging Britain. Princess Margaret enthusiastically embraced the mini-skirt, though never the micro, the twist and the music of the Beatles, which she says she adored from the start.

Tony had dropped almost all of his pre-marriage friends and, together, they had collected as eclectic a circle of characters around them as it was possible to imagine. Artistic, Bohemian, theatrical and sometimes downright bizarre, the faces now mingling for drinks in the giant drawing room at Kensington Palace were representative of the sexual freedom and open experience of the swinging sixties and were, for the most, household names. Yet Tony and Margaret had virtually no *real* friends at all. The people they socialised with and invited into their home were transient neighbours on a constantly revolving, new society carousel.

Some, like Peter Sellers, Rudolph Nureyev, Mary Quant and Edna O'Brian, were introduced by Tony who had met them on photographic assignments. Some they met at parties and others, like the Aga Khan and Stavros Niarchos, who played host to them on his private island, were just international socialites.

However, always at the centre of attention – shining more brightly than any of the stars – was Margaret. Peter Sellers said she was more of a sex goddess than his new, second wife, Britt Eckland, and her movie contemporaries could ever aspire to be.

They were heady and enchanting times but, despite the considerable outside stimulation and excitement, something began to go very wrong between the princess and her husband.

Annual holidays in Sardinia and Italy continued and, in 1965, they enjoyed rave reviews in a tour of America and were wined and dined by President Johnson in the White House at the first such social event since the assassination of Kennedy. Glimpses were still to be seen of the dynamic couple of their early years together but, far more frequently, they were being remarked on for their apartness and their growing vindictiveness towards each other. Their tastes and their respective circles of acquaintances were diverging and each seemed daily more ready to hurt or belittle the other.

'Whatever happened to the man I married?' Margaret was heard to ask one day. 'Tony was so charming. So easy to be with. Where has he gone?'

Once, when Tony returned with a modern American painting, Margaret told him frankly: 'I don't see anything in that at all.'

'Then I'll hang it in the toilet,' Tony told her crudely. 'You'll be able to contemplate it at your leisure and learn to appreciate it!'

If he arrived home and found Margaret entertaining some of her older friends, he would sometimes ignore them completely and go straight to his office area in the basement.

Margaret showed herself equally capable of such embarrassing tactics. At a party in a London club, given by Peter Sellers, the couple arrived together but, from the first moment, Margaret left Tony's side and spent the entire evening talking to her friends. She ignored him for three hours. It was a dangerous tactic and it failed to work for, shortly before the party ended, Tony left without her and she had to make her own way home.

At another society party, thrown by a newspaper proprietor, Tony approached Margaret towards midnight and suggested they leave. 'I'll leave when I decide,' she told him and dismissed him with a wave of her cigarette, without so much as a glance in his direction. Tony stood his ground. 'I've already decided we're leaving,' he told her quietly. 'If you're not ready to go in five minutes then I intend leaving ayway.'

Margaret did not answer. True to his word, Tony left five minutes later and, once again, Margaret had to rely on another guest to drive her home.

It was when Margaret was being at her most imperious

and completely ignored anyone who didn't observe full, royal formality in her presence that Tony became most irritated. If she believed she was not being treated with sufficient reverence, she would icily dissect the offending person with vicious sarcasm. Like the Queen, she could, unblinkingly, cold stare someone down in response to any remark she took offence to. If she were in the wrong mood, this could be the most innocuous comment.

Once, when two pals were being given the full treatment at Kensington Palace, Tony announced: 'It's colder in here than in a Siberian winter. Let's go downstairs where it's warmer,' and he led them away.

Said one of the Snowdon circle:

'The breakdown in their relationship was very dramatic. One moment they couldn't keep their hands off each other and the next they were sniping and stabbing at each other like lifetime enemies.

'Any kind of peace or co-operation that had existed in their home was being remorselessly destroyed. They had become like strangers living under the same roof.

'On one occasion he returned from an assignment abroad and, as he walked through the house, the colleague who accompanied him asked: "Aren't you going to say hello to your wife?"

'"Good heavens, no", replied Tony. "She won't want to see me."

'He gave the impression that he didn't care if he never saw her again. Both of them were drinking more heavily and that, as usually happens, only exacerbated things.'

On 27 January 1966, after a two-year illness, Tony's father, Ronald Armstrong-Jones died of cancer. It was a body blow for Tony who had worshipped his father. His resistance seriously depleted by grief, Tony felt unable to cope with the appalling bickering at Kensington Palace and persuaded the *Sunday Times* to organise an assignment abroad.

Shortly afterwards, he was on his way to India. Behind him in Kensington Palace he left a lonely, deeply unhappy, confused and affection-starved wife. And, knocking on the door, came Anthony Barton.

As a friend of that time put it:

'Tony had encouraged their friendship. He had even asked Barton to act as a companion to Margaret should he be working abroad.

'Everyone suspected that Tony was throwing them together to justify or compensate for his own activities with other women. But I don't think Tony suspected that she was actually falling in love with his friend. She became very deeply and emotionally involved.'

One member of the Margaret 'set' was quoted as saying:

'It was a very strange business. The thing only lasted three days. It was a flash in the pan. The marriage had been going wrong for some time. Margaret was flirting with anybody. She did it just to hurt Tony. She told all her friends about it. There was no way it could stay secret, or last very long. We all thought M was behaving very strangely. In the end it upset her too. She went and told all to Barton's wife.

'It was Margaret's first taste of adultery and she revelled in it. It didn't cause the reaction she might have expected. Far from wrecking the marriage, Barton and Eva stayed together stronger than ever.'

The first Eva knew of the affair was when Margaret confessed and said how sorry and guilty she felt.

As the friend at the time put it:

'Margaret felt that what she had done with Barton warranted a confession, although this could have been simply a ruse to get the information to Tony, who might otherwise not have known. But if she felt such genuine remorse then it was clearly much more than a reassuring kiss and cuddle.

'From what those who were in the know say, and judging how it shook their spouses when Margaret revealed all, the affair was a serious one, however short-lived.'

Surprisingly, the Bartons and the Snowdons managed to get back on speaking terms and, by July, they were dining together again, although joint holidays and invitations to stay in each other's homes were to be a thing of the past.

Tony's initial anger, explained the friend, surprisingly gave way to a new period of intense physical activity between him and Margaret. 'And no doubt Tony believed, too, that she owed him one!'

14

A House Divided

Tony had his own, painful experience to warn him of the terrible unhappiness that could be inflicted on children if their parents parted.

His own parents had divorced when he was just four years old and the shy, sensitive child was committed to spending the free time of his formative years divided between his mother and his stepfather in Ireland and his father and stepmother in England.

It was for this reason that he had waited until he was 30 – and believed he was sure the marriage would work – before he took the decision to wed, for he wanted his family to have all the lasting love and security that he had never known.

In the past two years, Tony had sadly detected some of the problems that had broken his parents' marriage arising in his own.

Anne and Ronald Armstrong-Jones had both found it difficult to adjust to the other's very different circle of friends. Ronald would often sit scowling and casting a chill on the atmosphere while his wife entertained her pre-marriage friends, such as Margaret was to do when Tony invited the chums of his photographic activities to Kensington Palace.

In his parents' case, it was Tony and his sister, Susan, who had eventually suffered when the marriage failed and he was determined that the same should not happen to his children.

Try as he might, Tony could not persuade Margaret to take a family holiday with the children apart from at Sandringham, Windsor and Balmoral, the royal residences that were, to Tony, more purgatory than pleasure. It was to be ten years – with their marriage already in tatters – before he would persuade her to take David and Sarah abroad with them on holiday.

It was for this reason, as much as any other, that he began refusing to join Margaret on her twice-yearly sun-shine holidays in Sardinia and the West Indies. Thus began her habit of taking holidays apart from Tony; a habit that was to lead to her seeking out other companions to replace him, culminating in her affair with Roddy Llewellyn, which rocked Tony completely.

In 1966, however, Tony was looking for family time and a place to spend it, so he jumped at the offer from his uncle, Oliver Messel, to take over the family's 500-year-old home in Sussex.

Old House was made up of a pair of Tudor woodsmen's cottages, knocked together, with a Georgian wing attached. Water was hand-pumped from the garden to a bathroom tank and the only lighting came from paraffin lamps. Here, in the 30 acres of woodland around the five bedroomed home where he himself had played as a child, Tony determined to establish a happy family home for himself and his children. If Margaret should wish to join them then so be it, but this was far from a prerequisite for success.

As it turned out, Princess Margaret had her own ideas about a family country home. She had taken a shine to Sunninghill, where she had briefly enjoyed water-skiing lessons on the lake. Apart from the natural beauty of the area, it had one paramount advantage for Margaret. It was close to Windsor, the Royal Lodge and the Queen.

She wanted their country retreat to be a home they had planned together from the start, not a hand-me-down from somebody else. Old House on the Nymans estate at Handcross (the grounds had been handed over to the National Trust by the Messel family) lacked the comfort and facilities Margaret was used to and she vetoed Tony's plan to renovate.

Having reached an impasse the Snowdons called in an advisor and asked him to choose the better scheme. He favoured building afresh at Sunninghill and Tony, ostensibly complying with this verdict, agreed to start drawing up plans with Margaret.

It never happened. Secretly Tony commissioned the expensive renovation work on Old House to go ahead at full speed. He had already obtained permission from the National Trust to make extensive changes and to create a lake in front of the house which would have a centrepiece of a pagoda on an island. Tony planned to pole out to this in a Venetian-style gondola.

He had earned a considerable sum from the sale of his latest book, *Private View*, and had been given a substantial pay increase at the *Sunday Times*, so money was not a problem, although much of the real donkey work was carried out by cheap student labour during the holidays.

When she found out he had reneged on their deal, Margaret said she felt 'crushed'. The damage done to their already rocky marriage was incalculable and, judging from the manner in which he did it, Tony probably knew of this effect from the start.

Nigel Dempster quoted Princess Margaret as saying: 'Tony broke up the whole marriage by going there. We were going to build a house at Sunninghill by the lake where we water-skied and then, without telling me, he went off and started Old House.'

Margaret went along to the opening ceremony, at which the Queen Mother cut a ribbon and the Queen led the cheering, but went again less than half a dozen times after that before refusing to return. She just didn't enjoy being there. It was fascinating that then, on one of these week-ends, Tony invited a mutual friend, club pianist Robin Douglas-Home, to stay. Within six months, Robin was to become Margaret's first major lover since her marriage, if one ignores the comparative hiccup of Anthony Barton.

Margaret's criticisms and open dislike of the place led Tony to comment wickedly that this proved, perhaps, that he had got it right. He had certainly wanted a place where he and the children could escape from what he called 'the unnatural atmosphere of a royal palace' and behave like ordinary people, free of nannies, servants and royal etiquette.

Thus began a gentle tug of war for the affection of their children that was to last into adulthood, for Margaret disliked the cramped conditions of the Sussex cottage, the lack of formality and the casual friends Tony invited to share his country retreat. She preferred to spend her week-ends at Royal Lodge, Windsor, the Queen Mother's home which had been renovated by her father before he became king. Here, with its liveried servants and formal meals, constant changes of clothes and everyone's deferment to her as the Queen's sister, the last real princess was in the environment she loved best – and the one most detested by her husband.

His most prevailing argument was that the children had to learn that not everyone ate off bone china with silver cutlery and drank out of crystal and gold. 'They must be allowed to be children and not mini-personages.'

As they grew older, David and Sarah tended to agree. They loved the freedom of Tony's country hideaway where they could run wild and escape from the chilly discipline of the royal households. As a boy, David particularly enjoyed fishing and lived for the hours when he could sit with Tony by the lake in the front garden. When he was eight, he was enrolled at Ashdown House, a £200-a-term boarding school just a few miles from the cottage.

Every free day the boy had from school, Tony, if he was in Britain, would spend it with him at the cottage. There they fished and Tony taught him to use a camera and also encouraged his son to assist in making furniture and other useful items in the carpenter's shop he had built.

Unfortunately, in the early days and on those rare occasions when Margaret joined them, the visits were frequently marred by the couple's quarrels. Her temper was such that Tony's friends would cry off their visits if they knew she was going to be there. 'It was therefore a relief all round when she decided to stay away entirely,' said one.

'Our marriage is in the mud,' Margaret told one friend.

The princess with her tragic, secret lover, Robin Douglas-Home.

Robin Douglas-Home at his wedding to beautiful English model Sandra Paul.

Top: Robin Douglas-Home's country home where he first made love to Princess Margaret.

Below: The nightclub pianist turned author in reflective mood in his quaintly decorated 'snug'.

Above: Princess Margaret dances with lofty Billy Wallace. Their romance led to a brief engagement in 1956.

Below: Princess Margaret represents the King for the first time at an official royal, foreign celebration.

Fashion is ignored by the royals when they dress to face the raw Scottish weather during their Balmoral holiday.

Princess Margaret and Tony Armstrong-Jones looking radiantly happy on their wedding day in 1960. But within a few years the marriage had become a sham.

Top: Lord Snowdon and his lovely, young mistress, Lady Jackie Rufus-Isaacs.

Below: Princess Margaret and Roddy Llewellyn, the last and youngest of her lovers, share a private moment on the beach of her island paradise of Mustique.

Left: Sophisticated and beautiful, the princess in formal pose for her twenty-first birthday.
Right: In more relaxed mood for a theatre outing in London's West End.

Just how deeply in the mud it was became painfully apparent when, towards the close of 1966, Princess Margaret took as her lover part-time club pianist Robin Douglas-Home.

It was to be another twelve years before her divorce from Tony was granted but, effectively, the princess's marriage ended then.

15

For Love of Robin

Princess Margaret's counter-reaction to the breakdown of her marriage was as typically selfish and headstrong as it was classlessly age-old. She embarked on a disastrously inappropriate love affair with a totally unsuitable man, someone who was even more emotionally unstable than herself.

She was 37 years old, overflowing with self-pity, subject to frequent bouts of extreme depression and occasional suicidal urges, lonely, neglected and bordering on alcoholic. Princess Margaret also seemed to apportion all of the blame for the collapse of their marriage to her husband.

As daughter and grand-daughter of king/emperors, the last princess to be raised in the unreal world of Victorian royal splendour, spoiled beyond redemption by her doting father, it has never occurred to Margaret to feel culpable when finding herself in a situation not to her liking.

She couldn't understand why Tony had grown to hate even being in the same room as herself. No one dared tell her what her breathtaking arrogance stopped her recognising in herself: that her imperious hauteur and rudeness were almost unendurable to most ordinary people.

Her marriage was suffering the worst imaginable seven-year itch, so Margaret scratched it.

Having another man to love and be loved by seemed to her the only acceptable antidote to Tony's vacillating, icy indifference or sneering contempt. Her choice of lover was prompted as much by convenience and as an instrument of revenge on Tony, as by yearnings of the heart.

He was a sometime friend of her husband and had, in the past, stayed with them at Tony's hideaway cottage in Sussex. Effete, increasingly raffish aristocrat and part-time night club pianist, Robin Douglas-Home was a hard-drinking, gambling womaniser who also viewed suicide as an acceptable alternative to personal problems.

A less suitable lover for the world's most beautiful and glamorous princess would have been hard to imagine, but Margaret knew that knowledge of her affair with Robin was guaranteed to drive Tony into a frenzy of outrage and jealousy. She also felt in charge of the relationship – dominating Robin socially, mentally and sexually. Said one palace observer who was close to her then: 'Without being able to admit it properly, even to herself, Princess Margaret desperately needed to be loved, even by somebody as degenerate as Robin. It was either that or go under completely. And I believe she came very close to that at the time.'

By the latter half of 1966, Princess Margaret's most regular bedtime companion had become a bottle of Scotch – which she drank alone – often while telephoning her friends until 2 or 3 o'clock in the morning, weeping inconsolably or ranting about the loveless life she was enduring with Tony. The more concerned, and one must say courageous, of her friends cautioned her of the possible perils of mixing copious quantities of whisky with some of the pills known to be contained in her Kensington Palace medicine cabinet. A concern they felt was fully justified when, early in 1967, during one of Tony's foreign assignments, she was rushed to the King Edward VII Hospital amid reports that she had taken a deliberate overdose of booze and pills. Not a serious attempt at suicide but a *'cri de coeur'* was the considered opinion. However, in Margaret's unstable state at that time, the one could so very easily have turned into the other without being intentional.

The Tony with whom Margaret was then living had become a stranger to her. To her utter bewilderment and distress, her once amusing, gentle, friend-turned-lover-turned-husband had become, she confided to her 'in' set, 'a monster', a heavy drinker at home who ridiculed her friends and her lifestyle or acted as though she did not exist.

When he was out on assignment, either in Britain or abroad, he deliberately refused to contact her, she complained, or even to tell her where he was staying, sometimes for weeks on end. Indignant phone calls from Margaret, asking after his whereabouts, became part of the daily routine at the *Sunday Times* after he started working there. She complained that when Tony actually did talk to her, he would taunt her with hints and innuendo about his possible romances while, at the same time, acting unreasonably jealous over almost any man she invited to Kensington Palace.

In turn, Margaret was convinced that Tony was having an affair with a close friend and colleague. The princess was also pryingly suspicious of Tony's relationship with a young photographer. 'I understand Tony better than anyone else,' she told a friend at the time. 'I also know when to worry and when not to worry about what he is up to.'

She certainly understood Tony well enough to know what his reaction would be when he heard that she was sleeping with Robin Douglas-Home. There were plenty of Margaret ill-wishers in London only too delighted to report her activities to Tony when he was away. And there were several who were eager to tell him what was going on with Robin. One insider recalls: 'His jealousy went into over-drive when he heard about Margaret's affair with Robin. He was furious but in public he kept his cool.

'There had been rumours in the American press that the royal marriage was in difficulties and when Tony flew to New York, after more than a month in Tokyo on assign-ment for the *Sunday Times*, he was pressured into making a press statement.'

The statement was made on 27 February 1967 in the New York offices of *Vogue*. 'Talk of a rift is totally unfounded,' he said. 'It's news to me and I would be the first to know. I am amazed.'

He said this knowing that his marriage was in a parlous state, that his wife was having an affair with his friend and that he had himself enjoyed more than one romantic fling on the side. He said it partly to protect his own pride but mainly out of loyalty to the royal family. Tony's loyalty to the Queen in particular was, and remains, absolute and he is still highly regarded and liked by her. In any case, divorce for the Snowdons was then considered to be out of the question so Tony saw little point in giving fuel to the rumours.

However, his coolness did not extend to the private domain. Margaret reported to Robin that Tony was 'hopping mad, more angry than I have ever known him. He never wants to see you or hear your name mentioned again'.

Ironically, as Tony was issuing his press statement in New York, Robin was driving through the gates of Kensington Palace on his way to join Princess Margaret.

How was it that these two men had come to share the love of the world's most beautiful and romantic princess?

Robin was nephew and heir-in-line to the Earl of Home – Alec – who renounced his titles to become prime minister in 1963. His father was a retired army major and noted ornithologist and he was also a distant cousin to a future emotional victim of the royal family, Lady Diana Spencer, the Princess of Wales to be.

Robin told me that he first became aware of Tony Armstrong-Jones about the time World War II ended. They were both pupils at Eton, although Robin was two years Tony's junior and certainly remained unknown then to Margaret's future husband. He remembered Tony boxing for Eton against Beaumont – and winning – and his triumph in the school finals when the fight was stopped in the second round in Tony's favour.

Said Robin:

'That was the first year we both saw Princess Margaret in the flesh for the first time. King George VI and the Queen and Elizabeth and Margaret came to Eton on an official visit to knight Sir Henry Martin.

'They came again two years later, for the five-hundredth anniversary of the visit to Eton by Henry VI in 1447 and Margaret, who was only a few weeks off her seventeenth birthday, looked a damned sight more attractive, even to a pimply youth of fifteen.

'Tony was back then, after a year's absence with polio. I suppose we may both have harboured a few, lusty, youthful fantasies about the beautiful and very well developed royal teenager but I, for one, never in my wildest imagining believed she would one day become my mistress. And I'm sure Tony didn't picture her as his future wife either.'

After leaving Eton, Robin infuriated the school's governors and staff by writing an article that was highly critical of the school's sadistic beating rituals in which he had several times been a highly reluctant participant. It was a precedent he followed a few years later when he wrote another highly critical report, this time of and to the War Office.

During a tour of active duty in Aden as a captain in the Coldstream Guards, one of his troop was killed by Yemen terrorists. Robin wrote accusing the War Office of risking the lives of British soldiers without any scruples. They were not impressed and Robin felt obliged to resign his commission. He said: 'They didn't think my attitude was sufficiently in line with the military policy of the day. An amicable parting of company was swiftly formulated. In other words I got out.'

Robin left the army a gifted and popular mess pianist and now began to play in a succession of night clubs which were frequented by Princess Margaret and her friends. 'She knew every popular song and tune,' said Robin, 'and she loved to sing along or play along with the pianist. She took a shine to me and I soon found myself being invited to parties where she was guest of honour.'

Margaret found him an amusing and entertaining addition to her 'set'. Although not one of the key members, like Johnny Dalkeith (Earl of Dalkeith), Sunny Blandford (Marquis of Blandford, son of the Duke of Marlborough), Lord Porchester (son of the Earl of Caernarvon), the Hon. Peter Ward (son of the Earl of Dudley), Lord Ogilvy (heir of the Earl of Airlie) and Dominic Elliott (younger son of the Earl of Minto), he became one of the favoured few like the Hon. Colin Tennant (heir to Lord Glenconnor), Billy Wallace (who inherited millions from his Tory Minister father) and David Pelham (razor blade heir and theatre impresario), who knew a warm welcome awaited them among Margaret's entourage.

At about this time the princess – who, from the age of twenty, had been involved in romantic flings with several male members of her set – was unofficially engaged to Billy Wallace and her already celebrated roving eye somehow passed Robin by.

Her turnover of boyfriends was notably high, both during and after the Townsend affair, which royal observers of the day said finished on her side long before her October 1955 'no marriage' proclamation.

A friend of that time revealed that Princess Margaret had a whole string of relationships throughout the fifties (her twenties), ranging from casual to very intense. Most lasted no longer than a few weeks; none more than a few months. Margaret made a revealingly wry observation to a friend, delivered, said the friend with considerable rancour, to the effect that every time she tried to develop a more intimate involvement with a man, he announced matrimonial plans within a matter of months. 'One kiss from me seems to send them rushing pell-mell up the aisle with someone else,' she is said to have remarked. Certainly, by the end of 1955 Dalkeith and Blandford were married and Tennant, Ward and Porchester were all husbands-in-waiting. 'I've been left on the shelf,' Margaret joked to her friends.

At that time, Robin Douglas-Home who, until the age of 24, had had little reputation as a ladies' man, was about to embark on his first great amorous adventure.

Robin's contact with royalty had not been limited to Princess Margaret. He also became friendly with the Duke of Kent and his sister, Princess Alexandra. 'There were a few possible sparks of romance between us,' Robin recounted to me years later. 'But they never ignited into a proper blaze. Pity, because she was far and away the sexiest and most daring woman in the royal family.'

Robin's reputation with the ladies was to change dramatically before his twenty-fifth birthday came around. In fact, his popularity rating with women was soon to become the stuff of legends. Dozens of them, young and old, married and single, blue bloods and commoners, were to tumble to his seductive wit and old-fashioned charm. Reminisced one society beauty who fleetingly enjoyed his bed:

'He was capable of directing all his attention at you – which so few men are. You truly believed at the time that what you were doing and saying were the most important things to him in his life. He was, one always felt, emotionally vulnerable and that made him, if anything, even more attractive.

'He had a weak mouth but it managed to say all the nicest things and was very good at kissing, I remember. He certainly knew where to press all the right buttons and was an excellent and imaginative lover.

'The only thing I found a bit off-putting was that he spoke with quite a high-pitched voice. He was almost fey and I know I wasn't the only woman who initially questioned his sexuality. He could so easily have been homosexual. He liked women in an intense way; the sort of way that homosexual men like us – experiencing with us rather than off us.

'Those may well have been the aspects which eventually appealed to Princess Margaret, because, apart from favouring men who were physically well endowed, Margaret was frequently attracted to men whose sexuality was – at the very least – questionable.

'At least one of her men was homosexually active before his relationship with the princess.'

However, at the end of 1956 the actual princess in Robin's sights was neither Margaret nor Alexandra. She was Margaretha, 22-year-old grand-daughter of King Gustav of Sweden ... and she was besotted with him.

Margaretha had been introduced to him by friends at a London party and had fallen immediately under his spell. At that time Robin's professed job was as a trainee account executive with a major advertising agency, but his preferred work was as resident night pianist in the cocktail bar at the Berkeley Hotel in Piccadilly.

After their first meeting, Princess Margaretha became a Berkeley Hotel cocktail bar *habituée* and it was soon very plain to waiters and regulars alike that she was in love. In fact that was a mild description of what she was experiencing. Margaretha was infatuated. She would sit gazing at Robin with calf-love eyes as he played her favourite melodies.

It was a love fully and genuinely requited by Robin,

although he was the first to admit that he did not possess the financial wherewithal to back his suit. However, that did not stop him, he later admitted to me, from taking advantage of her intense feelings towards him. He could, and did, invite her back to his London home where, behind locked doors and drawn curtains, he claimed, their romance blossomed. By the New Year, their love for each other was no longer in question and they had begun to discuss marriage. But, inevitably, friends of the Swedish royal family became aware of what was going on.

Equally inevitably, when she was told, Margaretha's mother, Princess Sibylla, was aghast and ordered her immediate recall. Her father threatened to throw Robin from the battlements of his palace if he ever showed up in Stockholm. In March 1957, the love-struck princess was hastily bundled off across the North Sea and placed in the protective care of relatives in Denmark.

Revealed Robin:

'The whole idea was to keep her incommunicado from me. They couldn't stomach the thought of their royal blood mixing with a drop of vintage club pianist brew. But I'm afraid they were a bit late for that.

'I rattled off a formal letter to her parents asking for Margaretha's hand in marriage though I recognised, right from the outset, that my chances of being accepted by the family were somewhat less probable than the survival of the proverbial cat in hell.

'I was given no opportunity to push my proposal in person for almost a year and, even then, under almost total watchdog conditions. We had privately swopped troths in London and I knew her love for me was utterly genuine. As was mine for her.

'But her whole family were lined up against me. She was left in no doubt by old King Gustav that she would forfeit all her royal rights if she married a commoner. She had that problem, as well as her love affair with me, in common with Princess Margaret.

'They both plumped for the rights and privileges when it mattered – and who, say I, could blame them.

'My uncle may have been the Earl of Home, Leader of the Conservatives in the House of Lords, Secretary for Commonwealth Relations and Lord President of the Council but I was still considered to be of pretty low stock by the Swedish royal family.

'Margaretha's mother, Sibylla, wasted no time in answering my proposal of marriage. The letter came back within a fortnight. The answer was brief and gave not the slightest possibility of but one interpretation. It was "No!".'

The public announcement from Count Carl-Reinhold von Essen, Master of the Swedish royal household, was equally as unequivocal. 'Mr Douglas-Home's suit for the hand in marriage of Princess Margaretha has been refused.'

The count added:

'Reports that Mr Douglas-Home asked for Princess Margaretha's hand are true. But the whole matter has been settled. It was a little innocent affair in London as so often happens between young people and the whole matter was ended with Princess Sibylla's reply to the Englishman's letter of proposal.'

The King did not write a letter of his own to Robin as a result of the letter of proposal, but the King's will was expressed in Princess Sibylla's reply. This reply was very polite but definite. The proposal was, from the Swedish point of view, to be considered as impossible.

Robin's mild-mannered father, Major H.M. Douglas-Home dismissed the affair as 'just a boyish romance. It is very silly to make such a fuss of it all,' he said, obviously thinking the matter not serious.

The romance may have been written off by parents on both sides as an innocent and childish affair but Margaretha and Robin were not prepared to have their relationship so easily and conveniently quashed. The princess was convinced that she was still in love with him, no matter how much her parents argued his total unsuitability. She still wanted to marry him. Margaretha's reaction was a forerunner to that of many other women who would give their hearts to Robin during the following decade.

Somehow, Robin and Margaretha contrived to exchange telephone calls and letters and, more than a year after Sweden's royal family had formally announced the rejection of Robin's suit, it was grudgingly announced that he was to visit the princess. Princess Sibylla was heard to mention engagement plans 'having to be postponed' – a far cry from her 'out of the question' edicts of the previous summer, although she continued to question publicly whether 'the sentiments Margaretha feels for Mr Douglas-Home are lasting'.

'Privately she was still telling Margaretha that she would forget me the moment someone decent came along,' said Robin.

In August 1958, Robin was a guest in King Gustav's palace. He lunched and dined with Margaretha and Princess Sibylla and King Gustav himself took the young couple for a drive in the country. He sat in the car while they walked along the banks of a frozen lake at Drottning-holm discussing their future together – or lack of it.

Soon afterwards, Robin left Sweden and quietly announced to friends that the wedding plans could now safely be considered off. It was he, he said, who had ended the romance and cancelled any arrangement they might have had for the future. He refused to discuss the romance after that but, until his death, a photograph of the princess signed 'All my love, darling. Margaretha' stood on his dressing table.

Shortly before his death, Robin did admit to me, with a very large and appreciative grin, that at their last meeting King Gustav had told him he would rather commit Margaretha to a nunnery than allow her to marry him. 'He told me very bluntly that I had "no fucking chance", said Robin. 'And I believed him. When kings make comments like that you know in your heart that they are not kidding.'

Princess Margaretha was finally married six years later, in 1964, to London businessman Mr John Ambler.

Robin did not let his experiences with the princess and the events in Sweden go entirely to waste. Thinly disguised, they provided part of the background to his second novel *When the Sweet Talking's Done*, published just a few months before his death.

Years later, when Robin discussed it with me, he said: 'She was the first princess to let me down.' He was monu-mentally subjective about everything. 'It hurt me very badly. Tore me apart inside to be rejected like that. What never occurred to me was that it might happen again – with another princess – and that the hurt could be even worse the second time around.'

FOR LOVE OF ROBIN

That second royal romance and rejection were still almost a decade away – a decade in which both Robin and Princess Margaret would find unexpected happiness in marriage, followed by appalling heartbreak as their relationships with their partners disintegrated.

Within a year of ending his relationship with Margaretha, Robin had married an eighteen-year-old international model, Sandra Paul, unquestionably one of the most beautiful women in Britain.

At the same time, that other British beauty, Princess Margaret – her almost farcical engagement to Billy Wallace behind her – was herself falling in love and beginning to contemplate marriage with Tony Armstrong-Jones.

Sandra Paul was earning up to £100 a week – a fortune in those days and equal to at least £3,000 today. Robin had spotted her at a fashion show and, purely by chance, then recognised her in the street a few days later. He invited her for a meal, took her to a cocktail party on the way, and, by evening, had decided he was in love.

He told me she was the most beautiful girl he had ever seen and that was good enough for him. Friends believe that he may never have taken account of her other attributes. She had a gentle, sunny personality and over-flowed with natural charm, but within was a character of purest steel.

Said one friend: 'I don't think Robin ever got to grips with the real Sandra Paul, the fabulous lady behind the initial shy smile and stunning beauty.'

Before their fashionable wedding in St James's, Piccadilly, Robin behaved impeccably; he formally asked her doctor father for her hand in marriage and bought her a diamond and ruby engagement ring. This time he was not told that he was too common.

201

Said the friend:

'Unfortunately for Sandra that's exactly how he acted after the wedding. Throughout their marriage he treated her in the most disgustingly offhand manner, even trying to convince her and others that her modelling success was due to her marrying him and being able to use his famous name. He seemed determined to undermine her confidence in herself in any way he could.

'Of course, having girls on the side was the most effective way of all. And he had those aplenty.

'The only point in his favour I could score him was that although Sandra was earning far more than him, he never used her money. He insisted on supporting them both, and their son, Sholto Alexander, who was born three years after their marriage, out of his earnings.'

They lived partly in London and partly in the country in a seventeenth-century farmhouse on the Surrey/Hampshire border, which he had bought when he believed his engagement to Princess Margaretha might still go ahead.

In the country, they were weekend hosts to numerous famous celebrities including Princess Alexandra. In London, they were essential guests at all the right parties. It should have been the ideal marriage, except for one major flaw – Robin himself.

He may have married the nicest and most beautiful woman on the London scene but, for Robin, when it came to sex, the grass in the other field was always greener. He couldn't resist any girl or woman who crossed his path. His adultery was so blatant and so frequent that it was impossible to keep it hidden from Sandra and he made little or no effort to try. On one occasion, he was caught, *in flagrante delicto* with a titled woman in the back of his car. He had a particular penchant for mobile sex and many of his conquests were on the back seats of chauffeur-driven limousines, hire cars or ordinary black cabs. He said that knowing there were wheels under him always turned him on. He was notorious for clutching ladies tightly by the cheeks of their bottoms while dancing and for groping them in the backs of taxis. Anything on wheels became a substitute bedroom in Robin's mind.

Sandra stuck it out for two years after the baby was born before leaving for New York and a trial separation. Robin chased after her and begged her to come home and try again. When she did, he perversely announced that he had now decided to leave her instead.

This immensely talented musician and writer seemed incapable of sustaining a normal, loving relationship with a woman and incapable, too, of being loyal to those who trusted him. It appeared that only by destroying the love and trust of those closest to him could he achieve any kind of reward or satisfaction.

Yet, everyone is agreed that his divorce from Sandra permanently scarred Robin. In the end, he agreed to provide her with evidence and stage-managed two adulterous scenarios, one involving a paid partner, a very unpleasant individual, he remembered, and one with an obliging friend. However, believing that the evidence of adultery would not be sufficient, Sandra Paul's solicitor sued, in addition, for cruelty. Robin's reaction to this petition was one of bitterness and bewilderment. 'It was as though a small bomb had gone off inside my head,' was his later recollection.

'It chapterised the marriage day by day and, incidentally, letter by letter, in the most vicious and unpleasant terms, with me as the aggressor and cruel one.

'Five years of one's life, say 70 per cent of which were very happy, reduced to a great wad of foolscap typed out by leering little clerks in solicitors' offices.

'I couldn't bear her to put a kind of tombstone on this marriage reading in the way that petition read.'

Sandra was granted her divorce in the Divorce Court on 21 June 1965 but she was never truly rid of Robin until he committed suicide three years later. He virtually hounded her into her second marriage, say friends, by telephoning her umpteen times a day, demanding her attention and time like some demented second child.

Robin extorted private meetings with her under the constant threat of his suicide. He would not accept that he was out of her life forever. Yet, at the same time, he was still sleeping with other women whenever the opportunity presented itself. With a charm honed to perfection during scores of romantic conquests, Robin succeeded in winning the close friendship of women who were far more recognisable on the international scene than even Sandra Paul. Somehow, he managed to break through the barrier of grief and suspicion inside which US president's widow, Jackie Kennedy had cocooned herself after the 1963 assassination. He became a close friend and confidante. So close, in fact, that, in 1966, he became the only man, up until then, whom Jackie had allowed to holiday with her and her children. He repaid her trust by selling everything he learned in a series of tabloid articles. This betrayal angered and saddened Jackie and, understandably, sent her already deep distrust of her fellow creatures plummeting to new depths.

Robin's friendship with Frank Sinatra was capitalised on in similar style after the crooner announced that Robin was one of the very few people he could trust to talk to. In return, Robin turned out a fast biography of the singer, except that this time there was no flak as Old Blue Eyes actually approved of what Robin had written about him.

Not so lucky was Richard Harris's wife, Elizabeth. Richard was in Hollywood and Elizabeth had returned to London, aware that their marriage was in trouble and not knowing if it would, or if she wanted it to, survive.

Robin had made an artform of seducing lonely wives whose self-esteem had taken a beating at the hands of insensitive and inattentive husbands. Elizabeth proved easy prey. After they were introduced at a dinner party, he invited her to tea at the Ritz. He plied her with charm and attention and she adored it. When their affair was over the ex-Mrs Harris, ex-Mrs Rex Harrison would ruefully admit: 'In nine years I'd never been unfaithful to Richard but I now developed an intemperate passion for an entirely unsuitable man.'

In her autobiography, Elizabeth wrote: 'My fear of Richard was turning to hatred. The animal quality I had once found so exciting now sickened me. I longed to be with a man who was quiet, gentle, and to return to London. One evening I met Robin Douglas-Home. He asked me to tea at the Ritz. He was amusing. Attentive.

'I had no experience of leading a double life and Richard became suspicious.'

However, Robin was a past master at leading a double life and once he was certain he had Elizabeth safely ensnared, he began his old game of sneaking 'quickie' affairs on the side. Some, he recalled to me afterwards, were so quick that they lasted only a few minutes. The thrill of the chase, the explosive confidence-fix of success-ful conquest were becoming, the ageing Lothario admitted, almost as essential to him as a full hypodermic syringe to a junkie.

Discretion had hardly been his forte when cheating on his wife but when it came to cheating on Elizabeth, which he did throughout their relationship, he rarely attempted the most rudimentary cover-up. He even telephoned his other women in front of her. Gone was the old-world charm. Even the pretence of love.

Tragically for Robin, it was not just in his attitude towards women that his behaviour was starting to unravel at the seams. He was drinking far more heavily and his gambling was beginning to get out of hand. Money from an early novel and press articles had long since dis-appeared and Robin found himself deeply in debt. It is a good measure of his moral degeneration by that stage that he turned to Elizabeth for the money. He had treated her incredibly badly, exposing her callously to his string of 'bits on the side' as he referred to his extra-relationship couplings, but he still persuaded her to bail him out of his financial jam.

Elizabeth recalled that she pawned her diamond bracelet and most of her rings to give him £2,000 – a tidy sum of money in the sixties. 'But that changed our relationship,' she wrote. 'We drifted apart.'

The affair with Robin did spark off one of Richard Harris's most spectacular rampages when he and Elizabeth were aboard the *Queen Mary* with astrologer Patric Walker, bound for New York.

On their first night at sea, when Harris became aggressive, Patric, who was seeing a new side to Richard, sensibly retired to his cabin. At the dining table, Harris was just getting into his stride, recalled Elizabeth.

'I was a whore, a cheat, a slut. Within minutes Richard had inflated my single adventure [with Robin] into a series of cheap affairs.'

Elizabeth excused herself and went to Patric Walker's cabin. He had been reading a book in bed and was consoling Elizabeth when Richard walked in.

'Patric was lifted out of his bed bodily and hurled across the cabin. He landed in a surprised, silken heap. Not daring to move a muscle, Patric looked on while Richard systematically wrecked the cabin. Flowers, silver picture frames, silk shirts, patent leather pumps, hosiery, bedside trinkets and mementoes filled the air in orbital fury. Then, just as suddenly as Richard arrived, Richard left – his anger spent.'

With Elizabeth out of his life, Robin turned again to piano playing to save the day. It, at least, provided him with some money, a steady supply of drinks and the chance to pick up girls. It was a month before Christmas 1966 and Britain was at the zenith of the swinging sixties when Robin Douglas-Home, now aged 34, took up occupancy of the horse-shoe-shaped piano at the Society restaurant.

Where once he had been a glittering star, Robin was now a slightly broken-down pianist from a vanished era. His consumption of champagne cocktails, always his favourite drink, rose, it seemed, in ratio to the lack of interest and applause from the surrounding tables. Most evenings ended with him weaving unsteadily into the night, his mind dulled by alcohol and wearing his depression like a cloak.

Princess Alexandra, still a friend and supporter, and her husband, Angus Ogilvy, dropped in with friends in an attempt to revive the carefree, funfilled nights of the fifties. Others from the Caprice, Mirabelle and the Casanova slipped in a couple of times to try to boost his spirits, but Robin's brand of music had given way to the Liverpool sound and even the royals were now dancing to a new kind of beat.

As Christmas approached, Robin found himself once more out of a job but with something, at least, to smile about. His writing was starting to generate a little money and he found he was, again, in demand on the social circuit. Suddenly he was, *de novo*, being fêted by the old members of the Margaret 'set' – regrouped to support the princess through the break-up of her marriage to Tony and surrounding her on her desperate nightly search for happiness in the fashionable clubs and restaurants of London's West End.

16

The End
of the Affair

Thus came for Robin Douglas-Home, after almost a
complete decade, that magic moment when he found
himself back at the princess's table. He had been a dinner
party guest at Kensington Palace during that time but his
direct contact with Margaret had been minimal.

Now it seemed as if time had stood still: the same
sycophantic faces in attendance, older but just as eager to
please; the same, almost endless ritual of lighting her
cigarette in its holder; the same whisky and water at her
elbow; the same, rather tacky, platform shoes on her feet,
still trying to boost her height by a couple of extra inches
from her genuine five feet two inches.

What was new was the sadness and the scarcely
concealed signs of desperation. Robin's finely tuned
antennae twitched, almost unbidden, into life. He could
recognise a disspirited and lonely woman sooner than any

man in London and before him was a classic example of the genre.

Robin's pursuit of Margaret was no different to that of scores of her predecessors. His charm and exclusive attentiveness were the two main weapons in his seduction armoury and he put them to work.

He told me long after their affair was over:

'It really surprised me just how like any other woman she reacted. She felt trapped in a loveless marriage and guessed that her husband was carrying on with other women.

'She wanted to strike back in kind but, just like so many other unhappy wives, she needed to do something which would bring back her self-esteem.

'She needed the reassurance that could only come from being totally loved and wanted by a man. She was fully aware that since the birth of her second child she had put on weight and that, at 36, she had lost some of the delicate beauty for which she had been so acclaimed in her twenties.

'Tony's insensitivity had also undermined her confidence. Any man she chose must be capable of loving her to the exclusion of all else. I felt that a further rejection would be unbearable. It would destroy her completely.

'Their real friends had been genuinely upset by the break-up of their marriage. At the start, she and Tony had been fantastic together and everyone had loved being invited to Kensington Palace. No matter how happy anyone else had been at their parties no one was as happy as Margaret and Tony themselves.

'When the two of them fell out of love, it seemed to

affect everyone else. Going to Kensington Palace when they were both there became a sort of nightmare. Friends found themselves taking sides and for anyone who liked them both it was an agonising choice to have to make.

'Tony didn't hide the fact that he was romantically interested in someone else apart from his wife. She was very brave about it but one could see that she was suffering enormously underneath.

'I was exceptionally fond of her and it caused me a good deal of unhappiness to see her looking so sad herself. I wanted very much to ask her about it and get her to talk but one must remember that she was the Queen's sister and it is hard to ask someone like that about the collapse of her marriage.

'To my utter astonishment it was she who broached the subject first.

'When she wasn't night clubbing, she had taken to inviting some of her friends to join her for quiet dinner parties at Kensington Palace. People like Dominic Elliott, Jocelyn Stevens and Patrick Lichfield were often summoned to the palace for dinner, usually at very short notice. She would get bored or lonely and suddenly get the urge to telephone a friend and ask him to go there.

'It happened to me several times. At first we just talked generalities about mutual friends and our common love of the theatre and music. She knew all the Cole Porter and Sammy Cahn songs and never forgot the words. I would play the piano and she would stand or sit next to me and sing.

'If Tony was at home, he would take very little interest. Usually, he would excuse himself and go down to his studio. But really one saw very little of him.'

On the night their relationship changed, Robin remembered that they had eaten at the oval dining table and Princess Margaret had got up from the table and was walking around the room as she talked. The lights were soft, there were candles burning on the table and she looked exquisitely lovely in a long, low-cut, pale blue gown. Her hair was taken up off her neck and she was wearing sapphire earrings which sparkled in the candlelight.

Then she was behind him, with her hands on his shoulders. Robin told me she said: 'You are such a great comfort to me. I don't know what I would do without you in these difficult times.'

There was no great declaration of love, he said.

'But it was an amazing moment, nevertheless. I reached to my shoulder and took one of her hands in mine. There was no resistance and I felt that I was walking on air.

'I had experienced this breakthrough with so many different women but this was the impossible – almost. I had hoped for affection from her. Believed it might come, even. But when it did it was almost overwhelming.

'When I left Kensington Palace I felt ten feet tall. I still didn't believe anything could come of our relationship. In her position she could never acknowledge a romantic attachment with me or anyone else. And however much they wanted it, I thought, she and Tony could never separate.

'I knew that if we went out to dine or to the theatre we would always have to have someone with us – as a chaperone. I certainly never anticipated things moving as quickly as they did.'

Robin made further visits to Kensington Palace and Princess Margaret lunched with him alone at his London home. He prepared the meal and served it himself. He would play the piano for her or read her some of his poems. Robin remembered that their first kiss came during one of these visits but, even then, he never imagined that their relationship would develop into an affair. He did remember her constantly playing her favourite record, 'This Guy's in Love With Me', a Herb Alpert song, whenever he visited Kensington Palace.

The change in Princess Margaret was remarked on by several of her friends but if they guessed the cause they did not make comments outside their circle.

The external evidence of Margaret's romance with Robin was, however, still contrary to the inner turmoil she continued to experience over the break-up of her marriage, and Tony's suspected peccadillos.

Her own romance caused Margaret to take considerable pains to restore her slightly worn exterior to its former perfection. A drastic diet enabled her to shed several pounds and a course of daily exercise began tightening up the sagging muscles in her arms, thighs and chin. As throughout her life, Margaret's weight, dimensions and fitness reflected the barometer of her sex life. By the end of January 1967 she was looking good but the sudden loss of weight had probably weakened her resistance. She caught three severe colds in succession and this left her spent and defenceless.

In addition, several confrontations with Tony, who was scheduled to depart on a long photographic assignment in Japan, had increased her tension and pushed up her consumption of cigarettes to chain-smoking proportions. Daily, she was estimated to be smoking more than 50 cigarettes and had developed a nagging cough.

Fearing that Tony's assignment was just a cover up for him to continue some secret affair, Margaret asked him to delay his trip. Indignantly, Tony asserted that the foreign job was genuine and the arrangements could not be postponed.

Explained Robin: 'She had telephoned me in the early hours and had obviously been drinking. She was very upset and sobbed that her life was in tatters. I could say nothing to bring her out of her depression.'

That day, Margaret was rushed to the King Edward VII hospital, for what was said to be observation and analytical tests. Cigarettes were banned and she was not allowed alcohol. Royal sources claim, however, that this was a cover-up for an attempted suicide.

Tony declared that he was not prepared to change his plans despite the public effect of flying off to the Far East while his wife was in hospital. He was severely criticised and fuel was added to already circulating stories that the Snowdons' marriage was in trouble.

For Robin Douglas-Home, Tony's refusal to cancel his trip was a godsend. He did visit Margaret in hospital and was one of her first guests at Kensington Palace when she was discharged. 'It threw her into my arms,' he told me. 'Tony was to blame. I was there to sympathise and comfort. His action turned what might have remained a simple romance into a full-blooded affair.'

Valentine's Day was looming and Princess Margaret

declared that she wanted to spend the weekend before that day alone with Robin. He had several times invited her to stay with him at his country house in West Chiltington in Sussex but she had demurred. Meeting at Kensington Palace and in his Cromwell Road town house had been in proportion to their romance until then. To stay with him in the country would put their relationship on a much more serious level. It would be a commitment to an affair. By inviting herself to spend the weekend in his home she was making a declaration to him that they were about to become lovers, he said.

On the morning of 10 February 1967, Robin said, the local police went to his home, Meadowbrook, in West Chiltington to vet it from a security viewpoint.

They found a long, two-storey, white-washed building behind high, white, double gates and a six-foot fence topped with barbed wire. Small, neatly trimmed lawns were bordered with beds of snowdrops and crocuses and a large section of the grounds had been left wild. A grassy area beneath trees was covered with a large aviary where Robin kept several dozen budgerigars and lovebirds.

Inside, the house was furnished in what Robin called comfortable country style: deep armchairs and sofas and open fires. In pride of place was a baby grand piano.

Princess Margaret arrived in her own chauffeur-driven limousine, direct from Kensington Palace. It was mid-afternoon but dusk was already creeping in when Robin greeted her in the front drive. It had all the appearance of a normal visit to a friend, until Margaret dismissed her chauffeur and sent him back to London.

Robin said that candles, which Margaret adores, were already alight and her favourite tunes, which he had pre-recorded on a special tape, were playing.

'It was the start', he said 'of the most exciting and extraordinary weekend of my life.

'We ate the meal I had prepared for us and then I played the piano for her. One item I played was "Spring is in the Air" which I had written and which had been played for us in the Travellers' Club when we had danced there recently. Later, she played the piano for me, and then we went upstairs."

That night they slept together and made love, he said. It was the first time he had seen her naked. 'She was like a goddess,' he said. And then he laughed.

'That sounds just like one would be expected to say about a princess – but she really was. Like a beautiful sculpted goddess. But there was certainly nothing cold about her. She was a passionate and uninhibited lover and I marvelled at her abandonment. She was very demanding as a lover and insisted on taking the dominant position. It was she who dictated the tempo.'

They awoke to the sound of Robin's exotic birds beneath the window and spent their first full day as lovers pottering around the house listening to music and talking.

'She told me she was in love with me and I told her I knew I was in love with her,' said Robin.

'We said all the silly things to each other that lovers say – though neither of us, at that stage, mentioned the future. It was as though there was an unofficial agreement not to talk of anything further than just days ahead.

'She told me that the sound of the birds reminded

her of when she was a little girl and her father, the late king, kept love birds and budgerigars in a cage.'

That evening Robin drove them to London in his white Alfa Romeo and they went to a jazz concert. Then it was back to Meadowbrook for another night of love.

On Sunday, they stayed in all day, listening to music, singing together while he played piano, and making love. Said Robin: 'She was incredibly demanding sexually. But she had to remain in control of things. I remember sitting at the piano with nothing on, playing, and she came to kneel next to me and urged me on by doing wonderful things to me. Giving pleasure and being in control almost seemed enough satisfaction for her.'

The following day – the 13th – he drove her back to Kensington Palace and went home to his little town house in Cromwell Road. 'She telephoned me half a dozen times that afternoon and evening,' he remembered. 'At two in the morning she called for the last time and told me she couldn't remember ever being so happy. And she wished me a happy Valentine's Day – reminding me that I had promised to visit her that night. As if I would forget.'

Just before midnight on the 14th, he drove into the guarded entrance of Kensington Palace in his Alfa Romeo. He said a torch was shone in the car and he was recognised and let through. Just minutes later, he said, Princess Margaret was in his arms.

As he was leaving she told him she had written him a Valentine's Day letter which he would receive later that day, at home. It arrived at his home just hours after he did – and was the first of several which she wrote to him. Over a year and a half later, a few days before he took his own life, Robin met a friend in the Tiberio restaurant. As always he danced with the girls, holding them by the cheeks of their bottoms. Although he said he had little money, he ordered champagne cocktails and then gave his friend two of Margaret's hand-written love letters. One day, at the right time, he said, he wanted people to know the truth of his love affair with Princess Margaret.

That first letter, written on her personal Kensington Palace writing paper surmounted by its coroneted M, made him cry.

It began:

Darling Robin,

Thank you for a

Perfect week-end.

It continued that, in the circumstances, her letter would sound like a grace or a new interpretation of 'All Things Bright and Beautiful'. She thanked him for the comforts of his home, which gave her peace of mind, and for the care and trouble he had taken to make everything delicious for her which, she said, had restored her heart.

She thanked him for the concert – the pleasure of which, she wrote, would remain in her mind forever. And she thanked him for his music, which had mended her nerve ends.

She wrote her thanks for making her live again and for standing (rather too little) no nonsense from her.

Then:

Thank you for being gentle when it was
unexpected which gave me back self-
confidence.
Thank you for everything nice which
everything was.
with best love.
M

With Tony away there was nothing to stop their love affair developing and Robin and Margaret conspired to spend several more nights together at Kensington Palace and the Cromwell Road house.

During these clandestine meetings, the forbidden was actually discussed – the possibility that one day they might be together for always. The word 'divorce' was even mentioned.

Margaret had become much more adventurous in their love making, he said and did not want to confine their sex sessions to the bedroom. One night, Robin claimed, this led to them being discovered in a very compromising position on a couch by one of the Kensington Palace servants who had assumed Margaret had gone to bed.

'It was excruciatingly embarrassing for me,' said Robin. 'But Margaret just stared at the servant until he left the room. Then she carried on as though we hadn't been interrupted. Though I found it very hard to continue after that I can tell you.'

However, just two weeks after they had consummated their love in West Chiltington, Margaret telephoned Robin in tears and sounded almost hysterical, he said.

Tony had surfaced in New York and had demanded to know the truth about rumours he had heard concerning a love affair between her and Robin. He was furious and had accused her of infidelity with their friend while he was away working.

'It followed exactly the pattern she had explained to me,' said Robin. 'He didn't seem to want her and preferred chasing other women, but he couldn't bear her to want another man.'

Margaret swore that she had denied anything other than friendship with Robin but said that Tony had refused to believe her. He had told her that Robin was never to be allowed into Kensington Palace again. None the less, Margaret and Robin did go on meeting – in Kensington Palace and at Cromwell Road – until the eve of Margaret's departure for America on 10 March.

Fleet Street, swirling with rumours of Margaret's attempted suicide, of Tony's more than professional attachment to a couple of ladies and the affair between Robin and Margaret, was convinced that the Snowdons' marriage was doomed.

Tony, in a spate of telephone calls from New York, told Margaret to order her friends to say nothing. He would issue whatever denials were necessary and the best rebuttal of all the rumours was for them to meet – quickly and in a romantic setting. She should fly to New York on the 10th where he would meet her at Kennedy Airport with a husbandly embrace and they would then go on to the Bahamas to stay at the home of Jocelyn Stevens on Lyford Cay.

Newspapers in America were already front-paging the story of the Snowdons' break-up and Tony told reporters in New York: 'Nothing has happened to our marriage. When I am away I write home and telephone like other husbands in love with their wives.' This particular lie hurt Margaret more than anything else Tony said because his failure to phone while he was away on assignment had long been one of the main bones of contention between them.

On 26 February, he told a *Daily Express* reporter at the Manhattan offices of *Vogue:* 'Talk of a rift is totally un-founded. It's news to me and I would be the first to know. I am amazed.'

The story appeared on the front page of the *Daily Express* in London, headlined: 'Tony Denies Rift With Margaret'.

'Don't worry,' Margaret soothed Robin. 'It has to be done this way for appearance's sake. I will never stop loving you.'

On the morning of 10 March, the last thing she did before leaving for Heathrow Airport to fly out with Jocelyn and Janie Stevens to New York, was to telephone Robin at his house in Cromwell Road.

'She told me that she was going but she was leaving her heart with me.'

'But things were never going to be the same between us again. We had enjoyed the most amazing 30 days of love. Margaret had opened her heart and

221

her soul to me and given bounteously of her love. I had kept a small item of her clothing which carried the scent of her and that morning after she had said "goodbye", I smothered my face in it and wept. I rightly believed I was never going to experience that glorious, heady aroma of her at first hand again.'

Tony and Margaret met, as arranged, as she changed aircraft in New York. They kissed warmly in front of the waiting cameras and, arm in arm, charade over, strolled to the plane waiting to fly them to the Bahamas. To press and public, the perfect reconciliation had been demonstrated but, in reality, all that had been agreed was that, with divorce an impossible alternative, Tony and Margaret accepted that they had to go on living together if only for the sake of their children, David, five, and Sarah, three. It was an inevitable decision but came only after two days of ferocious rows.

On returning to Britain, Margaret telephoned Robin and told him that they would not be able to meet again alone, that she had decided to give her marriage one more chance and try to make it work.

'She also admitted that she had never seen Tony so angry as when he had tried to make her confess to her affair. She said he had voiced the same questions over and over and had accused her of being unfaithful with Robin.

'She had been forced to swear on the Bible that we had not been lovers after he had berated her in the most awful language about her infidelity,' said Robin. 'She said she had sworn because she was too frightened to refuse. Tony couldn't find a Bible for her actually to place her hand on to swear but he made her say the words.

'She was sobbing all the time she was blurting out what had happened and I believe that she was genuinely frightened.

'He had called me a filthy, jumped-up little glory seeker. A despicable seducer of other men's wives who had gloated about our affair to his friends. He loathed the idea of ever having considered me a friend and deeply regretted ever inviting me to his country home in Nymans and to Kensington Palace.

'She said she was frightened of what might happen if we carried on meeting. We must confine ourselves to telephone calls and to meeting only in the company of other people.

'Perhaps one day we could be together again and she would pray for that to happen. But for the moment we must be content knowing that we were each loved by the other.

'Tony's jealously was well known among Margaret's friends. He no longer loved her but he couldn't bear her to have someone special in her life.

'Any other husband who believed the things about his wife that he accused her of would have left her. But he didn't seem quite ready to take that step.'

No more was Margaret herself. Divorce – separation even – was quite unthinkable then and Princess Margaret was not, never had been and never would be, prepared to do anything that would affect her royalness, her position in the line of succession, or of her just remaining Princess Margaret. Certainly no man and no love affair has ever persuaded her to jeopardise her position. Her feeling in this respect has always been the same.

Following her call of woe, on 22 March, Robin sat down and wrote a long and very emotional letter to Margaret, vividly describing his love for her and reminding her of their plans for the future. It was a forlorn gesture.

Her reply, although filled with her own love for him, nevertheless confirmed that, for the time being, although she wanted him desperately, their romance must continue at a distance. She wrote of Tony's temper and threats but, at the end, held out the possibility that she might, one day, come back to Robin. However, Robin knew their affair was dead. It hadn't been officially declared lifeless and might twitch on, grotesquely, for a while but it would never beat again with the glorious passion of those unforgettable 30 days.

'Robin of 30 days. That's what I'll go down in history as,' he said, giggling, slightly out of control. 'At least Anne had a thousand with Henry. And someone else did her the service of putting her out of her misery.'

On the familiar Kensington Palace writing paper, Margaret wrote on 25 March 1967:

Darling,

I have never had a letter like it, I don't suppose one like it has ever been written. The beauty in it and its poetry lifted my heart again.

She went on to explain how secure she felt in their love, between 10 February and 10 March, which was followed, after her reunion with Tony, by his attack on her over her affair with Robin. She continued that she was forced to deny their affair on the Bible, her only consolation being that there wasn't a Bible to be found for her to place her hand on. Tony seemed puzzled that an old friend could be so dastardly.

I think all the time of you

she wrote, adding how happy she had been to hear his voice again, knowing very well what lay beneath his every gesture, look and nod, cold as they might seem to others.

would do anything as you know and I make you happy and not hurt you.

Their hearts being divided was affecting her thoughts when she needed on her part to make a real effort to make her marriage work. She felt she could do this, curiously enough, more convincingly because of his love for her.

She wanted to keep the precious memories safe, which she claimed were more precious to her than perhaps Robin thought. They must make the most of this wonder that had happened to them so that people would marvel.

Only they with their secret source of inspiration would know. She would try to speak to him as much as possible but was in fear of Tony and didn't know what lengths he wouldn't go to, jealous as he was, to find out what she was up to, and Robin's movements too.

She asked his forgiveness for repeating Tony's hard words but thought it was better he should know.

And know always that I want you

she assured him, writing that it was only because she could not, that she would not, speak to him as much but told him it would always make her happy when she could do so.

Trust me as I trust you and love me as I love you. Our love has the passionate scent of new mown grass and lilies about it. Not many people are lucky enough to have known any love like this. I feel so happy that it has happened to me.

She asked if she could make him happy from a distance and thought it could work. And she asked him to promise that he would never give up. Given the chance, she said,

I will try and come back to you one day. I daren't at the moment.

THE END OF THE AFFAIR

She ended the letter

you are good and loyal, think that I am to whatever I may seem to do a day. All my love my darling.

The break up of his affair with Margaret was even more traumatic for Robin than either the end of his marriage or the breaking of his engagement to Princess Margaretha. He was shattered, heartbroken.

It was at this point that Robin agreed to record an interview for BBC 2's *Whicker's World*, to be called 'The Stresses of Divorce'. It was filmed at Meadowbrook in West Chiltington. He said: 'The only reason I did the broadcast was to help bring home to other people how awful, silly and expensive the whole divorce thing is.'

In the middle of the interview, while talking of the emotional agony his split with Sandra Paul and their divorce had caused him, Robin broke down completely and sobbed. This part was uncut and went out in full when the programme was broadcast in April.

'It was upsetting to talk about my divorce,' said Robin. 'But viewers could never have guessed at the real reason for my tears. They could never know that my affair with Princess Margaret had just broken up and that, while conducting the interview, Whicker had sat in the armchair which she had sat in after we had first made love.

'I was really crying for her and for me and for what I had lost. It was all too much for me to cope with.'

When he did manage to speak to Margaret on the

227

telephone, all she wanted to discuss was her plans for her new home which she intended to build in the West Indies.

Her self-preservation mechanism seemed to be functioning smoothly. Even amid her rows with Tony in the Bahamas, she had found time to telephone Colin Tennant and remind him of the wedding present he had offered verbally but never delivered – a plot on his private Caribbean island – Mustique.

On their return to London, Tennant had taken a large-scale map of the island to Kensington Palace and helped Margaret to pick out an ocean-front, ten-acre plot.

Knowing in her heart that her marriage to Tony was over and that any kind of reconciliation would be a sham and merely window dressing for the public, Margaret had begun planning a future to include as much independence as she could secure.

Tony disliked sun, sand and sea vacations in the Caribbean and would be quite content never to set foot on Mustique again. Whatever Margaret built there would be for herself and her friends alone.

'It was only May and I was already history,' Robin told me. 'She prattled on and on about the new house. Couldn't she understand that I was breaking into pieces. I had obviously served my purpose – provided my love and my body when she needed them – and now she had something else to occupy her.

'And someone else – so I discovered a couple of months later.

'Peter Sellers was back together with Britt Ekland after a separation but their marriage was still proving shaky. Tony had already proved more than attentive to the beautiful Britt and Sellers was rumoured to have set his cap at

Margaret – with some success according to the gossips.'

The foursome returned from a summer holiday in Sardinia where Margaret and Tony had, to the delight of the press, jointly occupied the Presidential Suite in the new luxury Cala di Volpe hotel.

Days had been spent aboard Sellers's 50-foot yacht, *Bobo*, where flirtatious Polaroid pictures of the foursome had been taken.

Margaret did not bother to call Robin on her 37th birthday. A party had been given in Sardinia by the Aga Khan – her host – and Robin surmised that she had been too preoccupied with her new beau, Sellers, to think about her ex-lover.

Robin somehow managed to complete a new novel (published in March 1968) which he admitted was partly autobiographical and pilloried the snobbery and hypo-scrisy with which the upper classes regard sex.

However, with his preferred profession, as pianist, he had less success. Famed gambler and zoo owner John Aspinall hired him to play in the early evening at his Clermont gaming club in Berkeley Square for £15 a night, three nights a week.

Being at the centre of things again could have been his salvation but his life's main flaw – the betrayal of his friends – once again got in the way of possible happiness. He was invited down to Aspinall's private zoo on his estate in Kent where he took photographs of his boss with some of his animals. The pictures were not intended for publication but, eager to impress his 'friends' in Fleet Street, Robin sold a photograph of Aspinall in his swimming pool with a young tiger to the *Daily Express* Hickey gossip column.

He was summarily dismissed the same morning that the picture appeared. 'Aspinall told me he didn't want me in the club any more, either as a pianist or anything,' said Robin. 'It was such a silly thing to get fired for.'

The last of Robin's romances was, if anything, more tragic than any of the others. He saw a photograph of 22-year-old Miss United Kingdom, Kathleen Winstanley, and instantly decided that he should marry her. He talked to friends about a possible engagement before he had even talked properly to the girl. All he had done was invite her down to West Chiltington to take pictures of her.

'Nobody was battering down my door to get me to play the piano for them so I had decided to take up photography again.'

Kathleen did arrive but when Robin tried to turn on the old charm he found, at the age of 36, that it had quite lost its magic. Gently, and with more kindness that he probably deserved, Kathleen explained that she had a boyfriend back home in Lancashire whom she loved.

'Everyone seems to have someone to love them,' Robin told me just two weeks before he killed himself. 'When that no longer is the case then it is time to go. Margaret said she was putting duty before happiness. That's what she's always said to get out of a romance. Ask Peter Townsend.'

Robin Douglas-Home telephoned Elizabeth Harris and Sandra Paul on the morning of 15 October 1968. He then lay on the bed where he had slept with Princess Margaret and took a fatal overdose of pills. It is not known if he telephoned the princess, but she did not attend his funeral.

17

Enter Peter Sellers

Princess Margaret's next love affair coincided with Tony's biggest amorous adventure to date.

The sophisticated princess went for long-time friend and Jewish-born comedy star Peter Sellers, freshly divorced from Britt Ekland and five years older than herself.

Adversely, Tony went for a member of the aristocracy, Lady Jacqueline Rufus-Isaacs, daughter of the Marquess of Reading and seventeen years his junior.

Tony had met Sellers on a photographic shoot and had introduced him to the princess. Margaret quickly became fond of the deeply sensitive, often morose, comedy genius. They were both exceptionally argumentative and, to everyone's astonishment, for she was inclined to become very bolshie when anyone disagreed with her, Margaret tolerated Sellers answering her back.

Said one royal observer:

'Above all, he was able to make her laugh and for that she would forgive almost anything, particularly during the mid-sixties when things had started to go badly wrong between herself and Tony.

'He enjoyed being around royalty. It reassured him about his worth and his position. Sellers could isolate slights and criticism even when he was being eulogised. His ego needed constant bolstering and his relationship with Princess Margaret – and, through her, with the Queen and Prince Philip – fed this desperate inner need.

'Sellers was also a great flirt, as was Margaret, and that was flirting in its true sense. By looks, by innuendo, by flattery and the giving of unexpected gifts – a game where no touching is allowed.

'That was sufficient for them both for several years, although Peter was infatuated with the princess and would have loved to have developed their relationship into something more physical soon after meeting her.'

One man who recognised the urge in Sellers for a more intimate accord with Margaret was renowned clairvoyant Maurice Woodruff. At this stage in his life, Sellers, an obsessive believer in astrology, spiritualism and clairvoyancy, was extremely influenced by Woodruff, allegedly the seventh son of a seventh son. He virtually could not face the day or take even a minor decision without consulting the homosexual, modern-day soothsayer.

Once, while talking with mutual good friend, *Steptoe* comedy star Harry Corbett, Maurice revealed: 'Peter is getting himself all in a twist over Princess Margaret.'

Leaning back on the settee and hugging his knees, he went on:

'Peter keeps hinting that he's on the brink of a big affair with the princess and wants me to give it my blessing. But I just can't see it.

'I've told him that all I can pick up is that he is exceptionally close to a woman at the pinnacle of society but that she isn't free to indulge herself as other women are.

'He admitted that the woman he had in mind was married. He's been here several times, both before and after his marriage to Britt and his heart attacks. I thought he would let it die after Britt came on the scene but it still bothers him.

'Once he bloody well gets something fixed in his head, it's almost impossible to dissuade him. I know he wants me to be more positive but I'm damned if I'm going to encourage him. I can't see it and I'm not going to make something up just to keep him happy.

'I only hope he doesn't make a fool of himself and it all ends in tears.'

Harry's reaction was typically down to earth. 'Well you can't knock the bloke's taste, Maurice. She's a gorgeous piece of stuff you've got to admit!'

According to Maurice, Sellers was even hoping to make Princess Margaret jealous when he introduced Britt Ekland to her. 'I can't wait to see her face,' Sellers told him.

After Peter Sellers's marriage to Britt, in February 1964, they became as near to being close friends of the Snowdons as anyone. Margaret and Sellers were happy to spend hours mimicking their friends and the famous personalities they knew, and weekends at Royal Lodge, Windsor were riotous get-togethers with Britt and Tony joining in as minor characters.

Prince Charles – a committed Goons fan – was particularly impressed when Margaret took the Sellers over to the castle to visit the Queen and her family. He loved playing Eccles to Sellers's Bluebottle.

After Sellers's heart attack scare and 90 seconds death (he had died eight times and been resuscitated eight times in the Cedars of Lebanon Hospital in Los Angeles) Sellers returned to Britain to recuperate in his country home at Elstead in Surrey.

Tony and Margaret were regular dinner guests and enjoyed the easy cameraderie of the Sellers and their show business friends.

On one occasion Margaret showed her ability to join in with a good joke when they decided to rib a late-arriving fellow guest. It was a black-tie dinner and Sellers suggested the men all sit at the table stripped to the waist, wearing only black bow ties.

When the missing guest arrived in full evening dress, Sellers told him: 'I only said black tie.'

'I think you're a bit overdressed!' said one of the others present.

'Margaret thought it was a hilarious gag.'

According to Britt Ekland, things began to get a little out of hand after the birth of her daughter, Victoria, in 1965. Margaret and Tony sent flowers and a cuddly teddy bear and Sellers reacted in characteristic style.

He would frequently hold what he called 'shower parties', which involved him inviting friends over and giving them costly items, mainly gimmicky electronic gadgets with which he had grown bored. As he grew richer and more famous, these 'toys' would become more expensive, although the time between acquisition and boredom decreased accordingly.

Now he began to shower gifts on Tony. If Tony happened to comment on a new piece of photographic equipment that Peter had bought, then he would insist he take it. That included cameras, flash guns, special lenses, anything. It became a 'shower party' for one. He presented Tony with an Italian Riva speedboat and sold him his spectacular custom-adapted silver-blue Aston Martin for a tiny fraction of its real price.

In her cruelly candid memoirs, Britt Ekland wrote that she would 'squirm with embarrassment' at the demeaning lengths to which Peter would go to please Snowdon and Margaret. She had heard it mentioned that Sellers was after a knighthood.

Friends of Sellers argue that the gifts were more likely to be what they knew as 'Peter's guilt offerings'. 'They may have been to make up for his lustful feelings towards the princess.'

At the end of 1964, while Britt was heavily pregnant with Victoria, Sellers and Margaret cooked up an idea for a surprise birthday gift for the Queen who would be 39 the following April. It was to be a crazy home movie, directed by Jocelyn Stevens and filmed by Tony and Peter Sellers. Tony was a one-legged golfer hopping about the fairway; Britt played a Hollywood vamp and Peter revived his Indian doctor character from the film *The Millionairess*, which he had made with Sophia Loren, with a parody on the 'Goodness Gracious Me' song.

However, the highlight involved Sellers and Margaret in an old-time music-hall act. Sellers, playing a quick-change artist, announced that he was about to do his famous impersonation of Princess Margaret. He then disappeared behind a screen and, moments later, various items of clothing he had been wearing were thrown over the top. Seconds later, Princess Margaret stepped from behind the screen, simpering and blowing kisses. After curtsying, she returned behind the screen and Sellers reappeared, praising himself for his sensational impersonation. He then went behind the screen a second time, having promised an impersonation of Queen Victoria, but reappeared in the same clothes saying: 'I don't know what Queen Victoria looked like.'

The film ends with the whole cast linking arms and singing 'We're Riding Along on the Crest of a Wave'. Sellers then paid for it to be edited and to have a sound track added in time for the party the following April.

The Queen's birthday began with a visit to the theatre to see Spike Milligan in his hit play *Son of Oblomov*. Margaret and Tony had organised it and invited Prince Philip, Prince Charles, Princess Anne, Peter Sellers and Britt Ekland.

Friends believe that Sellers stretched his friendship with the royals to the limit with an incredible cross-talk act with Milligan. It was certainly unscheduled and took everyone by surprise. 'And acutely embarrassed the Queen and Prince Philip, despite their public reaction at the time,' said one Sellers friend.

Milligan, in bed on stage, suddenly broke off from the play and shouted: 'Is there a Peter Sellers in the house?'

The other ex-Goon, sitting in the middle of the Royal party, shouted back: 'Yes'.

This was followed by an amazing exchange.

'Why can't a lady with a wooden leg change a pound note?' from Milligan.

'I don't know. Why can't a lady with a wooden leg change a pound note?' from Sellers.

'Because she's only got half a knicker.'

'I don't wish to know that.'

Then from Milligan: 'Why does Prince Philip wear red, white and blue braces?'

Sellers: 'I don't know. Why does Prince Philip wear red, white and blue braces?'

'To keep his trousers up.'

'He may have been playing the vulgar court jester some claimed him to be or he may have been trying to show that he was an equal of the royals,' said the friend. 'With such a complicated personality, God only knows why he did it.'

At Kensington Palace, the party was joined by the remaining ex-Goons Harry Secombe and Michael Bentine, prompting Prince Charles to declare it 'the best party ever'.

The highlight was the showing of the home movie, after which Sellers presented a copy to the Queen. This gesture, at least, was a hit as the Queen still occasionally shows the movie at family parties.

That summer, the Snowdons spent part of their summer holiday in Italy with Sellers and Britt who were in Rome making *After the Fox*.

By the following summer (1967), Sellers had recognised that the Snowdons' marriage was disintegrating fast. He had already experienced a separation and recent reconciliation with Britt and suggested that the answer for all of them was to team up in Sardinia and enjoy his new acquisition, a 60-foot, 50-ton motor yacht which he had christened *Bobo* after his latest picture.

It had cost him over £100,000 and he had ordered it fitted with twin V12 caterpillar engines, making it the fastest boat in the Mediterranean.

He was later to rename the boat *Victoria* after the film *Bobo* flopped. When he sold it in 1969, for £80,000 to a South American property dealer, it had hardly been used.

The party stayed in one of the Aga Khan's hotels on the Costa Smerelda and K hosted a lavish thirty-seventh birthday party for the princess. Kirk Douglas and his wife Anne, who were guests of Sellers, plus Princess Alexandra and Angus Ogilvy, were there and Margaret announced it her happiest night of the year.

Their days were spent on the *Bobo* where, it was reported, on one trip with only the Sellers and Snowdons on board, some rather *risqué* Polaroid photos were taken by Tony and Peter!

By 1968 Maurice Woodruff had changed his mind about Sellers's relationship with Margaret. 'Peter has come right out into the open and admitted he is in love with the princess,' he said. 'It is very worrying. He says he is splitting with Britt and has started an affair with Margaret. If so, then it can only end badly.'

Sellers came close to publicly confirming a close relationship with Margaret when he took her on one of several visits they made together to Ronnie Scott's jazz club in Soho. They had gone there with film director Brian Forbes and his wife Nanette after a visit to a Mayfair cinema to see the film Z.

Again, Spike Milligan was responsible for alerting the press to Sellers's royal connection.

Milligan wasn't present that night because he had 'flu but he had sent a poem he had composed, which Ronnie Scott read out over the microphone. 'Wherever you are, wherever you be, please take your hand off the princess's knee.'

Sellers later told the *Mirror*: 'There's only one thing I can say to Spike about Princess Margaret and myself. We are just good friends. You mustn't read anything else into this.'

'He knew exactly what he was saying and knew exactly what the implications were of using that phrase,' said a friend. 'He wanted people to think he was having an affair with the princess.'

Sellers had divorced Britt in December 1968 and, thereafter, he became a frequent weekend guest at Windsor Royal Lodge. He continued to tell friends that they were having an affair and explained that Margaret visited him, several nights a week, for romantic dinners.

The celebrated showbusiness writer Peter Evans, in his outstanding biography of Peter Sellers, *The Mask Behind The Mask*, quoted a friend as saying:

'To convince her detective that she was attending large dinner parties, Sellers, having discreetly dismissed the staff for the evening, would open the door disguised as a very old manservant in white wig and pince-nez eye glasses. In the background, on tape, were the sounds of a lively gathering of people, laughing, chatting. Having seen her safely to the door of the apartment, the detective waited downstairs, unaware that Her Royal Highness was entirely alone with the actor, enjoying "picnics" sent over from the Tiberio restaurant and, occasionally, from Mr Chow's in Knightsbridge.'

Sellers had acquired the lease on a £35,000 Clarges Street apartment and decorated it in modern Italian style, with ultramarine-stained wall fabrics, concealed wall lights and whole walls done in distressed mirror glass. 'It looked like a grand, though unlived in, hotel suite,' commented one observer.

On December 11 1969, Sellers invited the Snowdons, who were by now barely on speaking terms, to the charity première of his film *The Magic Christian* in which he co-starred with Ringo Starr. It was to be a night of bizarre couplings, at which Margaret's and Tony's lovers would be present and at which Britt Ekland would make off with the man who was to enjoy a future fling with the princess.

At the Kensington Odeon and later at Les Ambassadeurs for the party, Sellers's official escort was his ex-wife Britt Ekland. He and his new girl friend, Miranda Quarry, Lady Mancroft's daughter, had had a bust-up, so Britt was a last-minute stand in, he explained. Friends believed that it was because he did not want to confront Margaret with his new love, whom he was to take as his third bride the following year.

At Les Ambassadeurs Tony and Margaret separated almost immediately, as had become customary. Margaret sat between Patrick Lichfield and Jocelyn Stevens and Tony sat next to a tall, blonde debutante, who stood out as one of the most stunningly beautiful women present.

Cool, aloof and perfectly at ease in this distinguished company Lady Jacqueline Rufus-Isaacs had arrived at the exclusive Hamilton Place club with her brother, Lord Anthony Rufus-Isaacs. Lord Reading's son and daughter were there at the instigation of Tony. His hideaway cottage, Old House, bordered the Marquess of Reading's estate and was less than a mile from the peer's family home, the Grange. He had visited the Readings on several occasions and had become good friends with Margo, Lady Reading and her husband.

What they did not realise until much later – when the

affair became front-page news – was that Jackie, as she was known, had taken to slipping up the path from the Grange to join Tony secretly in his cottage, where they had become lovers. It happened the first time she visited. He had rowed her out in a gondola to his tiny island and showed her the Chinese pagoda-style summer house where he liked to entertain his friends to dinner.

However, no one, with the exception of her brother, was aware of their real relationship on the night of the Les Ambassadeurs party, although several people remarked on how closely Tony stuck to Jackie when the nucleus moved on for dancing at Annabel's. They were not the only couple whispering words of love that night. Britt Ekland, who was seated on Patrick Lichfield's other side, had hit it off immediately with the handsome photographer. When they finally left the party it was to return to Lichfield's studio house in Kensington, where they consummated their mutual desire in record time.

The most disgruntled guest was Princess Margaret, whose host, Sellers, disappeared before the end of the night with the intention of making it up with 23-year-old Miranda. If Margaret's relationship with Peter Sellers was on the point of petering out, Tony's affair with Jackie was just getting properly underway. Having learned, first hand, about Tony's affair with Jackie, Sellers came up with a Machiavellian scheme which might improve his relation-ship with Margaret by letting the cat out of the bag about Tony's peccadillo under the guise of 'only having a laugh'.

Wrote Sellers's biographer, Peter Evans:

'Impersonating Tony Snowdon, he telephoned Princess Margaret and embarked on a fairly raunchy confession of his burgeoning friendship with Lady

Jackie Rufus-Isaacs. Unfortunately, he had completely miscalculated Her Royal Highness's sense of humour, as well as her *sang-froid*: her attitude to that whole, delicate situation turned out to be considerably less "civilised" than Sellers had imagined.

'Realising the joke had gone badly awry, he ended the conversation hurriedly, without disclosure.

'He fretted about it for weeks. Finally, one evening at Laurence Harvey's apartment, he unburdened his dilemma. Harvey had a splendid air of *savoir-faire* that Sellers admired a lot. Harvey told Sellers to forget the whole business. "In my experience, dear heart," said the late Mr Harvey, "actresses and princesses have the most dreadful memories for trivia."

'Encouraged by the worldly Harvey's assurance and abetted by a joint of Acapulco Gold, Sellers confided cryptically: "The whole thing is, you see, she has the same size breasts as Sophia Loren. The same cup size exactly."

'Harvey, who preferred his women on more boyish lines, said blandly: "Large breasts and small husbands must be an irresistible *mélange* for some chaps."

'"They're my undoing," said Sellers, glumly.'

In Jackie's company, Tony discovered a happiness that had long since vanished from his relationship with Margaret. Despite the difference in their ages – he was seventeen years her senior – Jackie's easy laughter and intense interest in his work made Tony feel younger and more vital than at almost any time since his bachelor days.

Jackie told friends: 'He is a marvellous lover. Everyone else seems insignificant by comparison. He is considerate and exciting all at the same time.'

She knew about his relationship with Princess Margaret but, from the outset, never thought anything could come of their affair. She was willing to take whatever part of him he wanted to offer, or was able to.

Jackie had a flat in Cundy Street but her parents suddenly began to see a lot more of her than usual, especially at weekends – and of Tony too. He became a regular guest at the long, heavy, wooden table in the French Provençal-style kitchen where the family normally ate.

'The girl fell head over heels in love with Tony and that was that,' said a friend of the Readings. 'From the start they decided no hint of their relationship should be given to Jackie's parents. The third marquess was a member of the London Stock Exchange, a man of strong moral principles who would decidedly disapprove of a romance between his daughter and the Queen's brother-in-law.'

However, Tony and Jackie did trust one member of her family with their secret, her brother Anthony. He was cast in the role of go between and cover. Because Anthony ran his own television commercial company and had an interest in films, it was considered quite normal for him to be seen with Lord Snowdon. If Jackie joined them at restaurants and theatres, this was felt to be quite proper too. Why shouldn't a sister and brother be seen out together?

In reality, Anthony took very little part in their conversations, remaining, for the most part, a silent observer to the deepening romance. Several evenings each week, Tony would arrive at Anthony's basement apartment in Ennismore Gardens, where Jackie would be already waiting. Then Anthony would slip out or retire to a spare room and leave the lovers alone.

However, as the affair grew more passionate, even this

subterfuge was dispensed with and Tony took to driving directly to Jackie's own apartment in Cundy Street. Her flat was on the first floor of an old block and, frequently, Tony's car could be seen parked outside until after midnight.

Jackie's education at Southover Manor, Sussex and the International School in Geneva had provided her with a wide knowledge of art and music and the couple spent many happy hours discussing the projects of Tony's artistic friends. In their affair, she fully lived up to the Readings' family motto, 'Either do not attempt or complete'. Having committed herself to the affair, she held nothing back. Whatever resources of love and passion she had were directed totally towards Tony.

Throughout his life Tony, who is fairly short, had tried to avoid close contact with women taller than himself, but he never seemed aware of Jackie's six-inch height advantage.

To the delight of her parents, Jackie began spending even more time in Sussex, although much of this was spent in Tony's cottage rather than at her own home. Sometimes, so as not to alert her parents to the situation, Tony would invite other friends to Old House and, occasionally, the Readings, too, were asked to the cottage to watch a film show or dine with Tony in the island pagoda.

A year after the affair had started, Tony was talking openly of being able to obtain a divorce from Margaret. He had even confided in the Readings that his marriage was on the rocks because of Margaret's affairs with other men and had received great sympathy from that quarter. The Readings were not blind and had noticed that Margaret had not been near Old House for a year at least. Jackie certainly believed him and told Anthony that Tony wanted to marry her.

Tony's talk about divorce coincided with his relationship with Margaret reaching an all-time low. In private, they rarely met or spoke to one another and in public their estrangement had become a barely tolerated embarrassment to their friends.

Bu this time, too, because they were no longer making such a serious effort to keep their affair a secret, the relationship between Tony and Jackie had become known to many of their friends. The information that her husband was openly sleeping with another woman had also been passed to Princess Margaret. However, by this time such a gulf separated the Snowdons that it no longer upset the princess that Tony was being unfaithful. Of more concern was Tony's decision not to join the royal family for their traditional Christmas at Windsor. Instead, he told her, he planned to go into the London Clinic to undergo an operation for piles which had been troubling him for almost a year. He had been free to choose dates both before and after Christmas for his stay in hospital but she believed, and rightly so said his friends, that he had deliberately planned his hospitalisation to clash with the family's standing arrangements.

Margaret's concern was that this might be interpreted by the public as a deliberate snub to the Queen and the royal family, but Tony refused to alter his plans and, to demonstrate how annoyed she was, Princess Margaret went only once to visit him in his suite at the London Clinic.

Tony was delighted, for this meant that Jackie could spend parts of most afternoons and evenings by his bedside. Once again, Anthony provided the cover and then tactfully excused himself from Tony's bedroom to leave his sister and the patient alone.

By now friends had begun to speculate that Tony might

really ask for an official separation or even a divorce. It seemed an utterly pointless exercise to their friends that they should try to keep up the pretence that their marriage was still a happy one when everyone was aware that they were constantly at each other's throats.

In fact, the subject had been broached with the Queen earlier that year. It had been explained that Tony favoured an amicable separation and, perhaps after a few years, a quietly arranged divorce. He believed the divorce and remarriage of the Earl of Harewood in 1967 had set a possible royal precedent. However, the Queen is understood to have rejected this approach at that time and advocated that Tony and Margaret continue to live their separate lives discreetly and at all costs to maintain an outward appearance of unity.

Aware that Princess Margaret was enjoying a renewed romantic fling with old-time friend Dominic Elliott, whom he detested more than any other of Margaret's admirers, Tony may well have been contemplating a more direct approach to the Queen but events on the other side of the Atlantic were poised to take the decision about his future with Jackie out of his hands.

At the beginning of January, Jackie had driven to Switzerland with her elder brother, Viscount Erleigh, known as Sy. They were staying with friends at a chalet in Gsteig when the *New York Daily News*, quoting a close friend of the Snowdons, announced that Tony was in love with Jackie Rufus-Isaacs and was planning to separate from the princess.

British newspapers picked up the story and immediately demanded a statement from Kensington Palace. It was the situation the royals had dreaded. They could only pray that it was an unfounded rumour.

When contacted by the British press, Lord Reading, who had already spoken to Jackie and been given her denials, said he was outraged by the stories, which were totally untrue. He pointed out that the Snowdons were neighbours and they had visited each other's homes. Jackie was a friend of both and any suggestion of romance between her and Tony was ridiculous.

Reading had advised Jackie not to give any interviews. This was reiterated by a friend in Switzerland, even after she confessed that the story was correct and she and Tony were in love and wanted to marry. A phone call to Tony elicited the same advice: 'Don't say a word to anybody.' He would be going to Barbados where Princess Margaret would join him.

Just as after Margaret's affair with Douglas-Home, the Snowdons were about to put on a united front and what better way than a holiday in the sun, which the press could headline as another reconciliation or second honeymoon. Unfortunately for Tony, when pressed by her father Jackie was unable to stay silent. She confessed all. In a second, tearful phone call to Tony, she warned him that the Readings were appalled and furious. Having offered Tony their friendship and hospitality, they said he had repaid them with treachery and deceit. Her parents had forbidden her to speak to Tony ever again.

In a personal call to Tony, Lord Reading told him the same and accused him of seducing their daughter. He was warned never to try to set foot in the Grange again on risk of physical reprisal.

A week after Tony's departure for Barbados, on 21 January, Margaret flew out to join him, secretly delighted that it was his turn to be on the receiving end of a press attack. At Grantley Adams Airport, she dutifully kissed him for the waiting photographers, to show the world they were still a united and loving couple. 'Do we look as if we're breaking up,' was his later quote in a British newspaper.

As an interesting footnote, in February, after the other guests had departed, Jackie invited another friend to join her in the Gsteig chalet. It was Dai Llewellyn, and with him he brought his younger brother Roddy. According to Nigel Dempster, Dai said he had the marvellous idea of pairing Roddy off with Jackie. 'And it was a great success.' 'The morning after I had got them together, I had just made the Martinis when Rods came down the stairs, grinning sheepishly. I cheered! All Jackie would tell me was that they had formed an "understanding" but there was no doubt in my mind that something had happened."'

Tony's ex-mistress and Margaret's future lover! The totally bizarre nature of this scenario was not lost on Tony.

18

Joy with a Toyboy

The Snowdons last holiday together was spent in Sardinia in August 1973. They had their children with them and it was a disaster. They had been leading separate lives for several years and the charade of maintaining appearances placed an intolerable strain on both.

Margaret's previous holiday – in Mustique – had been with second-time-around love Dominic Elliott, and she much preferred it to being on the Costa Smerelda with Tony. On this occasion, though, she proved far better at putting on a show than Tony. Almost from the day they arrived Tony refused to talk to her. The children would point out: 'Mummy is talking to you', and he would reply: 'I know', and wouldn't answer her.

At the end of a week, Tony felt it was useless carrying on the pretence and packed his bags and returned to London. Margaret continued the holiday alone with her children. When she returned to London, she told Tony she thought the time had come for him to move out of Kensington Palace. He agreed without argument and promised it would happen when it became practicable.

Inevitably, the romance with Elliott lost its impetus and Margaret turned to another old flame, her cousin Patrick Lichfield, for love and affection. When some of their friends appeared mildly scandalised Margaret tried to reassure them by commenting: 'Don't worry, we're kissing cousins.'

But these affairs were in no way expected to last. Her sex life with Tony had always been good, but she found sleeping in separate bedrooms, living at opposite ends of their home and only joining forces for official functions, which he diligently continued to perform, unsatisfactory.

She wanted a regular, caring lover. Someone with whom she could share her life and her interests. Colin Tennant had tried to introduce suitable companions into her life but without success and when he invited her to stay at Glen, where fifteen years earlier his own, embryonic romance with Margaret had briefly flowered, she declined.

Having escorted her children to Balmoral for the traditional Scottish holiday however, Margaret reconsidered Tennant's offer and decided it might be fun to go but take the children with her.

Her call to say she was taking him up on his offer threw Tennant into a blue funk, he admitted afterwards. There was no one to pair her off with. In sheer desperation he telephoned his great-aunt, Violet Wyndham, who, although getting on in years was a London hostess of considerable note and one who knew a wide variety of young men, one of whom might be suitable for this purpose. After a little thought, Violet put forward the name of one young man who might just fit the bill – Olympic show jumping hero Harry Llewellyn's younger son, Roddy.

Roddy had been introduced to Violet by South Kensington interior designer Nicky Haslam – a cousin of the Earl of Bessborough – and a self-confessed homosexual. Nicky, a highly precocious old Etonian had, as a teenager, been briefly befriended by Tony Armstrong-Jones during his Pimlico bachelor days.

In 1972, he, in turn, had befriended Roddy Llewellyn who was going through a sexual identity crisis. Roddy had twice tried to commit suicide while sharing a flat with his cousin, Colin Prichard, who had also been his partner in a mobile disco business which went bust.

'Roddy was going through a very emotionally difficult time,' said Haslam:

'The poor darling was having all sorts of doubts about himself sexually. He literally didn't know which way to turn.

'It was Jackie Rufus-Isaacs who brought us together. She was working for Piero di Monzi who used to throw little luncheon parties in the garden behind his shops. I was there the day she brought Roddy along. She had met him on a skiing holiday the year before with his brother Dai.

'He was very little boy lost. A lovely, sweet, angelic boy who was desperate for work and thinking of buying a flat which his parents were financing.

'He took me to see the place after we finished lunch. It was an awful, dingy, dungeon-like flat. Not suitable at all. Far better, I told him, if he were to move in with me.'

Roddy, who liked the charismatic Nicky on sight, jumped at the chance and moved in immediately. He was not put off when he discovered that Nicky's home was, in fact, just a large studio – with one wall of floor to ceiling glass – and no spare bedroom for himself. There was one big, high-ceilinged room with a raised gallery which contained a large double bed, and off this a small kitchen and bathroom.

Nicky described their year together there as, 'a little like *War and Peace*. We had some spectacular fights but we also had some wonderfully rewarding moments.'

In their year together Roddy became a sort of Nicky Haslam clone. Nicky was a fashion leader in leather – punk style with chains, and Roddy let him assist in choosing similar ensembles for himself. he also had his ear pierced and adopted an earring like Nicky.

They went to America together – Roddy's first visit – where Nicky had rented a friend's house in Los Angeles. When Nicky bought a Honda motorbike, they chose His and His helmets and the leather-clad duo became a familar sight around Kensington.

The friends they mixed with tended to come in groups of three sexes, the predominant one being homosexual. It was a world Roddy found fascinating and exciting and he revelled in it.

However, in the summer of 1973, just three months before Margaret's history-changing visit to Glen House, Nicky and Roddy had a more than usually damaging fight. Roddy turned up at his brother's flat minus tufts of hair, Dai remembered, and asked if he could move in for a spell. Dai told Nigel Dempster: 'They had terrible fights and we all disapproved of Haslam and what he did to Rods. There are certain things for which I will never be able to forgive him.'

So when Violet Wyndham called asking for Roddy's whereabouts, Nicky could only refer her to the Llewellyn family home in Wales. Calling there she learned that Roddy was holidaying with friends in Cornwall and eventually got him on the end of the line.

When told he was going to be a guest at a house party which included Princess Margaret, Roddy became very flustered. But minutes later a reassuring phone call from Colin Tennant persuaded him that there was nothing to panic about.

He was told to fly to Edinburgh and be at the Café Royale there at one o'clock sharp, because a table had been booked for lunch. The air fare would be taken care of.

When Roddy arrived for the most important meeting of his life to date, everyone else was already seated, with an empty chair next to Princess Margaret.

It was later confided that the princess immediately liked what she saw. This tweed-jacketed young man with the shaggy blond hair, soft voice and firm, but gentle, handshake looked like a boyish version of her husband, though taller at five feet nine inches. Margaret knew his father well and was able to put him at his ease with small talk about his family as she sipped her gin and tonic and, ignoring the other lunch guests, concentrated solely on Roddy.

Dempster quotes Tennant as saying: 'It was obvious something happened as soon as Princess Margaret saw Roddy. She was taken with him immediately and devoured him through luncheon. It was a great relief.'

When talk turned to Glen, the Scottish castle where they would be staying, and which Tennant had inherited in 1967 when his father went into tax exile, someone mentioned the large, outdoor, heated swimming pool. When Roddy admitted to not having packed his trunks,

Margaret insisted on taking him shopping, there and then, and chose a pair featuring a Union Jack!

After the children had been packed off to bed by Nanny Sumner and after a dinner which passed for Roddy like a dream when he realised Princess Margaret was actually holding his hand, the two monopolised the piano, singing show tunes and later love songs as the night wore on.

They ended sitting apart from the others, on a settee, sipping whisky and water and swopping stories of their pasts. When Margaret decided it was time for bed, long before her usual hour, no one seemed surprised when Roddy chose to retire as well and left the room with her.

Violet's choice had been inspired. The part-time College of Arms genealogy researcher, although perhaps sexually naïve, had just that right quality of vulnerability and helplessness which most appealed to Margaret. The 43-year-old princess, after several romantic relationships, had fallen instantly and possessively in love with the 25-year-old who was about to embark on his first serious affair.

The children, who had grown used to other men in their mother's life, took the lightning elevation of Roddy Llewllyn to pole postion in Margaret's affections in their stride. They seemed more than pleased to see her happy again.

However, not everyone approved of the princess's latest infatuation. Some of her older friends were deeply concerned and tried to warn her with stories about Roddy's past. Her reaction was completely the opposite of what they had hoped for. The more critical and detrimental the stories were, the more she supported him. Friends compared her to a lioness defending her cub.

She made it quite plain to his detractors that Roddy was her lover and he was here to stay. Life and circumstances had caused him to suffer in the same way as herself. They were kindred spirits facing the world together. And she forbade anyone to speak further ill of him under threat of banishment from her circle.

Just as she had before, with Townsend, Margaret relied on friends to volunteer their homes so that she and Roddy could meet discreetly to pursue their love affair, although one of these assignations prompted a phone call from Tony to Nicky Haslam. With venom in his voice, he warned him: 'Tell your friend to keep out of my house.'

Within two months of meeting the princess, Roddy found a flat of his own in Walham Grove, Fulham and moved out of his brother's home. Margaret found it very cramped but, aware of Roddy's enthusiasm for his first home of his own, she recommended decorators and builders and went shopping herself to buy things to brighten the rooms.

In the hours they spent together, Roddy told Margaret the sad story of his early youth. He felt he had never come up to his father's expectations, first learning to play the piano and sing while Dai did well at games, then failing to follow Dai into Eton by getting low grades in the entrance exam. Harry managed to get him placed at Shrewsbury but Roddy hated the games-oriented school and spent much of his time crying down the phone to his mother to take him away.

Whereas Dai had proved a dazzling ladies' man, Roddy was shy with women and found he preferred the company of his own sex. With her own, not always happy, memories of growing up, these anecdotes brought her even closer to her 'darling angel' as she had taken to calling him. Six months after their meeting, and still feeling as though he were living in a dream world, Roddy found himself in a light aircraft bound from Barbados to Mustique to join Margaret for what she had described as their 'honeymoon'.

The only other guests at Margaret's house, Les Jolies Eaux, which had been designed by Tony's uncle, Oliver Messel, after Tony had refused to have anything to do with it, and was now fully completed were Colin and Anne Tennant. With Margaret, they drove the two miles from the house to pick him up from the airstrip in the princess's Land Rover.

It was an extremely quiet holiday, for few island regulars were in residence. The days were spent swimming and picnicking and the evenings playing the piano and singing or relaxing with a board game. Margaret and Roddy were able to indulge their romance to their heart's content knowing there were no outsiders to spread the word to the press.

She was also proud to show off her new figure in a skimpy bikini. As always, she found it easy to shed weight when she was happily involved in a love affair.

On 16 March, Margaret flew home, leaving Roddy on Barbados to follow a day later. She was certain that her affair was unknown to Tony and these precautions seemed necessary to preserve their secret. However, when she reached Heathrow Airport Tony was waiting, with a mink coat and a cynical smile. He knew all about Roddy. There were plenty of people Margaret had slighted in the past who were only too willing to create problems for her by keeping Tony informed on the progress of her affair.

Back in England, Tennant took it upon himself to find Roddy a job that might improve his financial position which was desperate to say the least. He persuaded his good friend Algy Cluff, a millionaire northerner who was speculating in North Sea oil, to take him on, and Roddy suddenly found himself Cluff's personal assistant.

Tennant and Cluff might have thought they were being helpful but Roddy neither understood Cluff's business nor felt compatible with any of the other members of staff. He found himself embarrassingly out of his depth.

He also found that the strain of his affair with Margaret was beginning to tell – not so much her company or their outings together but Roddy was finding that the physical side of their relationship was becoming difficult to cope with. This completely unexpected downside to their idyllic relationship, coupled with his growing unease at working with Cluff, set in motion a panic attack which refused to go away.

After an anniversary visit to Glen in early September, followed by the couple's first weekend with the Llewellyns at their family home, Llanvair, Roddy found the pressures getting too much. He felt he had to get away and didn't much mind where to.

Only after packing a bag did he phone Princess Margaret and his parents and tell them he was going abroad. No, he didn't know where to, and no, he didn't know when he would be back. All he knew was that he had to get away.

Nigel Dempster subsequently reported that Roddy found himself on a plane to Turkey. He got into conversation with a fellow traveller and explained he was running away from an affair with a married woman and that sex with her had become a bit of a problem. After Roddy had admitted that he was short of cash, wrote Dempster, the other man, a sophisticated and well-connected homosexual offered to let him share the double room that had been allocated to him at the Hilton Hotel in Istanbul. Roddy accepted the offer with gratitude.

The following day Roddy bid his new friend goodbye and took himself off on a three-week bus journey around Turkey. Finally feeling that he could now face up to the situation in Britain, he flew back to London.

During his absence he discovered that Princess Margaret had suffered a nervous breakdown in November. Some people claimed, inaccurately, that she had taken a handful of sleeping tablets because Roddy had walked out on her. Although this was untrue, her breakdown had certainly been due, to a large extent, to his unreasonable and unheralded bunk. Understandably, when he got in touch on his return, he did not receive the warmest of welcomes.

Margaret told him that they needed a period apart for reflection. She wasn't ending their relationship but she felt it better if they did not see one another until her return from Mustique in February. Roddy would not be welcome there this year as the Queen was touring the Caribbean and it would be inadvisable to have him there if her sister called.

While Margaret enjoyed another traditional Christmas with the royal family, Roddy travelled to Wales and, it appeared, still acting far from rationally, told his father he would visit Sir Harry's house in Barbados, which was already up for sale, redecorate where necessary and find a purchaser. He would take a Welsh friend, Louise Macgregor, with him and, after tying things up in Barbados, they would move on to South America where they would spend six months touring.

In Barbados they discovered that the house had been stripped of furniture and had to borrow beds and chairs from neighbours in order to stay there. Roddy began to drink heavily and, after a few days, was on a diet of rum only. He was sober enough to cheer the Queen when she

258

visited the island on 18 February but soon became so strange in his behaviour that Louise consulted Janet Kidd, who helped to organise sessions with a local psychiatrist.

It was then that the first of two, world-exclusive articles I had written for the *News of the World*, about Margaret and Roddy, Tony and Jackie, was published. The edition sold like hot cakes on the island.

Roddy became obsessed with the idea of visiting Princess Margaret on Mustique and told everyone that she had sent for him, knowing, of course, that she had expressly forbidden him to be there. Her guests at that time were Tony's stepfather and mother, the Earl and Countess of Rosse. Everyone, including the princess, was shocked when Roddy arrived in jeans and T-shirt, hair unbrushed and smelling of rum.

Fortunately, Margaret was due to fly back to London that day and took him as far as Barbados on her plane. There she bid him goodbye and transferred to a London-bound jumbo.

In the next few days, he see-sawed in mood from being manically exuberant to staggering about like a walking corpse and Janet Kidd was persuaded to telephone Harry Llewellyn in Wales. Harry agreed that Roddy should be flown home and it was arranged that the psychiatrist who had already begun treating him, Dr. Patrick Smith, should fly with him and see him safely into a London hospital.

On a stopover in Antigua, Roddy bought a copy of the *News of the World* containing my second world-exclusive article – and he spent much of the rest of the journey wandering up and down the aisles pointing out his picture to bemused holidaymakers.

Roddy spent three weeks in Charing Cross Hospital

before being declared well enough to go home to his parents' care in Wales.

Princess Margaret did not visit him in hospital though she wrote encouraging letters to his home.

It was during the spring and summer, when Roddy was convalescing in Wales, that Margaret began to cultivate a man whose friendship she still enjoys today. Ned Ryan, property owner and, at that time, running an antique silver stall in the Portobello Road market, has had the most incredibly varied career, being at various times a barman and a London bus conductor.

Margaret had met Ryan, the tubby, balding son of a Tipperary farmer, in 1974, and had found him vastly amusing, loving his hilarious stories, told in a thick Irish accent, about his many jobs. She encouraged friends to include Ned Ryan on their guest lists when she was to be present and began using him as an escort. They were spotted several times very early in the morning, shopping for antiques in the London street markets.

Ned, Margaret told friends, was a necessary antidote to the gloom and tension of Kensington Palace. Tony had now admitted to her that he was in love with Lucy Lindsay-Hogg, who had been his assistant on a film project in Australia. Lucy had been married to then TV director Michael Lindsay-Hogg for four years until their divorce in 1971. She had worked in the TV and film business until Tony, who had known her since 1973, invited her to be his assistant on the eleven-week Australian project, where they had fallen in love.

Her flat in Kensington Square was only a short walk from the palace and Tony now stayed there most nights until the early hours. Said one friend: 'It was doubly galling for Margaret to have her own lover convalescing in Wales while Tony was coming home in the middle of the night, making lots of noise, after making love to his new mistress.'

In June, Roddy announced that not only was he perfectly fit but he had been offered shares in a new, 47-acre, commune that John Rendall and Sarah Ponsonby were starting up at Surrendell in Wiltshire. Roddy had been asked to help them pull it together and organise the gardens. He was to have one of the eight bedrooms in the main house.

For extra income, they would open a restaurant in Bath, the nearest big town, called Parsenn Sally, after an earlier commune. Margaret went for lunch, loved the enthusiastic informality, and invited herself back for a weekend. She went in the early winter and found it more spartan and cold than anything she had ever experienced. Although she wrote a glowing letter of thanks, she did not ask to repeat the experience.

The following February, completely back in Margaret's good books, Roddy joined her for the spring holiday in Mustique. All was as idyllic and tranquil as before, except for one detail. Staying at the newly extended hotel, and following up my exclusive story of the previous year, was top international journalist Ross Waby, a New Zealander working for Rupert Murdoch's News International. He managed to sneak a picture of Roddy and Margaret when they came to the Beach Bar – the first shot of them in the two and a half years they had been lovers.

When it was published in the *News of the World*, it provided Tony with the lever he had been praying for. He announced that he found himself in a quite intolerable position and no one questioned his right to ask for a separation.

His own, long-standing affair with Lucy was still a secret which, Margaret thought, unfairly placed all the blame for their split on her.

The right moment had now arrived for Tony to move out. His belongings were transferred from Kensington Palace to the Countess of Rosse's London home nearby as Tony flew to Sydney, Australia for an exhibition of his photographs.

A statement released on 10 May read: 'Her Royal Highness, the Princess Margaret, Countess of Snowdon, and the Earl of Snowdon have mutually agreed to live apart. The Princess will carry out her public duties and functions unaccompanied by Lord Snowdon. There are no plans for divorce proceedings.'

In a halting voice, and apparently on the verge of tears. Tony read out a brief statement at a press conference in Sydney.

'I am naturally desperately sad in every way that this had to happen. And I would just like to say three things. First to pray for the understanding of our two children. Secondly, to wish Princess Margaret every happiness for her future. Thirdly, to express, with the utmost humility, the love, admiration and respect I will always have for her sister, her mother and indeed her entire family.

Says Margaret: 'I have never seen such good acting.'

On the plus side, Roddy and his friends at the commune were able to benefit from his romance with the princess. They shared one payment alone of £6,000 and other sums changed hands as journalists from around the world vied with one another for an exclusive.

The next time Tony and Margaret met was at Viscount Linley's confirmation party at Windsor in April, but they did not speak. Shortly afterwards, however, at the Queen's fiftieth birthday party, they were seen to talk at considerable length. Margaret, who was staying at Royal Lodge, arrived with the Queen Mother. Tony drove down accompanied by Lady Rupert Nevill, a close friend of the Queen, whose husband was Prince Philip's treasurer.

Tony had regained some of the weight he had lost during the strain of the crisis of their parting and was very tanned from his Australian trip. Everyone remarked how much younger he looked. It was true that, since the separation, he appeared to have shed years along with his worries almost as rapidly as Margaret appeared to have gained them. All his old wit and vitality had returned. With his charm and brilliant smile, he was one of the most popular guests at the party.

He and Margaret spent almost an hour talking alone during the evening and there were many hopeful expressions among the royals when they heard Margaret's laughter as Tony recounted an amusing anecdote from his Australian business visit. Said one of the guests: 'They looked more comfortable together than I had seen them in years. And Margaret was making a big effort to please. She listened to what he had to say and seemed genuinely to be enjoying his company.'

Afterwards, Tony stressed to friends that it was his dearest wish that this amicable relationship with his wife continue, but he did not want anyone to entertain hopes that they might eventually be reunited as man and wife.

Roddy made a brief appearance in London to visit Princess Margaret, although many thought it was more of an opportunity to show off when he appeared in Tramp night club wearing a T-shirt bearing the words 'Roddy for PM'.

He returned to Wales but, on hearing that the commune was in trouble, despite the injection of press money, drove to Surrendell to collect his things and formally to give up his interest there.

His next move was to register for a one-year course at the Merrist Wood Agricultural College near Guildford. To show how seriously he was applying himself, he refused an invitation to fly with Margaret to Mustique to celebrate Tennant's fiftieth birthday. Occasionally, Roddy would drive to London and share a meal with Margaret at Kensington Palace but the early passion of their romance seemed to have dimmed and neither appeared anxious to resurrect their physical relationship. In 1977, Margaret finally invited Roddy to Windsor Royal Lodge and, surprisingly, in view of her grave misgivings about their relationship, he developed an instant rapport with the Queen Mother.

They did not return to Mustique and Les Jolies Eaux until November that year and Roddy had to wait in Barbados until after the Queen had made a visit to the island during a flag-waving tour on Concorde.

On completion of his agricultural course, and the receipt of his diploma, Roddy set up Roddy Llewellyn Landscapes Limited and, on their return to London, he began trying to drum up business. However, more lucrative financial rewards beckoned when Victor Malik, a leather merchant, suggested that Roddy should make a record and introduced him to Claude Wolff, husband and manager of Petula Clark. In January, it was announced that Roddy had signed a deal with Wolff who expected him to earn as much as £250,000.

Roddy did sing one duet with Petula Clark for French television, managing to get a good take after four attempts, but he left for Mustique in February 1978, before recording of his album proper had begun. A week later, he was rushed to hospital in Barbados after mysteriously haemorrhaging, although he recovered rapidly after a blood transfusion.

When he did arrive back in London, it was to another lucrative offer, to promote a new club in Battersea called Bennett. This time there were more suggestions that, perhaps, Roddy was being used to cash in on Princess Margaret's name. This time, too, the Queen's advisers were adamant that Margaret was being involved in publicity stunts and that this could only have an adverse effect on the status of the royal family. The fact that Roddy had signed a £1,000 a month management deal with Wolff and a long-term recording contract with Phonogram as well as a £150 a week contract from Bennett 'to look after their plants', did not alter official opinion. Roddy, they said, would be best off out of the country for a period. Now that there was the prospect of decent money rolling in, Roddy finally agreed to go Tangier under an alias.

Margaret, who had returned from Mustique with a heavy cold which had developed into flu, was by this time too ill to care. At the beginning of May, she was admitted to King Edward VII hospital suffering from gastro-enteritis and a mild form of hepatitis, or inflammation of the liver.

On 10 May, a Kensington Palace statement was released: 'Her Royal Highness the Princess Margaret, Countess of Snowdon, and the Earl of Snowdon, after two years of separation, have agreed that their marriage should be formally ended. Accordingly Her Royal Highness will start the necessary proceedings.'

Tony could still look forward to a rewarding future. He married Lucy Lindsay-Hogg just five months after the decree absolute was granted in July.

To Margaret, released from hospital the day after the announcement, the future did not appear very rosy at all. As she was driven away, her appearance shocked on-lookers. The 47-year-old princess's face had a greyish tinge and was heavily lined. She had been advised not to resume official engagements for a month.

Roddy, who was still in Morocco, decided for personal reasons to assert himself and announce his own decision about the future. He told journalists: 'I am saying cate-gorically that I will never marry Princess Margaret. Circumstances – personal reasons – would prevent it. I don't consider myself in any way responsible for the divorce. Of course I hope to see her again. One always likes to see one's friends.'

Margaret, a heavy drinker most of her adult life, was told by doctors that she would have to abstain totally from alcohol for a year because of the hepatitis. She took it incredibly well. 'As long as I can still smoke I suppose it's not too bad,' she quipped. When friends offered to go dry to ease her own enforced abstinence, she made them drink as normal. 'I have the situation under control,' she said.

In June it was announced that Roddy's record was completed and he appeared on a radio show in London to talk about it. The album, called *Roddy*, was released in October and had a brief success as the BBC's album of the week but then vanished without trace from the charts. The failure of his debut record made it a certainty that he would never cut a second. Roddy was said to have received a £50,000 advance from the record company.

In August, Margaret celebrated her forty-eighth birthday

at Balmoral and then went on to join Roddy at Glen for a fifth anniversary bash. Margaret, now fully recovered from her illness, was in sparkling form although it was remarked on that her relationship with Roddy lacked the fire of earlier encounters.

In September, Margaret flew to the South Pacific to represent the Queen at the celebrations marking the granting of independence to the island of Tuvalu, formerly Ellice Island. On her first night there, on board the New Zealand frigate *Otago*, she woke in the early hours in panic and rang for her private secretary, Lord Napier. He heard Margaret whisper: 'Thank God you've answered. I'm in great pain, I can't breathe.' She was found to be suffering from viral pneumonia. 'I very nearly died,' she admitted later. She was flown to the nearest hospital, in Sydney, nine hours away and stayed there for nine days, before carrying on with the rest of her programme.

In March 1979 she learned, courtesy of the *Sunday Express*, that Lucy was expecting a baby. Tony hadn't told her.

Lady Frances Armstrong-Jones was born at midnight on 17 July, less than seven months after the marriage. Everyone generously conceded that she was premature!

It was in that year also that Roddy was to meet the Queen for the first time. It happened one Saturday evening in Royal Lodge. The Queen was talking to a nanny in the nursery when Roddy burst in wearing only a shirt and underpants, hoping to have buttons sewn on.

'Please forgive me, Ma'm, I look awful,' he said.

'Don't worry, I don't look too good myself,' replied the Queen.

The next day they were formally introduced after both had attended chapel at Windsor.

The following year Margaret undertook tours to

America, the Philippines, Singapore, Malaysia and Canada. It was the year of her fiftieth birthday and fifteen of her closest friends, including Jocelyn Stevens and Ned Ryman, agreed to split the cost of a fabulous dinner and discotheque at the Ritz. It was held on 4 November, the most convenient date for all the royal family. This party brought to a head Roddy's acceptability by the royals. Naturally, Margaret wanted him to attend: the Queen made it clear that she did not expect to see him there at all.

When Dominic Elliott took the Queen's side, Margaret, in a fit of anger, told him that she never wanted to see him again. Elliott resigned from the committee and refused an invitation when it was sent, thus ending a 30-year friendship.

Eventually, after much discussion between the two sisters, the Queen agreed that Roddy should be allowed in for the dancing with 140 other guests but that he should not attend the dinner for 40 special invitees, which included all the royals. When Roddy did join in for the discotheque, he was forced to stand on the sidelines almost to the end and until after the Queen and Prince Philip had left. Only then was he permitted to dance with Margaret.

The consensus among the guests was that, after this exhibition of freezing out, Roddy was highly unlikely to remain on the scene for more than a few months longer. 'If he does then he has to have the hide of a rhinoceros,' said one.

Margaret had not even been present at Roddy's October birthday party, held in Stringfellows night club. The party had been laid on free by the club's clever, publicity-conscious owner, Peter, and Margaret was not going to be drawn into further controversy over publicity stunts using her name through Roddy. Had she been there, however, she might have been disturbed to see the affectionate way in which he treated one particular guest, Tania Soskin whom Roddy had known since 1971. Within weeks of Margaret's fiftieth birthday, Roddy was sharing a bed with Tania and telling friends that they were in love.

Margaret did know that Tania had accompanied Roddy on a trip to California but she didn't realise in what capacity Tania had gone.

On 13 February, Roddy joined Margaret on the customary spring jaunt to Mustique. William and Anne Buckhurst, two of Margaret's other guests, were on the flight. For reasons unknown to his fellow passengers, Roddy was withdrawn and surly, refusing to join in the conversation or to make any attempt to get in holiday mood.

After less than a week on the island, Margaret took Roddy on one side and asked him what on earth was the matter. His churlish behaviour was upsetting her other guests. His answer shocked Margaret to her very core. He told her he was in love with Tania and wanted to marry her. Said a royal observer:

'She hadn't had the slightest idea that anything like that had been going on. It was probably the most devastating thing she had ever been confronted with.

'She handled it with dignity and style and gave him her blessing but something probably died inside her that day. I doubt she will ever feel safe in giving her heart to another man again.

'There would be new boyfriends and new escorts, but no man would ever enjoy the sensuality and passion from Princess Margaret which Roddy and those favoured other lovers had known up to that moment.'

19

The Future

When, at the age of 50, Princess Margaret was dropped by Roddy Llewelleyn, it was a totally unexpected and stunning blow to her self-esteem and her sexuality.

Her sensuality – she has an enduring Marie Antoinette quality – remains undiminished at 63, but she just no longer seems interested in a physical relationship with her men friends. Companionship without commitment seems to be her current policy.

'Roddy was the last great love of her life,' says one Margaret watcher.

'Although the physical relationship had been falling off for the last few years they were together. It was almost non-existent at the end.

'But despite everything he put her through, she still cared for him deeply. Just how much was shown

when she refused to drop him even after being hurt
so badly.'

Always at her best in adversity, Margaret, as usual,
covered over the emotional scars of her lover's betrayal and
did the unexpected.

Most of her really close friends, who had been against
the toyboy match from the beginning, hoped that Roddy's
shabby treatment of her would finally sound the death
knell on their relationship. They were almost in despair
after she invited Roddy and Tania around for lunch at
Kensington Palace to celebrate their engagement. When
she accepted an invitation to the wedding, there were
some who openly questioned her sanity. However, and
most fortuitously, Roddy was obliged to change the
wedding date, and the new date, 11 July, coincided with
the princess's state visit to Canada.

Thus, to deep sighs of relief from her friends, she was
saved the ultimate embarrassment of being labelled the
spurned older woman in favour of the young bride – an
approach already prepared on every Fleet Street picture
desk and back bench and with every photographer aware
of the importance, not to mention the value, of a picture
of them together.

She sent them a silver cigarette box as a wedding
present. That should have been the end of it, according to
her friends. However, there were to be future meetings –
at the Chelsea Flower Show and sometimes at a meal in
Kensington Palace. She even had Roddy and Tania – now
the parents of three children – to stay at the house in
Mustique. Her fondness for her 'darling angel' remained,
although, thankfully, the love affair was over.

According to many of her friends, say royal insiders,

Margaret pursued her affair with Roddy long after she should have pulled out – that moment being when she became aware that the relationship was being exploited for publicity purposes.

They also criticise her for continuing in her role as wife to Tony long after the marriage was dead. Even so, it was Princess Margaret who paved the way for the following royal generation to be able to walk away from their marriage partners.

Having loved and lost on so many occasions, one could excuse the princess for giving up on the idea of 'happily ever after' but she says she would still contemplate another marriage 'if the right man comes along'. She has seriously thought about remarriage and ideally would like someone who really loves her to look after her and care for her as she grows older.

The unpleasant truth, however, is that there do not appear to be any serious contenders for the hand of the Queen's sister in marriage. Men find it very difficult to be often or for long periods in her company. It is said that many of her alleged friends dislike her and say hurtful things behind her back.

Margaret has a regal calm about her, which, mixed with her natural aloofness, makes her overbearingly imperious. She can be breathtakingly rude and it has been said that she sometimes wields her royal position like a sledge-hammer. According to writer Fiammetta Rocco, she can be difficult even with friends and needs a non-stop stream of conversation from whoever is with her. She expects to be entertained all the time and it's very tricky when one runs out of things to say. Fiammetta recalls one friend's anecdote which tells of the chairman of a major company coming to dinner. He was a good conversationalist but when he stopped talking and asked her opinion on something she snapped: 'If you'd just shut up for a moment I'll tell you.' The host reported that he nearly dropped his knife and fork.

She quotes an occasional date as saying: 'She can be unbelievably rude. Quite takes your breath away. I couldn't go along with her for very long. Going out with her was a novelty at first. But curiosity killed the cat and now I don't see her that much any more.'

She is feminine not feminist and expects all the observancies of her sex as well as her rank. She tends to ignore women in company and concentrate on the men. Said a royal insider: 'I don't think she has any awareness of how much a caricature she has become of herself. She is more imperious than the Queen. At least the Queen will occasionally put on a pair of wellies and get stuck in – but not Margaret. She is far too regal for that. She hates to get her hands dirty.'

During private or official functions, she will change plans when it suits her, no matter what effect it might have on her hosts or their friends. Last year in Italy, the bigwigs of Genoa offered a cultural guided tour of their city, under the personal charge of the District Prefect, Vittorio Stelo. After an hour spent waiting in the sun, the resplendent dignatory wrapped his robes around him, lowered the brim of his feathered hat and went home.

Her host later revealed that Margaret had chosen to go on a private tour rather than the guided tour. Very disappointing, sighed Vittorio, like many others in a similar position before him.

Wrote Fiammetta: 'One friend recently had her bedroom rewired so that the princess could use her rollers, while another felt forced to reopen an unused and enormous drawing room, raising the shutters and removing all the dust sheets after the princess sighed at having to sit in the new snuggery that had been made as an alternative.'

Her friends are expected to keep her adequately and imaginatively entertained and organise her holidays throughout the year. She expects to be at Balmoral in September and Sandringham at Christmas with her sister. In February it is Mustique. Summer holidays are taken in Turkey and Italy. That's when friends are expected to step in and organise the villa or hotel.

Most weekends are spent at Royal Lodge, Windsor or with friends in the country. The princess does not wait to be asked but telephones her friends and announces her arrival. Some tremble at the thought of having her for the weekend, but they would tremble even more if they found themselves axed from her circle. She is frequently referred to as 'the weekend visitor from Hell.'

There are still a few faces from the past but the years have made their inroads on the Margaret 'set'. The once-dazzling group of rich landowners, intellectuals and aristocrats who cheered up the drab fifties have been decimated by death, doting grand-parenthood or have become victims of Margaret's displeasure. It is doubtful if some of the new set and the old set would have hit it off. Several of the new chums who enliven her evenings at Kensington Palace are homosexual.

She will not stay with one of her oldest friends, Jocelyn Stevens, because of his divorce, although they are still close. She feels she would be appearing disloyal to his ex-wife Janey, who now has rooms in Margaret's Kensington Palace home.

THE FUTURE

Said a palace insider:

'She can be very cruel sometimes. She can be devasta-
tingly wicked with her tongue. She was terribly under-
educated but she has lots of native cunning and wit.

'She has a shit list and once you go on it you don't
easily come off it – if ever.

'The *Daily Mail* columnist Lynda Lee Potter suggested a motto for Margaret five years ago. It was
written by Thomas Fuller the seventeenth-century
clergyman: "If it were not for hope the heart would
break". I think there are many of those around her,
and who cope with her, who are far more deserving
of the motto.

'Margaret will not compromise. She is a king's
daughter brought up in an incredibly exalted and
unnatural way, but it's the only way she knows. She
actually revels in demanding extra police outriders to
zip her through the West End during the day. She
accepts things like that as being her right.'

Men do find her difficult and there is almost a consensus
among them that a little of her company goes a very long way.

One of her favourite regular escorts – for shared, sunshine holidays as much as for normal, London, social
events – is Norman Lonsdale. Two years older than the
princess and an old Etonian businessman who was once
the boss of the Peter Evans eating house chain, he has been
a friend since 1981 and accompanied her to Mustique nine
months after her bust-up there with Roddy. Lonsdale is a
widower whose wife died in 1979. They met when
Viscount Linley was nineteen and a boyfriend of then
eighteen-year-old Emma Jane Lonsdale.

Lonsdale has gone on to share several foreign holidays with the princess and remains a close friend, but theirs is a friendship which has never hinted at spilling over into romance, even though Lonsdale has had other romances in the past thirteen years.

The only other man who can be said to be 'regular' in her life is Ned Ryan the jolly Irishman, called her 'court jester'. And he is a confirmed bachelor. In 1993 they were on Mustique together and returned to Britain to go to a Rolling Stones concert. Margaret was Ryan's 'date' in February 1993 at his sixtieth birthday party at the Lanesborough Hotel. Other guests included Joan Collins, Anouska Hempel, Elle McPherson and her boyfriend Tim Jeffries. Viscount Linley was there with his future wife, Serena Stanhope. Ned Ryan is now her longest-serving escort, though he still tells people: 'I'm a nobody.'

Not all of Margaret's evenings are spent with her escorts or her new party set. Too often for her, she must be content with being alone, eating her dinner, drinking whisky, watching television or doing a favourite crossword – she is considered an expert at both *The Times* and the *Telegraph* crosswords.

Often she will telephone friends, asking, sometimes pleading, with them to go round and share her evening. They know it will be until the early hours because Margaret is still a late reveller and a late sleeper, and that's why the bolder ones will refuse, making a rapid excuse. Otherwise, they will be persuaded into an evening of royal hand-holding and made to become a one-person royal variety performance.

The alternative, of course, is to let her sit it out alone. Some manage an instant, or well-prepared, excuse but most are too kind to subject her to that.

THE FUTURE

A year ago Margaret finally managed to quit smoking, eight years after an operation to remove part of a lung, and she has stopped drinking wine at lunchtime, although the drinking of whisky at night continues. Drinking alone does not worry her, it is a habit she has practised all her adult life.

Margaret still attends an impressive number of royal functions each year, albeit second-string royal occasions for the most part. 'Still playing second best after all these years,' she quipped to one royal insider. 'I guess I'll be second best to my grave.'

However, new friends say the princess has recovered much of her old vitality and her sense of fun remains undiminished. Last year, while entertaining a group of younger friends after a night out, she was playing the stereo system very loud and a guest commented that it might disturb her royal neighbours, Margaret replied: 'Princess Michael even complains about the noise the cats make. Let's give her something to really complain about.' And, according to one of her guests, she turned the stereo system up to full volume and lowered one of the speakers out of the window. 'It was only when she decided she had given them enough that she hauled the speaker back in.'

That has been Margaret's way all her life. To do the things she wanted when she wanted and to hell with the consequences. That is the way she treated her men and, for a time at least, they adored her for it.

It is doubtful if, after thirteen years, there will be another lover to rouse the passion and desire in Princess Margaret which so often led to romantic disruption in her past. She has said as much herself. Yet she has been so unpredictable all her life that it might be unwise totally to rule out one last relationship. Perhaps a man of truly princely attributes will one day make a fitting Romeo to the world's very last real princess's Juliet.

Index

279

INDEX

INDEX

Gsteig, Switzerland 246-7, 248
Gustav, King of Sweden 197-8,
    199-200

Haile Selassie, Emperor 5
Hamilton, Dennis 172
Hamilton, Willie 172
Harewood, Earl of 246
Harold, Crown Prince of Norway 159
Harris, Elizabeth 205-7, 230
Harris, Richard 205, 206-7
Harrods 55
Harvey, Laurence 242
Haslam, Nicky 251-3, 255
Heald, Sir Lionel 51
Hempel, Anouska 276
Henley Regatta 87
Hicks, David 148
Hollywood 177
Hornby, Susan 15
Hostage, The (play) 152-3

Ingram, Bruce 84
Ivananov, Yevgeny 82-8

Jamagne, Marie Luce (later
    Townsend) 57, 81, 141
Jamaica 175
Jeffries, Tim 276
Johnson, President Lyndon 177
Juan Carlos, King of Spain 159
Juliana, Queen of the Netherlands
    29, 158-9

Karim, Prince *see* Aga Khan IV
Keeler, Christine 84, 87, 88
Kennedy, Jackie 204-5
Kensington Palace 52, 80; PM and
    AA-J's first house in 166; Clock
    Court house 171-2, 175, 177-80,
    190, 209, 210-15, 217-20, 223-4,
    250, 274
Kent, Edward, Duke of 130, 195
KGB 87
Kidd, Janet 259
King Edward VII Hospital 190, 214,
    265-6
Kings Cross railway station 135
Knight, Clara 2, 3

Lang, Dr., Archbishop of Canterbury
    2
Lascelles, Tommy 38, 44-5, 46, 47, 48,
    49, 50, 51, 52
Lazlo, John de 42
Legge, Raine (later Countess
    Spencer) 54
Legh, Sir Piers 24
Leigh, Major Francis 120
Les Ambassadeurs club 17, 33,
    240-1
Lichfield, Patrick 211, 240, 241, 250
Lindsay-Hogg, Lucy 260-1, 262, 266,
    267
Linley, Viscount (David Armstrong-
    Jones; son of PM) 171, 173, 183,
    185-6, 249-50, 254, 263, 275, 276
LLanvair 257
Llewellyn, Dai 248, 251, 252, 255
Llewellyn, Sir Harry 251, 255, 258,
    259
Llewellyn, Roddy 183, 248, 251-69,
    270-2
Lloyd, Christopher 111
London, West End 112-15, 142, 207-
    8: clubs 17-18, 32, 33, 56-7, 112,
    154, 229; theatres 54, 73, 111, 112,
    152-3; *see also place names*
London Clinic 245
Lonsdale, Emma Jane 275
Lonsdale, Norman 275-6
Lord and Lady Algy (play) 54
Loren, Sophia 242
Los Angeles 252
Lowndes Square, Belgravia 60

MacDonald, Margaret 3
MacDonald, Ruby 3
Macgregor, Louise 258-9
Macmillan, Harold 163, 172
Magic Christian, The (film) 240
Malik, Victor 264
Malvern water 118
Margaret Rose, Princess: birth 1-2,
    christening 2-3; childhood 3-13,
    90, 173; adolescence 192-3; early
    suitors 14-19, 21, 90; 'escort
    period' 32-40, 194-5; death of
    father 39-41; religion 42; romance

282

INDEX

with PT 13, 14, 15, 18, 19-31, 34-8, 42-5, 57, 58, 60-2, 68-70; opposition to romance 44-50, 51-5, 58-63; tours Rhodesia 49; renunciation statement 63-7, 68-70; engaged to Wallace 70-2, 94; in late *1950s*, 66, 72-3, 94, 96-123; and Prince Philip 82-3, 86; developing relationship with AA-J 72, 86, 88-95, 102, 103, 116, 117, 129-35, 136-46, 147-8, 151-4, 192-3; engagement 90-1, 123, 124-8, 148-9, 155-9, 169; wedding 90, 159-62; honeymoon 162-4; married life 89, 165-81, 182-7, 188-92, 211-14, 234-5; children 170, 173-4, 175, 183, 185-6; breakdown of marriage 244-5, 249-50, 255, 261; separation statements 262, 265; affair with RD-H 185, 187, 188-9, 191-2, 208, 209-27, 230; letters to RD-H 217-19, 224-7; and Sellers 231-42; and RL 253-60, 261-9, 270-2; and Ryan 260; since marriage of RL 80-1, 272-8

Margaretha, Princess of Sweden 196-200

Mary, Queen 2, 4

Mask Behind the Mask, The (Evans) 239, 241-2

McNeill, Jane 15

McPherson, Elle 276

Meadowbrook, West Chiltington, Sussex 215-17, 227, 230

Merrist Wood Agricultural College 264

Messel, Oliver 183, 256

MI5 83, 87

Michael, Princess 277

Milligan, Spike 236-7, 238-9

Milroy Club 33, 54

Montagu, Judy 53, 54, 56

Mountbatten, Earl Louis 9-10

Mountbatten, Lady Pamela 148

Music 72, 147, 207-8, 211

Musselburgh, Scotland 119-21

Mustique, island 163-4, 228, 249, 256, 258, 259, 261, 264, 265, 269, 271, 274, 275, 276

Napier, Lord 267

National Trust 184

Nevill, Lord Rupert 65, 171

Nevill, Lady Rupert 263

New York 191, 192, 220-1, 222

New York Daily News 246

News of the World 259, 261

Niarchos, Stavros 177

Nureyev, Rudolph 177

O'Brien, Edna 177

Observer 175

Ogilby, Lord 194

Ogilvy, Angus 207, 238

Olaf, King of Norway 159

Old House, Sussex 183-6, 240, 244

Otago (ship) 267

Paris: *1949* 30

Parsenn Sally restaurant, Bath 261

Paul, Sandra 201-4, 227, 230

Pavlov, Anatoly 87

Pawle, Rosemary *see* Townsend

Peake, Iris 104, 105, 114-15, 129

Pelham, David 194

People newspaper 47-8, 167

Philip, Prince, Duke of Edinburgh: meets Elizabeth 9-10; engagement 26-7, 28; marriage 18, 28; and PT 36-7, 42, 44, 51, 58, 60, 62; Prince Consort 53; *1963* 82-6; relationship with PM 82-3, 86; and AA-J 136-7, 138-9, 156, 157, 165; and Sellers 236-7

Phipps, Rev. Simon 171

Photography 91-2, 102

Piccadilly, London 2

Pimlico Road 92, 102, 152, 153-4

Plunkett, Lord Patrick 49, 54, 57, 103, 111, 117, 152, 171

Ponsonby, Sarah 261, 262

Porchester, Lord 54, 57, 72, 194, 195

Portal, Sir Charles 'Peter' 24

Potter, Lynda Lee 275

Press 46-8, 56, 57-8, 61-2, 63, 65-6, 73, 153; US 46-7

Prichard, Colin 251

Private View (book by AA-J) 184

Profumo, John 84, 87, 88

INDEX

Tramp night club 263-4
Travellers' Club 216
Tribune 53
Turkey 257-8, 274
Tussaud waxworks 165
Tuvalu island 267

Uckfield House, Sussex 65-6
United States: ER tours; press 46-7

VE Day 13
Vogue 91, 92, 191, 221
von Essen, Count Carl-Reinhold
  198-9

Waby, Ross 261
Walham Grove, Fulham 255
Walker, Patric 206-7
Wallace, Barbara 71
Wallace, Billy 14-15, 18, 21, 38, 54,
  57, 103, 111, 112-14, 116-17, 141-2,
  194; engaged to PM 70-2, 194
Wallop, Jean 72
War Office 193
Ward, Peter 57, 72, 194, 195
Ward, Stephen 82-8
Warwick, Christopher 171
Waterhouse, Keith 102

West Chiltington, Susses 215-17, 227,
  230
West Indies *see* Caribbean; Mustique
Westminster Abbey 157, 158, 160
When the Sweet Talking's Done
  (R. Douglas-Home) 200
Whicker's World (TV programme)
  227
Wild One, The (film) 134
Wills, Jean 61, 62, 65
Wills, John 61, 65
Windsor, Duke of (formerly King
  Edward VIII) 2-3, 5-6, 68
Windsor, Duchess of (formerly Mrs
  Wallis Simpson) 5-6, 68
Windsor 245; Adelaide Cottage 25-6,
  42; Castle 10, 11, 43; Great Park 29,
  42-3, 118; Royal Lodge 115, 117-18,
  186, 263, 274, (PM's childhood 3),
  (AA-J at 131-3, 134-5, 143-6, 149-
  52, 165), (RL at 264, 267), (Sellers
  at 234, 239), (PT at 74)
Winstanley, Kathleen 230
Wolff, Claude 264-5
Woodruff, Maurice 232-3, 238
World War II 10-12, 21-4
Wyndham, Violet 250-1, 253, 254

285